C E L L O P H A N E

PA J   BOOKS

Series Editors

Bonnie Marranca and Gautam Dasgupta

A   PAJ   BOOK

THE   JOHNS   HOPKINS   UNIVERSITY

PRESS

BALTIMORE   AND   LONDON

PLAYS BY MAC WELLMAN

cellophane

FOREWORD BY MARJORIE PERLOFF

The Johns Hopkins University Press
2715 North Charles Street
Baltimore, Maryland 21218-4363
www.press.jhu.edu

Library of Congress Cataloging-in-Publication Data
Wellman, Mac.
   Cellophane: plays / Mac Wellman ; foreword by Marjorie Perloff.
      p.   cm. — (PAJ books)
   ISBN 0-8018-6719-3 (pbk. : alk. paper)
    I. Title.   II. Series
   PS3573.E468 C45 2001
   812'.54—dc21   00-066418

A catalog record for this book is available from the British Library.

Page 401 constitutes a continuation of the copyright page.

Contents

Foreword

*At the basis of the whole modern view
of the world lies the illusion that the
so-called laws of nature are the explanations of natural phenomena.*
—LUDWIG WITTGENSTEIN,
Tractatus Logico-Philosophicus

It is not interesting *at this point in
human time to portray the real world
as it seems to be in its own terms; but
it is interesting to unfold, in human
terms, the logic of its illogic and so get
at the nut of our contemporary human
experience.*
—MAC WELLMAN,
"Poisonous Tomatoes:
A Statement on Logic and the Theater"

"POISONOUS TOMATOES," which appeared as the preface to Mac Wellman's earlier collection of plays, *The Bad Infinity* (Johns Hopkins, 1992), makes the case that *naturalism,* with its premise that the stage is a "true to life" replica of the coherent "real" world outside its frame, has lost its efficacy as a form of theater. But in dismissing the naturalist theater with its petty "topical" plays as a "minor province of journalism" and opting for the "logic of illogic," Wellman could not have known just how quickly actual events would confirm his suspicions. At this writing (November 2000), the U.S. electoral process has totally broken down, thanks to the giant media glitch involving exit polls, a "confusing" Florida "butterfly" ballot, and the unprecedented and unbelievable closeness of a presidential race between two candidates whom Ralph Nader, for one, has defined as interchangeable Republocrats. To read the plays collected in *Cellophane* against the "debates" currently in progress on the TV screen or in the *New York Times* is to marvel at Wellman's uncanny ability to capture the deep structure of contemporary experience in all its absurdity and illogic. Perhaps this is why Wellman calls himself "a pessimist but a cheerful one." Living, as he says we do, in a "low and contemptible time, . . . a time when ideals are mocked and scorned, when the merely human is expendable, when those in position of official trust have put aside any pretense to disinterestedness and practice openly the grossest kind of self-aggrandizement," the arist's "collective act of imagining" becomes all the more important.

The ten plays collected in this new Wellman volume are prefaced by "A Chrestomathy of 22 Answers to 22 Wholly Unaskable and Unrelated Questions Concerning Political and Poetic Theater." The obscure word *chrestomathy* is carefully chosen: according to the *Oxford English Dictionary,* it combines *chrestos* (useful) and *matheia* (learning) to designate "a collection of choice passages from an author or authors, esp. one compiled to as-

sist in the acquirement of a language." *Useful learning* that helps us acquire
a "language": here is a good description of Wellman's own conception of dramatic art. True, such science fiction Westerns as *Harm's Way* have been
linked to the theater of Sam Shephard, who was an early influence, even as
Wellman's dense verbal surfaces and cross-purpose dialogue recall Beckett and
Pinter as well as the language poets—Bruce Andrews, Charles Bernstein, Steve
McCaffery—who are his contemporaries. But Wellman's uniqueness may well
be his preoccupation with chrestomathy, *useful learning,* or, more properly,
Useful Knowledge, as Gertrude Stein called her fascinating book of 1928.

Stein's "useful knowledge" has to do with such notoriously non-useful
topics as "Wherein Iowa Differs from Kansas and Indiana" or "The Difference Between the Inhabitants of France and the Inhabitants of the United
States of America." In a similar vein, Wellman's teachings are never the obvious lessons. In the playful sections of his "Chrestomathy," with its head-
ings like *"perot* (rhymes with 'parrot')," Wellman dissociates himself from
the "false moralism" of contemporary PCdom, even, even that of the
"earnest, politically committed theater downtown in New York." PC, he
posits, stems from the fear that "communication with the widest possible
audience has failed" and hence the playwright frantically tries to please the
"public" by preaching this or that PC dogma rather than engaging the "low
politics of actual people, living their complicated, actual, ridiculous lives."

In a Wellman play, the "low politics of actual people" turn out to be as in-
structive as they are hilariously funny. Consider the opening dialogue between two suburban neighbors in *Albanian Softshoe:*

SUSAN   I can't believe it.

NELL   You can't imagine how difficult this is.

SUSAN   Oh, yes, yes . . . Still, I'm stunned.

NELL   I saw him do it. Could've called the police you know.

SUSAN   It's not that I don't want to believe you. It's just.
             Oh darn. I'm just so disappointed.

NELL   All I can say is that I thought more of Harry.

SUSAN   Oh, he thinks the world of you and Bill.

N E L L	Can I trust you to do what has to be done?
S U S A N	I'll confront him with it, what you've told me,
	tell him he needs help, that we'll need a lawyer.
N E L L	If Bill had his way Harry'd need a pack of lawyers.
S U S A N	But I know he never *meant* any harm.

This exchange is at once wholly familiar and yet as "strange" as the "sunny afternoon" of the stage directions. "I can't believe it," Susan exclaims, evidently having been told by her "best friend" next door about the nameless crime her husband Harry has committed. Nell must tell it all for Susan's own good; Susan is appropriately "disappointed" and "stunned." But next thing we know—and this is a Wellman trademark—the tone has shifted. Harry "needs help"—the standard contemporary cliché about psychic trauma (everyone, it seems, needs "help") but it turns out that he needs, not a shrink, but a lawyer, indeed, in Nell's malicious words, "a pack of lawyers." And this despite the fact that—again, the cliché—"But I know he never *meant* any harm."

Pinteresque as this dialogue is, it quickly turns Gothic in the next scene, in which Susan tells Harry, "It's about Jill." Jill, we assume, is Nell and Bill's daughter (note the rhyming names); and it's only after an unapologetic Harry says, "I keep thinking about it, how much I wanted it, how good it felt," that we learn that the "fucking bitch" who's "been asking for it for months" is not the young girl next door—not, for that matter, any woman—but literally a bitch—that is, the neighbor's dog, whom Harry enjoyed running over and reducing to a "pancake" in the driveway. When Susan responds, "You need help, Harry. You're sick," hechanges the subject by confessing to her that something else is wrong: namely, "I keep finding myself following people."

It's a delicious grammatical twist. A harried husband might well tell his wife, "I'm finding myself being followed," but invert the passive construction and you have the absurdity of "I keep finding myself following people." Such locutions suggest that Harry is suffering from what he refers to as "metal fatigue," and as the play continues, that fatigue transforms Susan and Harry into Rachel and Fred, then Ginny and Art, a couple busy putting "tens and twenties" into the clothes drier even as they continue with their New

Age self-help talk. And before we know it, the suburban scene morphs into science fiction adventure, replete with extraterrestrials, sinister Albanian characters, and a fairy tale ending in which Wolfert (Man) marries an Ora ("No one but him ever saw her") and "They were very happy."

Here and in such plays as *Cleveland,* another brilliant send-up of suburban life, in which Mom has bumped off Dad the Trotskyite and the senior prom is full of "Mirandan whispertalk," Wellman's aim is to expose the sheer terror and irrationality of everyday life as cycled through the euphemisms of mediaspeak. Perhaps the masterpiece in this vein is the site-specific theater piece *Bad Penny,* designed for Bow Bridge in Central Park—a poetic drama that subtly questions the meaning of representation itself. "Sometimes," says First Woman, "the sky reminds me of the / sea, or sometimes it doesn't remind / me of anything at all, much, and / I pay no attention and sometimes / the sky looks like its own reflection / in an oily puddle of rain water. . . . Sometimes / I think the sky is only pretending to / be the sky, or that it's a fake image of / the true image of the sky, like what you / see in a puddle, and that in fact there's / no true sky at all."

First Woman continues in this vein. The plot thickens as First Man explains that he's in Central Park because he has "to change my goddam tire. There's no goddam gas station / over there (*Points east.*), so I figure, what / the hell, I walk across the park, maybe there's / a gas station over there (*Points west.*). Here is his description of the abandoned car: "It's a Ford Fairlane 500. Candy apple red. Two / four-barrel carburetors. Four on the floor. / Montana plates. Three hundred pounds of rock / salt in the trunk. Parked on 69th between Lex / and Park. Parked illegally. I hate parks." This wonderfully "site-specific" description is now questioned by the second and third men on the scene who argue that (1) Ford doesn't make the Fairlane any more; (2) if the First Man had a Fairlane, we wouldn't park such a fancy car on the street; (3) there are plenty of gas stations on the East Side; and (4) no one could lift a car up without a jack, wrench, and tire iron. And so it goes, all the characters now interrupting one another, bickering, remembering real or invented incidents from their past, and becoming increasingly aggressive until First Man is carried off by the mysterious Boatman of Bow Bridge. The remaining men and women now constitute a mock Greek chorus that pronounces on what has happened:

What you don't know can't hurt
you; make hay while the sun
shines; soon ripe, soon rotten;
if every man would sweep his
own doorstep the city would
soon be clean; the dog returns
to his own vomit; the exception
proves the rule, do as I say,
not as I do; dead men tell no
tales; call no man happy
till he dies . . .

and so on, in what is a wonderfully mad catalogue of contaminated proverbs and aphorisms, culminating, after another twenty lines or so, in the finale of First Woman, who concludes on a note of religious incantation—"For the Way is ever difficult to discover"—that recalls T. S. Eliot's *Family Reunion* or *Murder in the Cathedral.*

Bad Penny ("A bad penny always turns up") exemplifies Wellman's very special fusion of allusion, skewed aphorism, advertising copy, and everyday speech. Other dramatists have parodied contemporary political and media jargon, but I don't know of another who has Wellman's learning, command of language, and range of exempla. He can introduce the Greek tragic note ("call no man happy / till he dies") because he has laid the groundwork of his Central Park West site so carefully and conscientiously, that the "moral" at the end of the play is both true and untrue. At the same time, his characters often sound exactly like the people one really does overhear talking on the park bench; their arguments and disagreements are wholly familiar. Again, if you think Wellman is exaggerating, just think of the November 2000 discussion about "chads"—those four little connectors holding the punch-out circles of the Florida ballot that determine whether a vote was or was not actually cast.

But Wellman, far from being merely trendy, is also a very classical playwright. Consider the final play in this volume, *Cat's-Paw*, which is Wellman's Don Juan play, or rather, as he says in his headnote, Don Juan combined with Faust. He tells us, "I wanted my Juan to be an absence, not a presence; so I made two rules, and two rules only: there must be no men in the play, and further, there must be no talk of men in the play. My *Don Juan* was, thus, a play impossible to write—almost." Impossible to write because even the most female and feminist of plays—think of *The Trojan Women*—refer continuously to men, if only to revile them, deny their worth, or cut down their power.

Wellman's "Don Juan in Hell" has four characters: "the Mother, Jane Bub's mother, visiting from the Midwest; Jane Bub, her Mother's daughter; Jo Rudge, Jane Bub's best friend; and Lindsay Rudge, Jane Bub's best friend's daughter." Its first three scenes take place on great heights: the observation deck of the Empire State Building, the observation deck at the World Trade Center, and the Statue of Liberty, as if to say that women alone must exist in a purer, more spiritual realm. Only in the last scene do we shift to a dark hallway in Federal Superior Court in Lower Manhattan, where Jo Rudge is to be tried for trespassing inside the Statue of Liberty's raised arm.

Fathers, brothers, lovers—these don't exist in *Cat's-Paw*; only very occasionally do we hear of public men like Lenin, Bob Dole—and Don Juan himself. But Wellman's world of mothers and daughters, daughters and their friends, older and younger generation, is nothing if not poisonous. Cut off one sex completely, the play implies, and you have the "hell is other people" situation Sartre never dreamt of when he wrote *No Exit*. Yet it would be unfair to call *Cat's-Paw* sexist, for the implication is that an all-male world would be equally horrifying. It is the elimination of half the human species that creates the sense of "only air and misery" to which Jane and Jo refer.

The most experimental play in *The Bad Infinity* was surely *Terminal Hip*, a monologue created from what Wellman calls "the undiscovered continent of bad writing." Its idea came from H. L. Mencken's *The American Language*, which gave the poet-playwright the idea of creating the most awful combinations possible like "If I hadda been, I mighta could," and following them to their logical conclusions. "For two and a half years," writes Wellman, "I wrote a page or two every day, pages full of clumsy constructions, double (and triple) negatives, demented neologisms, and every conceivable combination of out of fashion, dated, or wholly artificial slang. Not to mention argot, cant, the tortured language of the workplace and the pitchman. I explored verbal detritus of every kind."

The second half of the resulting manuscript became *Terminal Hip*. The first half is the title play of this new volume, "a spectral portrait," as Wellman calls it in the headnote, "and chronical of America through the medium of bad language." As such, *Cellophane,* like *Terminal Hip,* is perhaps more poem than play, a long monologue or poetic sequence divided into sections and subsections, that impose great demands on the actor who speaks it all. Such monologue does not, of course, make for easy reading and before I actually saw *Terminal Hip* and *Cellophane* performed, I had my doubts about them. Could Wellman sustain the dramatic impulse through pages and pages of univocal speech? Could one character hold the audience's interest?

The answer is a resounding yes, given that these monologues are not, in fact, lyric but insistently dramatic and curiously theatrical in their address to the audience. Indeed, these "bad language" monologues consistently posit one or more interlocutors to be questioned, bullied, or cajoled. *Cellophane's* first part, "From *Mad Potatoes,*" begins with the passage:

AIN'T I SOCIETY, YOU SAY,
You ain't seen nothing yet hardly.
Not nobody don't chew no tobacco nomore nowheres here.

And section 6 begins:

Say them potatoes been longtime round say
At cat.
Whyfor not?
Allatime did.
Once the dog are you got pearly X.
Place upon a put why.
Globs of it.

"At cat" is the leitmotif of this section—an amazing debasement of the most primary of grammatical constructions. The rhyming monosyllables *at* and *cat* each belong to a hundred commonplace phrases—"at home," "at sea," "at rest," "at bat"; or again, "the cat," "a cat," "my cat," "pussy cat," "hungry cat," and so on. But the one arena in which *at* and *cat* can't exist is together. All the more reason why the simple "at cat" becomes so memorable. In section 3 of the second part, "From *Hollowness,*" we read,

Fire trash causes fire tracks.
Track fires stop fire trains.
Throw your trash up in the air.
X . . . (Y) . . .
Place where gas.
Sheer drop.

This sounds like a shorthand or defective version of a computer printout or web page providing rules for some industrial or household process. "X all the way to Crazy Day on Power Corn." It sounds so familiar.

How does Wellman keep the momentum of the piece for the hour or so of performance? Read *Cellophane* and you will note that, as in any artful poetic text, individual items are carefully related. The word and grammar pool is in fact quite restricted, so that when we come to the Elizabethan inflection of "Have you hat enough for this, or canst?" we want to reply "At cat." Or again, the X's and Y's (X and Y chromosomes?) recur throughout, culminating, at the piece's end, in "As if X on fire kilt the bar. / Won't, bore, detonate, cream in one's pants, / offer chew to mysterious stranger. / Go on being as if you didn't blow it." We can almost picture this "scene," the blowout occurring under those cellophane wraps.

At the heart of Mac Wellman's theater is the paradox that the exempla of "awful" word combinations heard onstage can help us to acquire the language we need to negotiate our daily lives. But this "useful learning" is never didactic or tendentious; it is, on the contrary, hilariously funny and hence enormously entertaining. Wellman is our latter-day Brecht, providing the *Verfremdung*, the "making strange" that makes us see what has been before us all along. Indeed—and here is a second paradox—reject naturalism as he may, Wellman, in the final analysis, can be understood as the most clear-eyed of realists. The limits of his language measure with exactitude the limits of his—and our—world.

MARJORIE PERLOFF

CELLOPHANE

A Chrestomathy of 22 Answers to 22 Wholly Unaskable & Unrelated Questions Concerning Political & Poetic Theater

I encountered the term geezer theater at a symposium in Los Angeles on the subject of playwriting. One of my Angeleno colleagues offered the term as quoted from a young person when asked why he (or she) never bothered to frequent the theater. A "furball" is literally a ball of fur coughed up by a cat after completing the daily feline ablutions. In my play *Sincerity Forever*, two furballs from Belial and Abaddon (places in Hell) make their appearance. These furballs are demonic creatures, given over to the joys of mockery. The furball alphabet begins much like that of ancient Greek, but soon wiggles off strangely.

Night rests like a ball of
fur on my tongue.
—RITA DOVE

What man, god or hero
Shall I place a tin wreath
upon?
—EZRA POUND

He can only behold
With unaffrighted eyes,
The horrors of the deep
And terror of the skies.
—THOMAS CAMPION

α *alpha*

AN INCOMPLETE dramatic action figures forth a shadow, or limb, that completes itself variously—like the flinch response to a pulled punch—in the imaginary space of an audience member's active awareness. Whether this kind of response is entirely successful dramatically, the one the author intended and would claim responsibility for, is another question. (Says furball: Go on. Just try and ask it! [Slasher plays. Gut-wrenching "drama." Son enters, carrying Dad's bloody spleen.]) Whatever happens, the equilibrium of events will be restored, entropy achieved, the action completed, the first act pistol fired, the angry ghost avenged, the final breath exhaled, what you will. The question left hanging should be: Is the inspiriting chaos the full or the blank kind? The void of plenitude, or that of nullity? The emptiness of Lear, or the little lost boy within of our contemporary American ho-hum classics? From Miller to Mamet, and so forth, to Foote and beyond.

β *beta*

THE HO-HUM classic takes place in the simple time of clocks, not the Wild Time of nonlinear narrative. The Wild Time of poetic theater can bend, slow, break, or fork. Narrative is not destroyed by the nonlinear, it is merely disguised. Disguised as something else, which is where the poetry comes in. The new science of chaos with its use of fractal geometry, for instance, reveals some interesting things about narrative, about the way breaks in the shape and flow of a narrative event, breaks that disrupt the flow of energy or information and redistribute it elsewhere, confirm the presence of deep structures we do not normally perceive, because they do not function in linear time. For chaos as architect manifests itself as other (and more) than a merely trivial messiness. Like the time-honored messiness of the typical American ho-hum classic.

In theater we sense the presence of these deep structures any time an actor on stage, within the role of character, does something—anything!—that truly surprises us or takes our breath away, any time the narrative takes a left turn out of the homilies and monorail moralizing of "geezer* theater" into the strange world of pure appearance, a land beyond the forest of symbols (where Little Red Riding Hood really went, where Dracula waits for us all, where Baudelaire was headed before he discovered the little boy within).

γ *gamma*

TAKE THE GREEKS. In Hesiod's *Theogony* there is an ancient debate concerning the meaning of the word *chaos* (χαοσ). A comparison of variants would seem to indicate that the cosmic region represented thereby cannot be either the earth or the sky, but is the gap between these. This suggestive notion points to one quality of what is considered to be formless, disordered, i.e., chaotic, namely that it shows what the boundaries of things *really* are— by the mere fact of its existence. Chaos, as a negative force, a boundary phenomenon, figures forth a positive shadow.

Chaos has been banned from all the better class of human endeavor in the West because it is a fundamentally subversive idea. (Occasional outlaws, like Alfred Jarry or John Cage, turn up now and again, but they are distinct aberrations. Geezer would like to romanticize them; geezer would not like to ponder their ideas.) What if form doesn't follow (obvious) function? If some

---

*The term *geezer* is impossible to define, because the only poetic thing about a geezer is a passion for disguise, a passion disguised as the voice of experience; however, the bedrock of Geezerdom may be the assumption that time itself is a uniform, evenly distributed throughout the universe, and may be told from clocks; the soul of a geezer is a clock.

things are *devoid* of purpose, hovering all too near the angelic *pleroma* of total meaninglessness? If some other things are intrinsically useless? Inexplicable? Ineluctably themselves? Scary, furry things? Terrifying . . . (!)

This kind of knowledge might be too much at odds with our political and aesthetic shibboleths: that aesthetic and ethical givens inform all art, indeed inform the more basic categories of coherence and identity upon which all higher human endeavors are based.

δ delta

DISORDER occurs in all the arts. And the argument against an "organic" conception of art goes back to the pre-Socratic philosopher Heraclitus: ". . . nothing in nature more beautiful than a random assortment of unrelated objects." But what I'm talking about is not this. Because even in "classic" aesthetics a certain amount of disorder must always be factored in. The most high-minded, rigid of these cannot wholly avoid it. But what, implies the demon (furball) Heraclitus, if the function of disorder goes further, deeper? And what if we conceive of it not negatively, but positively, as the fundamental, unseen architect of all that is orderly, possesses a shape, boasts a fixed structural configuration: the world of objects and their appearance? What if chaos should be the true determiner and shaper of representation itself? Whisper that across the table at the next theater communications group conference; or at the next meeting of the board of directors; or within earshot, at the back of the theater, of the dramaturgs, where they sit in the shadows, scheming. See how long it will take for those in charge to show you the door. We like our Greeks rational, "life-affirming," "human," "Classical."

ε epsilon

THE CONTINUOUS fracturing of events, their dispersal, reintegration, and final, absolute disintegration in the medium of time, whether it be clock or stage, seems to be the basis of theater narrative itself. Real continuities in a non-geezer narrative are easily confused with errant discontinuity, because time is bent, sped up rapidly, or radically slowed, to move focus accordingly, shifting from one kind of character display, event-cycle, or energy field to a related but very different one—all for the elaboration of the narrative.

All this is as old as the description of Achilles' shield and its peculiar relation—or seeming nonrelation—to the plot of the *Iliad*; or as the power and strangeness of Beckett's oddly obsessive gestural minutiae and Pinter's illustrious pauses; or as—more recently—the intricate frame-within-frame of Len Jenkin's plays and Stuart Sherman's antic abbreviations in much of his work. An episode in a work of art may appear confused because focus has "popped" up or down to a radically different landscape of scale. What appears to be mere "noise" may be the meat of the matter, the essence of the argument. That's why I always look where I'm not "supposed to" when I go to a play. Time's arrow sometimes errs and lead us astray. The unities are for Aristotle, and the avatars of geezer theater, those who run most of the big institutions and will admit disorder into their own scheme of things only if it is safe: the touching prologue of the "memory" play, or that odious figment of geezer wishful thinking, the flashback.

▽ upsidedown

DOES IT REALLY matter, theoretically speaking, whether the events which constitute the drama *King Lear* are a representation or a presentation simple? Or those which constitute the drama *Street Scene*, or those of *Dress Suits for Hire*? Of course not. All that does matter is that, at some level, i.e., "scale," these be taken for what they are; as events proper, more or less intriguing, more or less revelatory of the human condition, more or less engrossing. As events—not nonevents, the geezer building blocks for a theater designed to tidy up our collective moral depravity and make us more clean-living citizens, more responsible members of whatever human community. (When I hear the word *community* in the dog-eat-dog world of theater I know someone, usually a community leader, wants something from me. And probably something I might be loathe to part with if they would spell it out. Something like my personal idiosyncrasies, my dignity, or my soul—certainly my dollars.)

Theater begins in a state of theatricality that is the repudiation of a split between presentation and representation, between performance and illusion, between making a show and "drama" (conceived of as the better class of the-

ater). The "meaningfulness" of events on stage need not be conditioned totally by a lot of antiquated rules of character, conflict, exposition, resolution,
denouement and the like. *Peripeteia, anagnorisis?* Please, I prefer simple
χαος—which figures forth invisible vectors of strangeness, charm, and
thrill; vectors of voodoo, rage, desire, and hatred, throughout the entire theater. In fact, a whole new vocabulary may be necessary to do justice to the
"hot," unstable, poetic theater of our time—as well as the "hot," unstable
theater of all time. I am talking about low-rent poetic furball theater. Pan
time and space. Texture rather than structure; framing and fire escapes versus ancient conventions of the geezer theater establishment and geezer
academy. The world conceived of as a panicked space-time continuum
irradiated by theater rays. Exorcism of the drama virus. Belasco possessed
by the spirit of Spinoza; Spinoza possessed by Groucho.

Isn't this layering of fictions the way real life actually *feels* most of the
time? Isn't it what we deeply suspect as comprising, both provisionally and
ultimately, "the way things are" anyway, really? Aren't we all employed
mostly in the act of more or less imperfectly impersonating ourselves? Scary
thought—scary, furry thought! (The rubric of the "poetic" itself may be too
tame, too much a word spoiled by muttering geezer associations. Toothless
geezer rambling. Gummed phlights of phantasy. Too close to that ghastly
anachronism, the "poetical.")

 moo

INDEED, it seems central to the notion of theatricality *per se* (as opposed to
theater itself) that it repel distinctions of presentation versus representation
as spurious to its central aim, which is to make something happen, show forth
for what it is, in a given space. In theater the end of this appearance, this activity, is awe, wonder, and the sophisticated pleasures so lovingly chronicled in
traditional criticism: pathos, identification, empathy, and the "cleansing" of the
audience's emotion. Concretely, complexly, chaotically. And this is because—
however its forms evolve, its human or unhuman passions are adumbrated—
theater *narrative* is born by and of chaos, out of the materials of chaos, and this
narrative appearance is the most wonderful thing we know. (Further, furball
knows what geezer never suspects: it may be the only thing we know.)

➤ *woop*

WHAT WE HAVE instead is the Theater of Good Intentions. The theater of the nonevent. (See below.) What is especially ironic about all this is that, just as performance culture has emerged from na(t)ive American Naturalism, so that naturalism seems to have derived from the efforts of a whole generation of supposedly tough-minded leftist screenwriters and playwrights, Odets, Trumbo, Miller, and Lawson among them. These writers were led to naturalism for obvious reasons: originally it was art on behalf of the poor, the disenfranchised; also they wanted to transcend the geezerdom of their time: wacky, fake-elegant Broadway. They wanted as much of the gritty truth of real-life America as they could load into their work. Lawson in particular seems to have recognized the difficulty of reconciling an objective social theater with the interiorizing bias of the Stanislavsky system (at least as practiced in the States), but he could see no alternative. American actors were trained in that way, and one had to use them.

The paradox is that the leftists' political agenda may have led them to concoct a kind of theater that would eventually mutate into just the sort of mindless and trivial sensationalizing "entertainment" they despised. Naturalism possessed by its intention of approaching the grainy, textured rawness of "real-life" ends up sacralizing the nonevent. Geezer theater. But in the context of American culture this is easily comprehensible. The need for little epiphanies rapidly escalates into a hunger for ever larger fixes of the stuff.

 gums

THE NONEVENT (as described by Daniel Boorstin, cited in *Naming Names*, by Victor Navasky [1980, Viking], pp. 322–23.):

1. It is not spontaneous. (Someone has planned, planted, or initiated it.)
2. It is planted for the immediate purpose of being reported or reproduced.
3. Its relation to underlying reality is ambiguous. (A train wreck is real.)
4. It is a self-fulfilling prophecy.

rabbit

THE PERFORMANCE culture of our time sacralizes nonevents because in performance terms they demand a manipulated response. The nonevent contains an image of itself, is possessed by its own significance. How many well-intentioned plays have we seen that are so bewitched, so mesmerized by their own profundity that they feel more like the reanimated corpses of plays than plays proper? No wonder the young hate (geezer) theater. The laugh track on TV sitcoms is no more egregious than the canned spontaneity of so many of our most highly touted contemporary plays. Laughter, tears, gut-wrenching emotion, and publicly induced hysteria: all generated, as if by magic, on demand ("cried so much the tears curled the pages of my *Playbill*": geezer knows he/she is alive because his/her face makes water). Geezer—whether a producer, critic, or audience member—is never interested in a theater that might be the occasion for reflection, or introspection.

Accordingly, the kinds of theater and playwriting that have found favor most in These States are devoted to art as social conditioning. A theater of the nonevent. The *real* event, which is supposed to be what naturalism and even political theater are after, must always vanish in this context. This is because the real event, being real, is also elusive, spontaneous, unpredictable, and freely (chaotically) determined; hence it can never be an occasion for that species of performance that is totally assured of its meaningfulness, and so outlandishly complacent in this belief. The real event usually happens on our stage only by accident, as when an actor has had to replace another and goes on stage script in hand (I'm thinking of Bill Raymond in the run of *A Lie of the Mind* some years back). All this sounds foolishly paradoxical; but paradox is at the heart of our theater and our culture.

XX *exxon*

GEEZER = theater of the nonevent.

J [*willowy*

<small>P O E T I C</small> theater is not, like geezer, a V.M.O. (*very massive object,* a term from astronomy).

❞❞ ❞❞ *tigertiger*

<small>P O E T I C</small> theater pieces consist of surprising texts, in surprising contexts. When well produced, they are surprising as only the genuinely new can be. (The geezer of Theater History, however, seeks perennial [hegemonic] stability and always tells me the same thing: "It can't be done." Then, when I do it, geezer replies: "It's been done before." You can't win with theater geezers.) Often the textual and gestural elements feel separately tracked, to reveal another dark truth known to furball but not to geezer: people don't always know what they mean when they say something, people tell lies, kid themselves, are mistaken, self-deceived, ill-spoken, at a loss for words at the critical moment (the Billy Budd syndrome). Sometimes people don't even know—literally—what they are saying. Or doing. Really. This happens: what man, god, or demon could have dreamt up that ultimate geezer, Ross Perot? Go figure.

The poetic is intrinsically political. It flies up in the face of the unpolitical and squawks (Furball whinnies: if it's obvious, it's obviously *wrong*). The poetic escapes the tyranny of the ostensible (i.e., warm and clutchy issue-oriented plays) by treating them as V.M.O.s, to be cracked and split open. The demonic ironist (possessed by demonic furball ironicity) writes plays that mimic—up to a point—the products of geezer theater. Then, treating its sleek regional theater host as a fat, insensible V.M.O., it erupts from within, howling, like an alien chest-burster. No wonder the gray eminences who preside over geezerdom are suspicious of poetic theater. They should be.

❋❋❋ *silvery*

<small>P O E T I C</small> theater lacks two things indispensable for geezer theater: patience and reverence. Poetic theater is seriously *silly.* Furthermore, poetic theater takes impossible and ridiculous shortcuts, makes a mockery of the Aris-

totelian better class of narrative. It redescribes narrative as a field of mutable loci, an unstable topos of strangeness and charm (in the physicists' sense), where reference and cross-reference fission throughout; where meanings radiate simultaneously in all directions, creating a text like a Sierpinski carpet—infinitely sparse and infinitely populated—with significant chimes and rimes of reason. This is complex complexity, and it resembles life itself more than the products of "realistic" theater because it, unlike them, is Real Life itself. On stage, for all to hear, see, and feel. Its deck is not stacked in the interest of a univocal, authorial geezer muse.

The poetic recapitulates the rough-and-tumble of the actual creative moment. Since an important component of this creative moment as it elongates through time is choice—choice among options, choice of image chain, association path, possible narrative outcome, etc.—an audience is always involved with choice *per se,* is always confronted with a delectiary of potential choices, aesthetic, ethical, and ultimately political. Thus, it is the open-ended character of poetic theater that so enables it with optional richness—often in the form of answers to questions no one has heretofore bothered to ask. And this in the midst of apparent chaos.

Poetic theater is hilariously based on the tragic sense of life, in the realization that no one stands outside the dialectic of choice and responsibility, futility and fatefulness that the truly engaged life affords and compels. The poetic is seriously silly. *Seely:* soul-full.

✳ thistle

A DEFINITION of *seely*—silly (OED):
I: Observant of due season; punctual.
II: Happy, blissful; fortunate, lucky, well-omened, auspicious.
III: Spiritually blessed, soul-filled.
IV: Pious, holy, good.

▢ hubert

THE PROBLEM is not with talent or with ideas. There are plenty of talented people, people with wonderful ideas, working within the confines of the

theater V.M.O. It may finally be a question of passion—something theater people take for granted (in themselves)—or what we regard as passion. Somehow, however, the context for this curiously compartmentalized theater betrays its aspirations. It's as if the ideas, the ideals of those involved, mean literally nothing. Over and over, geezer theater, when it tries to get serious, entombs interesting ideas—alarming, complex, intriguing, even *new* ideas!—in the hokey framework of story theater, thus repudiating content in the name of a reassuring but totalizing form. How many boring plays about brilliant scientists, thinkers, artists, and philosophers can you think of without even trying? The nonevent gobbling up the true with Pac-Man vengeance. Why are we so resistant to the truly provocative in our theater?
Geezer—V.M.O.

banana

THE LITTLE lost boy within = a geezer waiting to happen.

<> *perot (pronounced "parrot")*

IT'S HARDLY headline news to say that the false moralism of American theater is a form of thought control. On the other hand, it does need to be quietly and firmly stated. Whether it be the terminally upbeat product developed by the more ghastly of the Broadway regional sausage machines or what passes for earnest, politically committed theater downtown in New York or other supposedly sophisticated places, like San Francisco or the Twin Cities, false moralism ignores context, stresses the ostensible, and in particular forces a valorization of the real event by reducing it to mere performance—a suspect signifier.

►⇢↗ *phood*

NOW CERTAINLY it must be granted that, as Tony Kushner has argued, it is, in fact, a good thing to be "politically correct," i.e., politically sensitive to others, enlightened, and responsible for one's choices. (Tony K: great playwright, author of the only current Big Play with Big Ideas [*Angels in America,* a true gullywhumpus of a theatrical V.M.O.] that both furballs and the Heraclitean, demonic ironist of this tract can truly get behind.) the dangers of PC all but disappear when compared to the Truly Evil lies and distortions of the mainstream right-wing media. That being granted, it must still be admitted that theater PC of the dry-rot academic and institutional kind—the truly venal and spiteful variety—stems from a strange species of dread and self-loathing, and, in particular, from the fear that in our time, communication with the widest possible audience has failed—and is, in fact, no longer a transaction with much to offer. This fear is a pervasive one in our society, and not merely in the world of the arts. You will find it on the Right, on the Left, and in the vast realm of ethically in-between—wherever the shadow of the geezerly has fallen. What it boils down to finally is a deep suspicion of, and distaste for, democracy.

Of the political correctness of the Right I have nothing to say at present; it deserves a far more massive and meticulous discussion than I could ever manage in a few pages. The PC of the Right is almost literally the air we breathe, and there is no doubt that the air is poisoned. The question I prefer to address here is whether the PC of the cultural Left (as opposed to the political—a substance always, and mysteriously, in short supply in These States) has not crippled itself by an oddly misappropriate focus on correct language *per se,* a focus which is only too easily co-opted by the forces of corporate (geezer) theater.

Professor Brian Hansen, in *Theater: Dynamics of the Art,* has written of the theater experience as a Lockean-Rousseauian contract arrangement between show and audience. So, in these terms, the PC of corporate (geezer) theater acts as if it regarded the contract as a broken one. The wider audience is the enemy, an object of suspicion; the theater itself, a house of pain. Why? There are a number of issues here, all of them complex. One has to do with the way idealistic young theater artists grow up, as it were, in this culture. Often as not, they are driven out by sheer economics. Poor people do not often choose to make a career in the theater, for the very good reason that there is rarely if ever a career to be made, without embracing careerism itself, in the most crass and vulgar sense. Theater survivors, thus, are often persons disabused of the practical substance of their youthful political and social ardor but nostalgically connected to the sentiment of the old rhetoric. Economic reality impels them to seek refuge in the corporate rather than the improvised models of earlier days. Thus is the passionate young theater artist slowly self-embalmed by ever larger doses of corporate double-talk until the hideous transformation (into full-blown geezerhood) is complete. The "progressive" and socially "aware" theater that is produced satisfies neither the deepest longings of the individual artist in question nor the nebulous yearnings of the subscription audience— not to mention the board of directors. It may simply be that American (geezer) theater is like the perennial nerd who wants to be liked a little too much for any self-respecting audience to really stay interested.

The audience is another complex problem, because it is neither very enthusiastic nor are its concerns very enlightened. This audience has been unable to "get" what progressive theater has been about, at the least, since the '30s, what with the Group Theater, Brecht, and the subsequent blacklist period (decisive for American theater and its timorous notion of what constitutes risk-taking).

Thus, the geezer theater doubts itself and its mission, senses it has failed to get its point across, whether it be an ethic, a vision of the calamitous horror of the recent past (war, slavery, imperialism, more war, the holocaust, yet more war), or a possible way out of the nightmare of history through a new, wholly secular transcendence. Failed in the sense of inspiring a common notion of "we." Failed in the most basic sense: of operating purposively on any level of what it perceives as meaningful historicity.

Accordingly, geezer PC, out of a sense of injured merit, has both promulgated and accepted an unavowed fate, consisting of the narrowest, most spiritually impoverished, and least wiggly of narrative lines. It enacts this doom, an act of self-flagellating prophetic immolation, by self-censorship, self-referential cross-talk, and a refusal to engage either political foes or the public at large in a way either can understand. Uniformity of opinion becomes an absolute, real discussion a threat, aesthetics a deeply suspect project, not to mention the realm of potential usurpers, Quislings, and the politically unenlightenable. The (corporate) PC geezer seeks control through language games and fatuous attempts at radical redescription through a cleansed terminology. A terminology cleansed of poetic multiplicity, and the danger of wayward narrative inference. But the world thus redescribed (like the sad places ethnically "cleansed" in former Yugoslavia) is a phantom world—a world of ghosts. Such activity is as much nonaction, in political terms, as the nonevent described above by Boorstin. Poets and furballs have always sided in this dispute with William Blake, who preferred crooked roads "of genius" to the straight-arrow, improved variety, because the latter lead directly, not to the Emerald City, but to the concrete abutments of geezerdom—whether PC or not.

That the terminology of Marxism seems stale, morally nil—if not reprehensible—does not mean socialism itself is dead. Surely, the age-old vision of a secular *paradiso,* with room for all peoples, of all races, ethnicities, and cultural propensities and affiliations is still an overwhelming one. If, as Isaiah Berlin has often pointed out, all political and ethical ends may not be ultimately compatible, it does not follow that more in the way of a general reconciliation is not possible. Equality, the dream of a better world for all, with a concomitant reduction of human suffering, and the increase of the means of happiness, are not silly pipe dreams. And if they are *silly*—they are so in that curiously neglected, old sense of the word: light-hearted, joyous, full of the bright playfulness of the soul.

ϑ *wiggle*

CHAOS. The gap between Earth and Sky. I would like to live in the Land of Chaos—between the tyranny of the Angels of the Upper Aire, who control all the institutions of the Ostensible, the Visible, the Obvious, and that of the spirits of the earth-bound, who want to control and censor our thought with their chronic and chthonic suspiciousness and obsession with age-old hatreds. I want to live among the few who actually enjoy the company of people who are different from themselves.

◯ *dumpdidum*

IDENTITY POLITICS overlaps significantly with the vast empire of geezerdom. But the notion of Identity Politics prevalent in the theater is as compromised as the one conditioning PC, for the higher politics of corporate theater geezerdom has only a passing familiarity with the low politics of actual people, living their complicated, actual, ridiculous lives. Geezer theater has co-opted the rhetoric of IP for its own banal and careerist ends; geezer theater, too, suborns and undermines ideals of diversity and multiculturalism in order that its institutions may survive and prosper, survive the unspeakable invasiveness of the Other. IP rhetoric allows the corporate a wiggly disguise. I mean, in particular, the big cheeses of the better class of funding industries, the foundations and the academies.

Big Cheeses believe Big Money ought to go to PC geezers sensitive to IP so they will create lots of theatrical V.M.O.s. The Big Play as V.M.O. must have one Big Idea per play to qualify as both PC and sensitive to IP. The tip-off is that those who benefit from this kind of tactic are rarely "minority" individuals, whether they be African American, Native American, gay and lesbian, or whatever; institutions do, houses of pain forever inured to the myriad (chaotic) inner lives of the individual, houses of geezer sensibility— places where productions may come and go but the parking lot remains for all time. ("Minority": ghastly geezer moniker for the person geezer would suborn with snake-oil salesman smiles and back-pats.)

We as individuals may recapitulate the experience—mores and morals too—of the cultures we spring from, but that is not all we do. We also communicate with, and have commerce with, others who are decidedly, ineradicably, different from us, different in myriad other ways than the special half-dozen or so deemed decisive by PC geezers, ways that in myriad specific instances may be much more decisive than these.

△ Velveeta

H O W   O D D and laughable this would be were it not that real issues, of great ethical import, are at stake. My own feeling is that the weapons of PC discipline, terms like *racist, sexist, fascist, —— abuser, homophobe, gay-bashing* (at least when used euphemistically) ought to be used as little as possible, as a last resort. Terms like these are our trump cards. They lose power if employed promiscuously, and the fact that currently they are bandied about so carelessly is only one more demonstration of the desperate futility and self-hatred that pervades the Left. The problem with PC terminology is that it is fundamentally literal-minded and trivial—unpoetic; to the extent that it trivializes the abuses it seeks to redescribe, it does all who attempt, in their own lives, true political correctness, a great disservice.

We, as individual artists, do not need to be told who we are by the geezer authorities of PC institutions, any more than by the geezers of the Upper Aire, the sky people who rule us with their money. (Are they *that* different in the long run? Furball thinks not.) Furball knows too that the wonderful thing about theater in These States is that it is a *weed:* unkillable, bone-headed, demonic, democratic, and inherently diverse—in a word (world), SILLY.

☐ boxkite

POETIC THEATER is no respecter of values other than the wayward beanstalk of its own silly, but sensibly silly peregrinations. This is because poetic theater is simply more versatile than either conventional geezer or PC geezer theater, two similar chunks of the same old wedge of stale American (corporate) cheese.

Poetic theater's very refusal to stay put and be nailed down to a unitary point of view enables it to shift quickly from one narrative strategy to another, from one set of perceptions to another, from one vocabulary or set of vocabularies to others in a fashion that exponentially increases the ways of apprehending both text and world. This seems appropriate, given the times. All I would argue is that we need a place for poetic theater in our culture, because it offers us insights into ourselves and our world that seem unavailable otherwise.

If the denseness, idiosyncratic nature, and general unpackageability of its final products have pretty much precluded wide acceptance among American institutional theaters, so much the worse for them. By its very nature a truly poetic theater can never settle into the mold of geezer theater. The poetic always eludes the banality of the received idea, the time-honored, the enshrined, the "classical," the nonevent.

Poetic theater is not about correcting other people's bad thoughts; it is about the life which flows through all of us and which we barely understand. This life embodies an ethic which may not always be neatly paraphrasable, or even in palpable evidence, but without which we are only so much raw material for those who would redescribe us for their own ends, for the energy that is the carrier of this ethic implicates us all in its doings and we are all complicit in its waywardness.

Albanian
Softshoe

A little Naturalistic Family Play.

As an Entertainment for the

Dwellers of the Ice Moons of Saturn.

Heideggerian Flapdoodle and the

Search for Pancake. The Tale of

the Man Who Married an Ora.

Sometime in the mid-eighties I happened to pick up a Victorian travel book written by one of the many fearless English ladies chronicled so wonderfully by Eric Overmyer in his *On the Verge*. The author had journeyed throughout Albania, then a virtual *terra incognita*. Soon I was devouring whatever folklore and history I could find. The music, especially, I found mesmerizing, for I had never heard anything like it. Why Albania? Part of the attraction for me lay in that people's refusal to accommodate themselves to either Western or Eastern civilization. The Albanians seemed a nation of brigands, bandits, and outlaws, a people without even a written legal code because of their distrust of all things lawyerly. An Orientalist fantasy? Of course; but I

PERFORMANCE NOTES

The appearance of an asterisk within a speech indicates that the next speech begins to overlap at that point.
    Musical scores for "Anthem" and "Methane Cliffs" follow the text of the play.

decided to make creative use of my Orientalist illusion by using it to address a double agenda: first as the basis of a critique of the deceitful, lying, double-dealing ethos of my own time; and also as a means of addressing the topic of homelessness—but homelessness refracted through a strange lens, so that I might approach without it recourse to the platitudes of the so-called liberal press. Despite its oddities, *Albanian Softshoe* is one of my best plays (or because of them).

PERSONS OF THE PLAY

NELL FOX, later FOX PERSON and an ORA;

SUSAN WOLF, later RACHEL, GINNY, WOLFERT, and the MAN WHO
   MARRIED AN ORA;

HARRY WOLF, later FRED, ART, and a SLINKING FIGURE, an emissary of the
FALSE AHMED BEY, a *drangue* and a *calendar*;

THE MAN OF SHALA, an Albanian *comitadj*, or *bandit*;

WINGFOOT, another *drangue* and a *calendar*;

PANCAKE, a *drangue* of peculiar physiognomy;

a strange MAN;

THE ORA'S FATHER; and

ALBANIANS of all shapes and sizes and an AMERICAN FARMER.

Albanian Softshoe takes place at various locations within the planetary
system of Saturn.

Anthem
Oh we're back to the Balkans again.
Back to the joy and the pain—
What if it burns or it blows or it snows?
Oh we're back to the Balkans again.
Back where tomorrow the quick may be dead,
with a hole in the heart or a ball in the head.
Back where the passions are rapid and red.
Oh we're back to the Balkans again!

Act One

Scene one. A living room in the suburbs. Large unknown window center. A sunny afternoon, only strange. A strange fireplace filled with human bones. Doorway right. Elegant furnishings. Conventional—but strange—nature paintings on wall. A closet up left. Sofa, TV, etc. SUSAN WOLF *and her neighbor,* NELL FOX, *sit having coffee.* SUSAN *looks shocked.*

SUSAN   I can't believe it.

NELL   You can't imagine how difficult this is.

SUSAN   Oh, yes, yes . . . Still, I'm stunned.

NELL   I saw him do it. Could've called the police you know.

SUSAN   It's not that I don't want to believe you. It's just.
       Oh darn. I'm just so disappointed.

NELL   All I can say is that. I thought more of Harry.

SUSAN   Oh, he thinks the world of you and Bill.

NELL   Can I trust you to do what has to be done?

SUSAN   I'll confront him with it, what you've told me,
       tell him he needs help, that we'll need a lawyer.

NELL   If Bill had his way Harry'd need a pack of lawyers.

SUSAN   But I know he never *meant* any harm.

NELL   I know. I know. He just needs help, Susan. He needs it
       desperately. This is the only way.

SUSAN   He'll be home soon. You'd better go. I wouldn't want
          him to barge in on us like this.

NELL   Give me a ring. Or shall I call you?

SUSAN   You call me.

NELL   Okay.

SUSAN   I'm sorry, Nell.
          (*They embrace.*)

NELL   It's going to be all right, honey.

(NELL *goes out. Pause.* SUSAN *primps in the mirror. Turns on the radio.
Sits down and starts reading a magazine. The closet door opens. She
gets up and closes it, and returns to her reading. The door opens and
closes without her noticing. She looks up. Smiles.*)

Fade to black.

Scene two. Same as before. Night, only strange. HARRY *sits reading the
evening newspaper.* SUSAN *brings him a large drink.*

HARRY   Hey, Enver Hoxha died! How about that! The last real old-
          time Stalinist dictator.
          (*Raises glass.*)
          A toast to Enver Hoxha.

SUSAN   We have to talk, Harry. Nell came over. It's about Jill.
          (*He buries head in newspaper.*)

HARRY   What about Jill?

SUSAN   It's true then.

HARRY
          (*Lowering paper*)
          What are you talking about?

SUSAN   Don't lie to me, Harry. It's bad enough the way it is.
          Just come clean, for Christ's sake.
          (*She weeps.*)

HARRY What did Nell say?

SUSAN That if you don't seek professional help Bill'll call the police. Sue. The works.

HARRY I didn't do it.

SUSAN Please tell me the truth.

HARRY I've thought of suicide lately, Susan, and. I keep having this fantasy that I'm following this guy with a fez, and . . . Then there's the
obsession with Jill.

SUSAN Oh no.

HARRY Yes.

  (*Pause. He weeps.*)

  The guilt and the shame.

SUSAN So it is true

HARRY I couldn't help myself.

SUSAN What on earth do you mean?

HARRY I keep thinking about it, how much I wanted it, how good it felt.

SUSAN What about Jill's feelings?

HARRY It didn't matter. She's been driving me crazy for so long. So when I finally had the chance . . . Guess I just lost my head. It just happened.

SUSAN You could *do* something like that?

HARRY With relish. With animal glee. She was asking for it.

SUSAN You disgust me. They're right. They ought to throw the book at you.

HARRY That fucking bitch's been asking for it for months. There she was, sound asleep in our driveway. I looked in the

rear-view mirror. Popped the old tub into reverse and.
Floored it. Sent that dog one-way to dog paradise.
Floored it! Then forward, then back again. Then forward,
then back again. Till that evil, mangy hound was flat as
a pancake.

(*Steadies himself with drink.*)

No more dogshit in the pansies.
No more dogshit in the stringbeans, by God.

SUSAN   You do need help, Harry. You're sick,

HARRY   I'm not sorry, I tell you.

(*Pause.*)

There's something else, Susie. At work.

SUSAN   What. What is it?

HARRY   Nothing much. Some of the guys. Few missing checks.
And I keep finding myself following people. This man
with a fez . . .

SUSAN   Go on. I'm listening.

HARRY   I've talked to Hoskins. A good lawyer, Hoskins.

SUSAN   What's happening, dear?

HARRY   A little mix-up. Not much.

SUSAN   Can you be more specific?

HARRY   Not now. It's a delicate situation. Maybe a grand jury.

SUSAN   Did you do something illegal?

HARRY   Only a jot. The merest jot.

SUSAN   Explain.

HARRY   It's all legalese. Wouldn't make sense to you. Too
complicated. Contracts. That stuff. From overwork.
The strain.

SUSAN   Why'd you bring it up then?

HARRY   Well we might lose the house and car and stuff.

SUSAN   WHAT!?

HARRY   Don't get excited. It's not definite. I said *might*.
             Another drink?
             (*She goes out. He gets up. Paces. His tie clasp comes off.*)
             Metal fatigue in the tie clasp.

SUSAN
     (*Off.*)
             What's that?

HARRY   Tie clasp broke. Metal fatigue.
             (*She enters. Hands him the drink.*)

SUSAN   Let's hear it all.

HARRY   Some money disappeared. They say. Thanks.

SUSAN   Who say?

HARRY   Joe. Fred. Some of the guys in accounting.

SUSAN   How much.

HARRY   Four or five hundred. Thousand. Ah.

SUSAN   What does this have to do with you?

HARRY   I've been hitting OTB a lot lately. Bad month. Last
             year now! The fur coat, remember? Spain? All that?

SUSAN   I see.
     (*Pause.*)

HARRY   Basically we're, ah, wiped out. El facto.

SUSAN   You do need help.

HARRY   We're in this together, baby.

SUSAN   I'm not sure.

(*He starts pacing again.*)

> Metal fatigue in the tie clasp, ah . . .

SUSAN   What are you saying?

HARRY   It wasn't just me. It was George and Randy. And a few others. We've got a plan.

SUSAN   It better be good.

HARRY   We come down on them like a ton of bricks. Sue their asses before they know what hit 'em. Invoke the disclosures clause. Right.

SUSAN   What's that?

HARRY   It's all funny money anyway. Who cares?
(*He laughs.*)

> What am I worried about?

SUSAN   Is your name on the. Contract?

HARRY   It's on the prospectus. I think.

SUSAN   And anyone else's?

HARRY   Nope. Not that I . . .
(*Opens closet door. Looks in. We see the toe of a giant Albanian shoe.*)

> What's this? Some kind of summer gourd?

(*She looks.*)

SUSAN   That's odd. Cleaning lady must have left it.
(*She touches it gingerly.*)

> It looks vaguely Caribbean, doesn't it?

HARRY   Well, never mind.
(*Closes the closet.*)

> The industry still has a great future. Star Wars. Chips. All that stuff.

SUSAN   The car too?

HARRY   The car too. Everything. Lawn mower. All of it.

SUSAN   So where do we go from here?

HARRY   I'm not beaten, Susie. It wasn't my fault, I swear.
Ask anyone. Ask Sam. Ask Bill. Don't ask Bill. Anyone
else. Can't lay a finger on me.

SUSAN   You're immune, eh?
(*Goes to the kitchen to pour herself a drink.*)

HARRY   That's sarcasm, Susan. I distinctly heard sarcasm in your
voice. That's not called for.

SUSAN   You dumb bunny!

HARRY   Are there any attorneys on your side of the family?
Dick's an attorney, isn't he?

SUSAN   Corporate. He doesn't know aerospace.

HARRY   You sure? I though he knew aerospace.

SUSAN   He doesn't know aerospace.
(*Pause.*)

HARRY   Oh. Is dinner ready?

SUSAN   I had to clean up the mess in the driveway.

HARRY   Did I tell you I think I've been following somebody?
(*He gets up.*)
Let me see if there's anything for dinner.
(*Goes to kitchen.*)

SUSAN   It's getting dark earlier. Who did you say died?
(*He returns with a soft fork.*)

HARRY   What's going on around here. Look at this fork.
More metal fatigue. What the hell do you use
on the dishes? Sulphuric acid?

SUSAN   I can't explain it. It's the best Danish flatware.

HARRY   Ridiculous. Enver Hoxha died. President of Albania.

SUSAN   You sure you don't want to tell me about the money
        you've embezzled?

HARRY   Don't talk to me in that tone.

SUSAN   How should I?

HARRY   It's an interest-free loan from me to me in the name of
        the company. That's all. Standard practice. Those G.S.A.
        clowns.

SUSAN   What am I supposed to tell Nell? And Bill?

HARRY   Tell 'em it was an accident. And that
        I am already in treatment. Oh, by the
        way, there's something else.
        I'm in love with another man. Aside from me.
        I know I shouldn't've kept
        you from this—this from you.
        It's Doctor Wineskin.
        Unusually strong transference or counter-
        transference or whatever you call it.
        That's what he calls it, ha ha, a joke.

SUSAN   I don't know what to say.

HARRY   Don't look at me with those harsh, judging eyes.

SUSAN   Honestly, Harry.

HARRY   And I'm not a . . . fag.
        If that's what you're thinking.
        I'm just in love with another man.
        That's all. Aside from me.
   (*Pause.*)
        It just happened. I dunno.
   (*Pause. He looks out the window.*)
        Say, there's a man on the roof there. With a pitchfork.

(*Scene three. Same as before. Next morning—again strange.* NELL *and* SUSAN.

A large, wiggling box with air holes. Easy listening music on radio.

NELL   I'm glad to hear it.

SUSAN   Yes, he's seeking treatment.

NELL   Wonderful.

SUSAN   And since we changed our names and the phone number and painted the car we both feel a lot better. No more nasty calls. Hate mail. You know.

NELL   How smart of you.

SUSAN   More coffee?

NELL   Love some.

(SUSAN *pours. Box barks thunderously.* NELL *gets up and goes over to it.*)

Whatever kind is it? It's very large.

SUSAN   Albanian wolfhound. Very rare. We got you all the papers. Shots. It's been neutered.

NELL   What does it eat?

SUSAN   Raw meat. About fourteen pounds a day. Do you have a strong chain? It'll get bigger.

NELL   Bill will be delighted. What a nice way to patch things up.

SUSAN   The least we could do. Harry felt so bad.

(*Pause.*)

NELL   Guess I'll be off now. The man to fix the roof is supposed to show up.

SUSAN   You know, I've been meaning to tell you. I saw a man, a very *strange* man, standing on your roof. With a pitchfork.

NELL   Really? Doesn't surprise me. Someone's been up there. A dozen tiles came crashing down. Nearly brained me.

On the patio. Sunbathing.

SUSAN   It's not the first time. I really should've told you
             earlier.

NELL   Next time please do. I'm concerned about crime. Oh dear,
             I think I'll have to leave the dog till Bill and Harry come
             home.

SUSAN   Harry is Fred now.

NELL   That's right. How silly of me.
             (*The* MAN OF SHALA *appears in the window.*)

SUSAN   That must be the roof man.

NELL   So, thanks for the coffee. And I'll send Bill over.

SUSAN   Maybe, maybe the workman can carry it.

NELL   All by himself?
             (*The* MAN OF SHALA *smiles. They go to the door.*)

SUSAN   Hello. Are you here for the roof? Next door?

MAN OF SHALA   Roof repair. That house?

SUSAN   Yes, that house. But we were wondering could you perhaps
             help by carrying this box across the way?

MAN OF SHALA   Sure, lady.
             (*Box barks thunderously and moves about.*)
             You got some kinda animal in here?

NELL   Dog.

SUSAN   A large dog.

MAN OF SHALA   Night is the dog's time.
             (*Picks up box.*)

SUSAN   My, he's strong.

MAN OF SHALA   In my country there is a story.

(*Puts down the box.*)

    Heavy sombitch.

(*Pause.*)

    There is this very good lady. She so virtuous she can pick up monster boulder. And carry it whole shitass long way. From Shala to Scutari. She famous lady. Then she carry boulder where her boyfriend live. He stepping outside, give her the look. She put down the boulder, can't pick it up no more. This story prove no woman any damn good. Ha ha.

(*Picks up box and goes out.*)

SUSAN   You know what I forgot?

(*Holds out string.*)

    There was a lot of this out back. Looked like it was blown off your roof. What is it?

NELL   Looks like string.

(*A strange pause.*)

SUSAN   Well, so long.

NELL   And thanks. Bill's like a kid with animals. See you later.

(*She goes.*)

SUSAN   Bye.

(SUSAN *looks around and crosses to kitchen. Albanian dance music blares on the radio. She enters angrily and changes channels.*)

    That's not easy listening music!

Slow blackout.

Scene four. Same as before. Evening. SUSAN *is now* RACHEL. HARRY *is now* FRED. *Both wear wigs.* RACHEL *is on the phone. As usual,* FRED *reads the paper.*

RACHEL   Nell. This is Rachel. Rachel? Your neighbor. Used to be Susan. Right. There's a dead swan in your swimming pool. Oh, it's a nun? Fred, it's a nun. I thought I'd tell you because I think Jill has been eating part of it. No, tomorrow is garbage day. Fred is my husband. The same one. Different name. I know it's a little confusing. Done wonders for our sex life. Fred is no longer a homosexual. How about that? So long.

(*Hangs up.*)

FRED   Have you seen the cheese?

RACHEL   Which cheese?

FRED   The one I brought home last week. A real steal. Prokletiya. From the Balkans.

RACHEL   That's the overripe one?

FRED   That's the way it's supposed to smell.

RACHEL   I threw it out.

FRED   Rachel, why didn't you ask me first?

RACHEL   You were occupied. Repairing the document shredder. You always get so perturbed.

FRED   What did you do with it?

RACHEL   Left it out for the birds. They won't touch it.

FRED   You have no taste for the exotic, Rachel.

RACHEL   I think Jill, the dog next door, ate part of it.

FRED   Good idea. The Dog.

RACHEL   Wonderful. Bill and Nell love it.

FRED   I still feel suicidal though. Despite the new identity. A disquieting sense of the loneliness of infinite perspectives.

RACHEL   One day at a time Harry, ah, Fred.
        (*Slow blackout begins.*)

FRED   At least I'm not following that guy anymore. With the fez.

Total black.

Scene five. Same as before. Another strange day. NELL *and* RACHEL. *The former with her arm in a sling.*

NELL   Just a little puppy playfulness.

RACHEL   Must be painful.

NELL   Looks worse than it feels.
    (*Pause.*)
                I'm a little worried about Bill.

RACHEL   Whatever for?

NELL   Yesterday. I saw him out in the backyard. Sitting on one of the dining room chairs, doing something, something *strange* to a cat.

RACHEL   One of the neighborhood cats?

NELL   No. A stray. Never saw it before.

RACHEL   I wouldn't worry about it. As long as it wasn't one of the neighborhood cats.

NELL   Whatever do you suppose . . . skip it.
                Speaking of Bill, he wanted to know if we could perhaps borrow the shredder over the weekend.

RACHEL   Sure, if Fred's not using it.

NELL   Sorry about that mess in the pool.

RACHEL   It wasn't your fault.

NELL   Well it's all cleaned up.

RACHEL   Those tots.

NELL   Boys will be boys.

RACHEL   Getting darker earlier, isn't it?

NELL   Darker and darker.

RACHEL   *Goldfinger*'s on cable tonight. Want to come over and
            watch?

NELL   Sure.

RACHEL   Who are you?

NELL   Why, Nell, of course.

RACHEL   No, I mean, *really*. WHO ARE YOU?

NELL   I don't want to get into it right now.

RACHEL   Why not?

NELL   It's a creepy, little situation.

RACHEL   Think you've got forever? More coffee?

NELL   One life is quite enough. Sure, I'd love some.

RACHEL   I wouldn't worry about Bill.

NELL   I won't.
            (*Pause. It begins to get dark.*)
            What about the coffee?

RACHEL   What coffee?

NELL   You offered me another cup.

RACHEL   Did I? How silly of me.
            (*Pause.*)

NELL   I'd like one.

RACHEL   I don't think there is any.

NELL   Why don't you look?

RACHEL   Why don't you, I'm tired.

NELL   Okay.

(*She goes to the kitchen.*)

There's none in the pot.

RACHEL   Told you.

NELL

(*Off.*)

Where's the coffee?

RACHEL   I'm not sure there's any left.

(*Comes out of the kitchen with an empty can.*)

NELL   Looks like this is the end of it.

RACHEL   Sorry.

NELL   What about instant?

RACHEL   In the cupboard.

(*Pause.* NELL *goes out.*)

NELL

(*From offstage.*)

Something stinks in here.

RACHEL   The cheese.

NELL   Found it.

RACHEL   Prokletiya. From the Balkans.

NELL   Instant coffee was under the sink.

RACHEL   Really!? The cleaning lady.

(*Pause.*)

NELL   How do you light the burner?

RACHEL   First button on the right.

(*The light goes out.*)

Not that one.

NELL   Which one then?

RACHEL   The other one.
         (*The light comes on. Pause.*)

NELL   I'll just have it with hot tap water.

RACHEL   That's novel.

NELL   I used to in college.

RACHEL   In college I used to cook soup in an immersion
         heater. Right in the can.
         (NELL *enters with her cup of coffee.*)

NELL   Good coffee.

RACHEL   What else?

NELL   What else what?

RACHEL   I mean what else is there?

NELL   Not much I know of. Dark.

RACHEL   Moon and stars. Cold cup of coffee.
         (*They giggle.*)

NELL   Not much.

RACHEL   The movers are coming on Friday.

NELL   You're not packed.

RACHEL   Oh, the furniture's staying.

NELL   I don't understand.

RACHEL   They're just moving the house. Not us.

         Blackout.

Scene six. Furniture as before. No house. RACHEL *and* FRED *reading and watching TV. A starry night. Jupiter and next to it, Saturn. The bugs make beautiful noises, only strange.*

FRED   Is the wash done?

RACHEL   The tens and twenties are in the drier.

FRED   Nice night.

RACHEL   Insect noises. The best.

FRED   There's Jupiter, and there's Saturn.

RACHEL   Where?

FRED   There and there.
        (*Points.*)

RACHEL   Fred, I'm worried again.

FRED   It's the tremors in the fabric of the World Egg.
        (*Pause.*)
              Time to change our names again?

RACHEL   I'd feel more comfortable.

FRED

        (*Going back to his newspaper*)
              Fine with me.
        (*The TV bursts into flame.*)

Scene seven. Bright sunshine. The house, with furniture. FRED *is now* ART. RACHEL *is now* GINNY. *The latter fidgets. Looks tense.* ART *has his hand stuck in the coffee pot.*

GINNY   Art.

ART   Yes, Ginny.

GINNY   I think we have to have a real heart-to-heart.
              Clear the air.

ART   I guess you're right. I've been unwilling to admit a few
              things to myself. You know how it is. Get wrapped up in
              work. One thing leads to another.

GINNY   I think we'd better . . .
        (*Doorbell rings.*)

Who could that be?
(*She goes to the door.*)
Nell.

NELL   Ginny. Art. I need to talk.

ART   Sit down, Nell.

NELL   I guess I just feel so angry with myself.
For so many years. For so long.
Mom and dad. The beasts.
Discipline, summer camp. All of it.
Braces. Chores. Dancing school.
White gloves. Acne. WHY ME?
Can you believe it? Not one kind
word. When I was runner-up
in tennis. Not one word. Guilt.
Shame. Psychic murder. Once
in my goddam life to be taken
for what I am and not something
else. Not to be taken for granted.*
Not to be mocked. Spurned. One
lousy chance. That's all. Bill
doesn't see me. Doesn't know me.
Treats me like the fucking dog.
I don't eat fourteen fucking pounds
of horsemeat every day. I don't do
perverted things to stray cats in the
middle of the backyard in broad
daylight. I care for others. I am a
nurturing person. Have always been
tidy, neat and law abiding. And
just where did it get me I ask you.
Look at this fucking neighborhood.
Most of the people who live here
are so far beneath me they're above
me! Not one of them pays me the time

of day. I could've been a dancer,
in the theater, gone to graduate school.
My fucking LSE's were higher than
Bill's. You ask him. The nun, you ask,
what about the nun. It was a
sudden thing. An act of passion. A
person committing an act of passion
is only responsible for the passion
not the act, and the act I've done
I'll stand behind one thousand percent.
But if you let on I'll know you for
the finks you are, true finks. All those
years at Catholic school. All those
humiliations. This hardly makes up for
one week of that. But it's a start. Living
right is the best revenge they say and
they're right. I WANT MY SHARE, MY
PLACE IN THE SUN. I PITY ANYONE WHO TRIES
TO STOP ME. I'VE BEEN SWEET, RETIRING,
THE PERFECT, LITTLE PASSIVE HOUSEWIFE
UP TO NOW, BUT WATCH OUT. I'M LOOKING
OUT FOR NUMBER ONE, AND I'M GONNA GET
IT. I'M GONNA WIN. I'M NOT ASKING
ANYMORE, I'M GONNA TAKE WHAT I WANT
BECAUSE I NEED WHAT I WANT AND IF YOU
GET IN MY WAY YOU WILL SURELY DIE.

(*Sits down and sobs.*)

ART   Okay. Okay. I hear you. I know what
you're saying, Nell, you're saying
we're responsible because we live
right next door, right? I mean like
what do you want? So I killed the
dog. I got you another dog didn't
I? What do you want? Blood? Well
blood you will not get.* Because I

have suffered enough giving way
to assholes like you and Bill. With
your fancy swimming pools and
Buicks and high and mighty attitudes.
I am involved in aerospace, lady,
fucking Star Wars, and I don't mind
telling you I am one important guy.
Sure, Mom and Dad weren't
exactly great to me. They never even
gave me the rubber duck in fourth
grade, when I SAID I WANTED THE
RUBBER DUCK and so it cost a dollar
thirty-nine, Jimmy Lyle got a rubber
duck and his folks were poor. I mean
certifiable poor. You should hear what
Doctor Wineskin told me about the
sources of my conditions. The emotional
deprivation. The sadistic behavior,
particularly on the part of my old man.
When he croaked I was so happy I
jumped up and down for an hour
and a half. He was the meanest son-of-a-
bitch I ever knew. And my mother?
The biggest ballbuster in town. You
wonder why I have this weak character,
and this shifty system of values
and this *labile* personality? She fucking
suffocated me with fake warmth, fake
loving, fake everything. Nothing real.
All she was interested in was herself,
and she'd still be calling me up here every
day to tell me what a miserable fuck-up
I am if it wasn't for me changing
our phone number five times in the
last six months. And I will not be
the patsy for all that hoohah down

at the office, I was only doing my
job, I was one of many, most of the
guys are more into the lucre than me,
and in fact if it hadn't been for me
it would've been a lot worse, I can tell
you. I'm a young man yet, there's so
much I wanna do, learn languages,
go places, have fun. Sorry about the
dog, Nell, listen to me, I was outa my
mind at work, the pressure, the worry . . .

(*Paces and waves the coffee pot.*)

GINNY   Well blood I fucking well want, Art.
What've you ever done for me except
drag me away from Delray Beach where
everyone knew me and loved me, and
I mighta become someone and drag
me off to this hole, with this miserable
crowd of losers, alcoholics, petty thieves,
dreamers of the small dream, Harry,
Art, whatever your name is. You think
I like facing the neighbors after you
maliciously run over their rotten
cat? [ART: Dog.] Dog then. You think
I like having no roof over our heads?
You think I like your sleazy bunch
of aerospace embezzler friends
who haven't got balls enough to
follow through with what they start
with any assurance of success? You
think I'm an idiot? Certainly you
treat me like one. I mean,
my father's 96 and he's taking Creative
Writing courses, mother's gaga but she
still has to go for photosynthesis at the
Botanical Gardens every other day.
Florence Nightingale, Joan of Arc I am not.

All you do is talk about what you
want, but all I do is bust my ass
for other people and what thanks do
I get? Absolutely none.
When do I get to be creative?
When, I ask you!
I dream dreams, big ones, and
all I get from you is cheese.
Prokletiya cheese from the Balkans,
from the "Accursed Mountains."
I'm sorry you have to hear
this, Nell, it's not pretty,
but I have to get this out.
It's been eating at me.
If you don't let it out
you can give yourself
cancer. I've seen it happen.
Except my mother, fucking
94 years old and no cancer.
Just gaga. Always was
gaga. Stop crying, Nell.
The truth hurts. I know.
A bitter pill. And you, you
lout, all I have to say to
you is. I've thought it
over. I wanna make a
new start. Be brand new.
Try out my wings and fly.
I know I can do it.

(*A shot rings out.* ART *falls, mortally wounded.* GINNY *cradles him.*)

GINNY   Art, what's happened?

ART

(*Choking*)
Moons of ice. Cheese. Puppets.
(*The* MAN OF SHALA *enters in full Albanian dress. Fustenella. Fez.*

Strange, pointy Albanian shoes. He carries a Martini carbine. Opens the chamber, removes the expended cartridge and tosses it near the dying man. ART *sees him.*)

> Destroy the cheese.

(*He dies. The* WOMEN *react with horror. The* MAN OF SHALA *walks out.*)

The entire set is flown out during a five-count blackout.

Act Two

Scene. Nightfall on Iapetus, the eighth moon of Saturn. The ringed planet is visible in the distance. Applause for the puppet show. OLD WOMAN *bows. The puppets bow. Their little theater is a miniature replica of the first act set. The puppets are miniature versions of the characters presented there. So, Act One has been a show for the amusement of the characters of Act Two, the dwellers of the ice moons. These include several* ALBANIANS, *the Turkish-garbed calendar* WINGFOOT, *a mysterious* SLINKING FIGURE, WOLFERT, *and* FOX PERSON. *The last two are not impressed by the show.*

WOLFERT   Dumb.

FOX PERSON   Real dumb.

WINGFOOT   Act Two. Nightfall on Iapetus, the eighth moon of Saturn. Glowing softly in the night sky is the ringed planet herself, some two million two hundred thousand miles away. The little puppet show you have just witnessed has been an entertainment for the exiled dwellers of the ice moons.

WOLFERT   What's it about?

FOX PERSON   What's it mean?

OLD WOMAN   It's about the dragons and the drangoijt. The man who was killed was a dragon. The one who killed him a drangue—

FOX PERSON   What's a drangue?

OLD WOMAN   People with little wings under their arms.
            You have them in your country too. You
            can tell them when it rains: they rush
            indoors—

WOLFERT   Afraid they'll get their wings wet?
    (WOLFERT *and* FOX PERSON *chuckle.*)

OLD WOMAN   No, they're not afraid of anything. When
            they hear the dragon they go home to be ready
            in case they're called to fly, and fight the
            dragon. Even the babies fly home grasping their
            cradles. There is no drangue so young it could
            not scratch the dragon—

FOX PERSON   People like that don't exist.
    (*The* SLINKING FIGURE *approaches* FOX PERSON.)

SLINKING FIGURE   Pardon me . . .

OLD WOMAN   How do I know? I am stupid. I gather wood.
            Anything can happen in the mountains of
            Albania.
    (*She goes.*)

SLINKING FIGURE   Pardon me.
    (*Gives a gold coin to* FOX PERSON.)

FOX PERSON   What's this for?

SLINKING FIGURE   It is the balance of the half Napoleon
            from your supper of the other night.
            The price was too much. The owner
            of the establishment has been . . . punished.
            You will please come with me to see my
            master, Ahmed Bey. . . . You are new, perhaps,
            to the ice moons?

WOLFERT   Shitass no. Been here years.

SLINKING FIGURE   His residence lies there, in the Great Smudge.
Cover your eyes and nose. The soot of the
Great Smudge of Iapetus causes health problems.
(*Wind and dust. A vast dark landscape opens strangely before them.*
Dead people covered with soot. A screen, Arab lamps. FALSE AHMED
BEY *wears a fez. Moustache. He offers little cups of coffee to the two.*
The SLINKING FIGURE *discreetly retires.* WINGFOOT *appears, armed*
with a yataghan [*sword*] *and stands guard. Pause. They sit.*)

FALSE AHMED BEY   You are perhaps wonder why I have summon you
to this place. I am Ahmed Bey. Vizier of all the ice moons.
You may bow.

(*They bow.*)

Actually I am not Ahmed Bey. I am a person of no importance
attached by happenstance to the Sublime Porte of the Vizier
of the Sanjak of Ops. *He* is Ahmed Bey. But I am a true
Calendar, like my colleague Wingfoot, and a true drangue,
as portrayed in the moving piece of theater presented by our
Fatima, who was just here. Know that several years ago some
cheese was stolen from me. Presumably by an impersonator,
a false calendar. Who knows where this fiend now lurks?
All this laborious to explain—

WOLFERT   You got any chew, you know, Mail Pouch, Red Barn?

(FOX PERSON *slugs* WOLFERT.)

FALSE AHMED BEY   Being a true calendar, I was saved from further
humiliation and injury by another member of our secret
society, one Pancake. Also a drangue. Now I wish to repay
Pancake. Hence this gift of cheese you will so kind as to
deliver, in person, to Pancake.

(*An uneasy pause.*)

WOLFERT   Ah . . .

FALSE AHMED BEY   If you oblige me in this matter your exile on the
ice moons will be considerably mitigated, I assure you.

WOLFERT   The tub is broke.

FOX PERSON   (*Aside*)
                  Oh, shitass, no.
        (WINGFOOT *glares at them.*)

FALSE AHMED BEY   We encourage your patience. The gift in question
        is to be delivered to the person in question—

FOX PERSON   Mister Pancake . . .

FALSE AHMED BEY   That is correct, Mister Pancake. And this person
        is known to be dwelling somewhere among the ice moons.
        There is, however, a further complication. The cheese is
        false cheese. A replica. The real cheese, has, alas, again been
        stolen. This time by the Shquipetars, Sons of the Eagle,
        Children of Kombi, Arnauts—Albanians. They are a nui-
        sance in these parts. You must find the cheese first. But if
        you do not find the true cheese you must give Pancake the
        false cheese. Pancake will not like the false cheese, but if
        there is no real cheese then the false cheese must suffice. It
        is the thought that counts. Pancake may become angry.
        Now the cheese should be easier to locate than Pancake for
        Pancake is a very famous man on the ice moons, and
        cheese is all but unknown. Therefore it will be obvious
        when you have encountered a cheese that it is a true
        cheese. You will perhaps encounter Albanians as you ap-
        proach Saturn. You are authorized to venture as far as the
        cloudtops, even to our fastness at Tohu Bohu, on Ann's
        Spot. But Pancake will not be there. Although he might be
        there if he is no place else, for if he is no place else, indeed,
        it stands to reason he is there. But I don't think so. It is
        more likely for Pancake to be skulking about on Mimas or
        Enceladus or Tethys or Dione or Rhea or Titan (which
        smells of catpiss) or Hyperion or even Iapetus, where we
        now stand. This is the gift.
    (*Hands it to* WOLFERT.)

WOLFERT   It looks like cheese.

FALSE AHMED BEY   It looks like cheese but it is not cheese.

WOLFERT   Feel it, Fox Person, it's cheese.

FALSE AHMED BEY

(*Arising*)
    Wingfoot is a calendar. I will go now.
    He will explain some things to you you need to know.
    He will find you a guide.
(*He walks off into the Great Smudge.*)

FOX PERSON   The tub is broke.

FALSE AHMED BEY

(*Calling back*)
    The tub will be repaired.
(WINGFOOT *snaps his fingers and the* MAN OF SHALA *appears. Pause.*
He smiles.)

MAN OF SHALA   I am the Man of Shala. On a dare, and as a favor to
    Wingfoot, I have agreed to take these two through all the
    ice moons, to the cloudtops of Saturn, if necessary. They are
    looking for a man named Pancake. For what reason? I don't
    know and I don't care. The ice moons are all Shoshi land. I
    am of Shala. The Shoshi and the Shala are at blood. But be-
    cause these two are women I will not be harmed. It is our
    custom. When they offer us hospitality I will make fun of
    the Shoshi. It is a very good joke I think.
(*Pause.*)
    These Americans are ghost, a homeless people.

WOLFERT TO FOX PERSON   You got any chew?

FOX PERSON   You knowed if I got any chew
    I wouldn't give it to you.

WOLFERT   So you don't got any chew?

FOX PERSON   That's what I said.

WOLFERT   Guess I heard you right.

FOX PERSON   That's right.

WOLFERT   Yup.
> (*Pause.*)

WINGFOOT
> (*With passion*)
>> Sky. Yarth. Gods. People.
>> All such like and kinda am.
>> All kinda hoohah.
>> You shall all kinda numerous and diverse hoohah
>>> am.
>> Which was and shall have been.
>> Boring hoohah and him very intriguing one.
>> Big one and one colored green.
>> Yet it will hardly kinda no as be.
>> For it am all one kinda flapdoodle.
>> Most it go kinda scratchy.
>> Somehow it be glued together.
>> Mosthow it go on for awhile and grow ugly and
>>> fall apart.
>> Mostly it lie there on the floor all tore-down and
>>> falled over and scrunched-up and awful looking.
>> Sometime it sit up and take notice.
>> And allatime what is be sitting there big grin on
>>> himher
>>>> face scratching himher feets.
> (*Pause.*)
>> You have to got did.
>> You have to get going.
>> You have to get it over with.
>> You have to get back at X in the name of Y.
>> You have to get ready to wastebasket.
>> You have to jell.
>> You have to taxi.
>> You have to auto.

You have to typewrite.

You have to electrocute.

You got to plumb.

You got to jam.

You got to barb.

You got to elocute.

You got to ush.

You got to perc.

You got to demagogue.

You must have to simonize.

You must have to slenderize.

You must have to fletcherize.

You must have to backwardize.

You must have to customize.

You must have to customerize.

You must have to belgiumize.

You must have to respectableize.

You ought to scenarioize.

You ought to debunk sure.

You ought to delouse sure.

You ought to dewax sure.

You ought to dejelly sure.

You ought to debamboozle sure.

You had better give some thought to write the biography of,
    to protest against, to give momentum to, to ballyhoo, to
    lobby-display, to railroad, to signaturize, to pan, to
    steamroll, to get the drop on, to get sore at, to get even
    with all them who did what.

You gotta moronize.

For it got a case of the screaming barf.

Wind among the elephant bones.

People on all fours in himher head.

X in the name of why.

Such and mostsuch illusory hoohah shall have done
    been did.

For who is I at, you ask.
I is at cat longtime freestanding.
Be similar.
Be born.
Be at cat near the shadow of Crowe's Y.
Be born again as a garbage-eating quadruped.
Be safe am.
Tote that hoohah! Slam that Whangdoodle!
All one freestanding hunka hoohah shall
    will have been are.

FOX PERSON   You think if we ignore him he'll go away?

WINGFOOT   Didn't I never tell you, you ain't got no right to go out and
    chase after no ball when nobody ain't watching you?
Nor do not saw the air?
Scarce am I are and I gets foozled.
Cause of how the sky am.
All manner hoohah clear from X to X′ and allaway from Y
    to Y′ and all kinda bunched-up and turned likeso inside-
    out and rightside-up do there be.
Blame it on the labernath I do not.
We are all
At cat
    too and shall have been done to as we have did done
    in a most awfuller manner come what may shitass no.
For hewho saw the air hetoo am
At Cat.

(*Pause.*)

So what you say.
So what am precisely what I'm saying.
You don't catch no ball without you have no ball even if you
    got no base neither.
It am a law of nature do.
Cause of how like the air am filled with empty dumpty.
All
At Cat.

Clear across the blackdress X to X′ a whole helluva way
past the piles and heaps of hoohah to where what the
crowe's eye.

Cuts.

Only himher two-foot hoohah to himher are hardly been
done when it shall be did gets done to who was paying no
nevermind dontcha know.

World a hellish awfullest place be.

(*Pause.*)

By the slenderest of strands the sky am.

By the slenderest of strands all that pertains to the sky shall
have been done did.

Yarth too am by the slenderest of strands and all manner of
hoohah as shall be done did in Yarth's name except
himher hoohah as is

At Cat.

By the slenderest of strands them gods been done did.

Even at the door of the labernath.

By the slenderest of strands do them people go and be did
even if'n they never got no base on balls without no
bat neither.

All equidistant is was.

Sky full of things in X.

Sky full of other things in Y.

Simple and complex hoohah.

Moving and ponderous one.

One small one with bright eye and fast talk and big dumb
one who never say nothing as long as the moon and stars

Shake flour over his face by the slenderest of strands.

(*Pause.*)

WOLFERT   (*To* WINGFOOT.)

You. You got any chew?

(*Pause.*)

FOX PERSON   Let's rev up the tub.

(WOLFERT *summons their spacecraft with a duck call. View of Saturn from Hyperion.*)

FOX PERSON   View of Saturn from Hyperion. Roughly 921,727 and four-
fifths miles.

(*Sharply angled ground. They all tilt [*FOX, WOLFERT, *and the* MAN OF SHALA; WINGFOOT *has vanished]. The first two have set up the card table that accompanies them on their journey. The* MAN OF SHALA *sets up an old gas can painted white. This is to keep off the Ssy Kec, or Evil Eye.*)

WOLFERT   Hyperion looks like a brick. It's covered with the same kind
of gunk that covers one side of Iapetus. Looks like someone
knocked it cockeye. Wingfoot took off. Said something to
the effect he'd be back if we ever found Pancake. The Man
of Shala sits and smokes cigarettes, drinks *rakeia*, Albanian
red-eye and don't say much. It's about 410 degrees below
zero and me with no newspaper for my boots and no chew.
No cheese and no one ever heard of no Pancake.

(*Long, bored pause.*)

MAN OF SHALA   What have the men of Tirana been doing?
I am the son of the mountain eagle;
I do not give up my nest while there is life
    in my claws;
I do not yield to the Gendarmes!
I will drown them in their own blood.
Rise, rise and go to the door.
There is a sergeant with twenty soldiers.
Ho! Ho! Sergeant, I am not the man you think!
I will not bow and be led to the slaughter.
I will not be killed like a lamb
    for the men of Tirana.*
I am a goat and I will fight.

WOLFERT   Hey, you, shut up.

MAN OF SHALA   I am thinking of the buried treasure.

WOLFERT   Sure, and we have the maps.

MAN OF SHALA   You have secret maps. But they will do you no good.
Those maps are from the Turks. I can smell them.
Moslems stink. When you want to declare war on the
Moslems you throw a dead pig into the mosque.
(*Long, bored pause.*)

FOX PERSON   How do you suppose this place got to be shaped like
this?

WOLFERT   A cow kicked it.

MAN OF SHALA   I know a good joke. There is this cow. (*Cracks up.*)
It fell off a cliff. (*Cracks up.*) Was smashed to pieces.
All over the place. But then. (*Cracks up.*) All the bits
and pieces jump together and make a new cow. (*Wild
laughter.*)
(*The others do not respond. Pause. The* MAN OF SHALA *becomes suddenly serious.*)
The oras guard our secrets. Foreigners with strange maps
want to steal our treasure. But our land is a fortress of
mountains, and the secret places are hard to discover.

FOX PERSON   Call the tub.
(WOLFERT *calls the tub. The giant red sphere of Titan glides by. We
hear the voice of*)

FOX PERSON   Titan. Ammonia and Methane. Great big fuzzy red
pumpkin.
People used to say Titan's Earth in an icebox. Don't you
believe it! It's more like, like a deep-freeze cat box. Pure
cat piss! Wouldn't land there for all the ho in Hoboken.
(*Sings "Methane Cliffs."*) Pee you.
(*Sound of the duck call. View of Rhea as they approach for a landing.*)

WOLFERT   Rhea is bigger, dumber, and emptier than Iapetus. Covered
with junk,

litter, hoohah. View of Saturn from Rhea. A strange man
approaches.

SLINKING FIGURE   Pardon me.
(*Presses a gold coin into* FOX PERSON'*s hand.*)

FOX PERSON   What's this for?

SLINKING FIGURE   It is from the other night. Your supper? The price was
too much. The owner of the establishment has been
punished.

MAN OF SHALA   Sometimes we kill many all at one time.

FOX PERSON   You shoot Moslems, but steal their names.

MAN OF SHALA   When I am dead who cares about my soul? I won't live
long. Shala is at blood with Shoshi, Plani, Nikaj,
Krasnich and Goshi. Besides, they have good names.
(*The* SLINKING FIGURE *mutters to the little group and casts a spell. A
bowl of water appears in his open palm.*)

FOX PERSON   He told us about the man who dealt with the devil. He
asked for a bowl of water and performed charms over it,
and asked the Pasha and his friend what they'd like to
see. Malta, they said. Malta they saw. Complete with
a little steamer in the harbor. Have I permission to
depart? Certainly, says the Pasha. The man put his
finger on the water, and disembarked for America. They
poured the water into the stream and the man never
returned.
(*The* SLINKING FIGURE *touches the water in the bowl and both he and
the bowl disappear.*)

MAN OF SHALA   It is useless to dig for buried treasure unless you know
the proper spell.
(*An* ALBANIAN WOMAN *appears. Stands off a ways.*)

WOLFERT   Rhea, junk planet. Look at this trash. No way around it.

FOX PERSON   We prepared to leave for Dione. Two years. A woman

came up to us before we left. She gave us honeycomb
and asked for a new constitution.
(*The* WOMAN *bows and disappears.*)
If I was Pancake I wouldn't put up here.

WOLFERT   You aren't Pancake. Pancake has his hidden reasons. Ask
the Man of Shala.

MAN OF SHALA   Sometimes we kill eighteen or twenty, all on one day.
(*Duck call. View of Saturn from Dione. A large blast, fireball, smoke,
fumes. A group of* ALBANIANS *in the distance slowly approaches. These
are the Shoshi.*)

FOX PERSON   Dione. We had kind of bumpy landing. Whole shitload
of Albanians there to greet us. Wolfert lost it. Wolfert
lost it totally.

WOLFERT   Wingfoot said "Try Roncevaux Terra."

FOX PERSON   Wingfoot said many things.

WOLFERT   Darksome place.

FOX PERSON   We're on the dark side.
(*The* MAN OF SHALA *sees the Shoshi and thumbs his nose at them.*)

WOLFERT   Downright gloomy.

FOX PERSON   Hey, you've got the wrong map.

WOLFERT   WHADDAYA MEAN WRONG MAP?

FOX PERSON   That's a map of Iapetus. We're on Dione.

WOLFERT   SHITASS NO. TELL ME: IS THAT THE GREAT SMUDGE
OR NO?

FOX PERSON   Only looks like it. We're on Dione.
(*Sees the Shoshi.*)
Ignore them. Maybe they'll go away.

WOLFERT   FUCKING ALBANIANS.

LOOK AT THAT HAT. (*Points to the* MAN OF SHALA.)
LOOK AT THOSE SHOES.
GROTESQUE.
Have you noticed?
They're following us.

FOX PERSON   That's our guide. The Man of Shala.

WOLFERT   NO, HE'S NOT. HE LOOKS DIFFERENT.

FOX PERSON   He's the same.

WOLFERT   OF COURSE HE'S THE SAME.
THEY ALL LOOK THE SAME.

FOX PERSON   But he's different.

WOLFERT
(*To* SHALA.)
YOU, COME HERE.

FOX PERSON   Don't. Don't.

WOLFERT   YOU ARE THE MAN OF SHALA I SUPPOSE?

MAN OF SHALA   I am the same.

WOLFERT
(*To* FOX PERSON.)
Tell him to go away.

MAN OF SHALA   What can I do?

WOLFERT   GO AWAY.

MAN OF SHALA   Homeless. A nation of ghost.

WOLFERT   HEY! WHY THE STRANGE HAT?
WHY THE RIDICULOUS CLODHOPPERS?
WHY THE CORNBALL MOUSTACHE?

MAN OF SHALA   It is our custom.

FOX PERSON   See? He's the same.

WOLFERT   WHAT DOES THAT MEAN?
"HE'S THE SAME"?
I'M THE SAME.
YOU'RE THE SAME.
MAYBE THEY'LL GO AWAY.
IGNORE THEM.

(*Pause.*)

GET A LOAD OF THEM SHOES!
HEY, THEM MARTIAN SHOES!?

MAN OF SHALA   I am the Man of Shala. Pplum, my friend, once sheltered a runaway wife of the Shoshi. Her husband was cruel. He met the husband on the trail and was shot by him. Pplum shot and killed the husband, and then died. He was a hero, for there was no blood. The slate was clean for his son. This blood (*Nods at the Shoshi.*) came later.

WOLFERT   No blood, ha, blood and no blood.

SHOSHI MAN   Day and a half hospitality for the Shala murder. Then I shall lead you an hour's journey (so we cannot conjure you) all the way to the Palatine Chasmata. I will say to you: "Go on a smooth road. There is a *besa*, an oath of peace, between us for a day and a night because you are my guest. After that I will follow you all my life, until I kill you." That is what I will say and that is what I will do. Come and eat with us and drank coffee and *rakeia*.

(*They do so. Much cordial talk. Stories. Anecdotes. Useful information.*)

FOX PERSON   It is the unwritten law of the Albanians, the Law of Lek. Even a blow delivered by accident must be avenged.

ALBANIAN WOMAN   If a girl refuse to marry her betrothed she must remain virgin all her life. If her father sells her to another that causes *two* bloods: one between her family and her betrothed's, and one between her husband's and her betrothed's. Should she run away there is a triple blood, as her family is at blood also with her husband's.

FOX PERSON   Lek both ordered blood vengeance to be taken and
               condemned
                   the taker of it to be severely punished.

MAN OF SHALA   My friend Pplum had only been shot twice. That is
               too few
                   shots to kill a healthy man. This leg? Took four shots.
                   I dig the bullets out with a knife. I clean the wound with
                   rakeia. Bind it. The leg is good as new. Only short. This
                   finger was shot. I clean the would with *rakeia* and bind it.
                   Perfectly good finger. Only short. I clean a head wound
                   for another friend once. Part of the skill was missing.
                   I replace the skull with a piece of bottle gourd.
     (*Pause.*)
                   One night a group of us we're looking at stars. Someone
                   said: "That's the biggest." "No, that one!" "Liar!" "You
                   call me a liar?" In an hour seventeen men were dead.

FOX PERSON   The tale of the Mirdite woman married to the Scutarene.
               He sold her brother to the Turks. They slew him. She used
               her yataghan on her husband. Then slew her children: "You
               seed of serpent, you shall never live to betray your people."

SHOSHI MAN   I know a story, one more terrible, about my friend
               Ramiz. Ramiz walked by the river one day and saw a
                   beautiful girl.
                   She was an ora. As was our custom, he fell in love
                   with her on the spot, she was beautiful, very beautiful,
                   with long golden hair. He wanted her for his wife, so
                   he took her home, and there he made her his wife. But
                   after this she refused to speak to him. Even after the
                   customary time, six weeks. Ramiz was very much in love
                   with the ora, and this refusal to speak made him very sad.
                   He thought he would please her by cooking rare delicacies,
                   which he did, and by bringing her little gifts, which
                   he did, colorful scarves and things of beaten gold and
                   carved ivory. But none of these things pleased the ora.

She ate in silence, made love in silence, and worked in
silence, beside him. But this refusal to speak made him
very sad.

(*Pause.*)

A year later she gave birth to a small child,
a boy. This, too, she accomplished in silence,
and she nursed the baby silently also, and this
refusal to speak made him mad with grief.

(*Pause.*)

So when she had gone out to market one
day and left the child with him, he had
an idea. He hid the sleeping baby outside
in a basket of wheat. He caught a chicken,
wrung its neck, and bloodied the baby's
clothes and cradle. Then he bloodied his
knife, and awaited her return. When she
appeared at the door he stood up
in the darkness and spoke. He said
if you do not speak to me now, I
will kill the child. And he waited.
She looked at him and said nothing.
He stabbed the chicken, and she
could see the blood on the swaddling
clothes, and the blood on the knife.
When he was done she said, if you had
only allowed me three more days
I would have made you king of the world.
And she bent over and then she arose
and went out the door.

(*Pause.*)

Three days later the unharmed chid
died, and Ramiz went mad and now
he lives in the mountains, the
"Accursed Mountains."

(*The* SLINKING FIGURE *enters. Goes to* WOLFERT *with a golden coin.*)

WOLFERT   What's this?

SLINKING FIGURE   Don't you remember the other night? This is the balance
of the half Napoleon. The price was too much. The owner
has been strung up in a tree. We slit open his belly. And
let the pigs feed on his entrails while he was still alive.
All this for you.
(*Pause.*)
You and I—brothers in enlightenment—all the others are
poor, low trash.
(*Sees painted oil can and runs out.*)

MAN OF SHALA   A horse's skull is also very useful against the Evil Eye.
(ALBANIAN WOMEN *rush up and touch* FOX PERSON'*s straw hat.*)

ALBANIAN WOMAN   Why do you wear wheat on your head? Is there a
law about it? Or is it for pleasure?

FOX PERSON   I wear it because of the sun.

ALBANIAN WOMAN   Why because of the sun?

FOX PERSON   Where I come from the sun is very hot.

ALBANIAN WOMAN   No it isn't.

FOX PERSON   I wear it because I do. It is our custom.

ALBANIAN WOMAN   It is better for a village to burn
than for a custom to fall. Do you have
oras in your country?
(WOLFERT *and* FOX PERSON *exchange glances.*)

FOX PERSON   I have never seen one. Nope. I guess.

MAN OF SHALA   You do not see oras, you hear them.
(*Pause.*)
I knew a man who was followed
by an ora all his life. She had
long golden hair and wore a

shining white gown. When she left
he knew it was time for him to die.

(*Long pause.* WOLFERT *sounds the duck call. View of Saturn from Tethys.*)

WOLFERT   Tethys is a smashed world. There is reason to believe
it broke apart and then reformed.

(*The* MAN OF SHALA *laughs.*)

Its structure is such that it might be quite fragile.
Tethys is located some 182,846 and four-fifths miles
from Saturn. Its diameter is 658 and two-thirds miles.
Tethys is composed almost entirely of ice and is a brilliant
white. We followed the huge trench system, Ithaca Chasma,
for hundreds of miles, nearly all the way around the moon.
We explored the interior of the vast impact crater, Odys-
seus, 248 and a half miles across. We didn't find Pancake.
However we did find a real American farmer.

(*The* AMERICAN FARMER *steps forth.*)

AMERICAN FARMER   Came here to get away from urban crime.
Negroes. No goddam
Negroes up here. Climate's too rough. 330 degrees below
zero. Not a damn thing grows up here. Fucking ball of ice.
Still, it's a whole lot of prime real estate. Justa laying there!
And you can take a deep breath of emptiness and smell
freedom.
No Negroes. Fair number of Albanians though. Almost as
bad
as the Negroes. Good with the bad, I figure.

(*He goes away.*)

WOLFERT   You got any, you know, personal chew?

FOX PERSON   "Personal" chew?

WOLFERT   Like secret, man. Hidden. For friends.

FOX PERSON   I don't have any.

WOLFERT   Friends or chew?

FOX PERSON   Neither.

WOLFERT   Don't suppose you never played no baseball neither.

FOX PERSON   Not likely. Whyn't you just buzz off?
        (*A little* ALBANIAN GIRL *runs up.*)

LITTLE GIRL   You gave my brother a handkerchief. It is not fair. Is
               it my fault I am a girl? Is it my fault I am too small
               to work in the mill? I go with the sheep. I carry the
               lambs. I climb the trees and cut leaves. I bring water
               from the spring . . .
        (*Beats her breast.*)
                 . . . and my brother gets new trousers, and also a handkerchief.
               I say to the world it is not just. I shall cry to the five
               ice moons, it is not fair!

WOLFERT   WHO THE FUCK ARE YOU? WE NEVER GAVE NO
                 HANDKERCHIEF TO NO BROTHER
               NOHOW SURE.

LITTLE GIRL   Aren't you Dumbbell and Shit-for-Brains?

FOX PERSON   We are Fox Person and Wolfert.

LITTLE GIRL   Are you sure you aren't Dumbbell and Shit-for-Brains?

MAN OF SHALA   I gave her brother a handkerchief.
               She shall have two handkerchiefs.
        (*She bows.*)

LITTLE GIRL
        (*To* SHALA.)
               Glory to your eyes.
        (*Turning to* FOX PERSON *and* WOLFERT.)
               Since you are foreigners you must be
               looking for the buried treasure.
               Do you have a map?

Ask the Man of Shala to tell you
about the Golden Man.
(*He shushes her and gives her a handkerchief.*)
Glory to your eyes.
(*She goes. Pause.*)

FOX PERSON   How come you know all these things?

MAN OF SHALA   *Jam comitadj.* For I am a bandit.
(*Uneasy pause.*)

FOX PERSON   Do you like it—banditing?

MAN OF SHALA   Yes. I like it very much.
(WOLFERT *summons the "tub." View of Saturn from Enceladus.*)

FOX PERSON   Scene 46. Enceladus. Same old boring hoohah. Looked for
Pancake in Diyar Planitia, crossed to Sarandib Planitia,
north over the ice floes all the way to Ali Baba, clear
across the Isbanir Fossa, Daryabar Fossa, and Bossorah
Fossa.
Volcanoes of ice. Fucking Albanian parking lot. No damn
Pancake
and no base on balls. Bright as a real Chromium hubcap.

WOLFERT   And no chew neither.
(*He sounds the duck call.*)

FOX PERSON   Fired up the tub and cleared out. Three years. Call this
a life.
(*View of Saturn rising seen from Mimas.*)

WOLFERT   Scene 47. Arrived on Mimas. 115,403 and a third miles
from the cloudtops of Saturn. Diameter 242 and a third
miles. Magnitude. Who knows? Albedo. Who cares? Mimas
is frozen solid. Nothing's happened here in five billion
years. Skated 252 miles across the ice-flats from Balin to
Morgan in twelve hours. Found no cheese and no goddamn
Pancake. Skidded off the walls of Modred into some low
hills. Broke a leg of our card table in Pelion Chasm. Long

haul past Merlin to Tintagel Chasm. The whole place's one big frozen "Camelot" comic book. No goddamn Pancake, and nobody ain't seen no goddamn Guinevere neither. Guinevere with the golden hair. Found human graffito "Diane sucks" and a phone number. Kept the phone number. It's dawn now. Saturn rising gets to be a little scary, and Saturn is always rising.

(*They sit and play cards.*)

Bors. Ban. Avalon Chasma. Pellinore. Oeta Chasm. And a huge crater, Arthur. One third the size of Mimas herself. Slid down inside and lost my Swiss army knife. Found Albanian PT boat frozen in the ice near the central mount. Huchwan Shanghai II class. 120 tons. Leaflets of Enver Hoxha defending official party line on the "suicide" of Mehmet Shehu. Also a copy of his *Memoirs*.

(*Opens book at random. An* ALBANIAN SOCIALIST *appears in a puddle of light.*)

ALBANIAN SOCIALIST   After the end of the Second World War, a considerable quantity of gold hidden by the German Nazis, who had looted it from other people, including the Albanian people, was discovered in the Merkers salt pans in Germany. A tripartite commission was set up to return this wealth to the countries where it belonged. . . . Later, too, the tripartite commission declared that our claim for 2,454 kilograms of pure gold was just. . . . But as this same commission informed us again, "this quantity was subject to a claim by a third party and the dispute over this matter was in the process of settlement." Blah. Blah. Blah. We have waited a long time for this lawful property of the Albanian people to be delivered to us, but to this day it remains in the claws of the dragon.

(WOLFERT *closes book and the* ALBANIAN SOCIALIST *disappears. Pause.*)

WOLFERT   Vast electrical storms visible on the cloudtops. Footprints of a biped on the slopes of the central peak. And a Classic

Coke can 5 cents deposit due. Named the peak Mount Catpiss. Where can you buy cigarettes on this dump? The Man
of Shala told us you divorce your wife by snipping off part
of her skirt with a pair of scissors. The Man of Shala told us
a stolen clock is worth more than a normal clock. Just between you and me, I don't believe a word of it. Where can
you buy shoelaces on this dump? Eleven months make a
year. One long yawn.

(*Back to the card game.*)

FOX PERSON   Four of clubs.

WOLFERT   You win. My deal. Got any chew?

FOX PERSON   Ultraviolet rays do wonderful things for my dream life.
You ever change your socks?

(*The* SLINKING FIGURE *enters and slides up to* FOX PERSON.)

SLINKING FIGURE   (*To* FOX PERSON.)
Psst!

(*The* MAN OF SHALA *gets up suddenly. Pulls out a Webley revolver.*)

FOX PERSON   Yeah?

(*The* MAN OF SHALA *grabs the* SLINKING FIGURE *by the shirt.*)

SLINKING FIGURE   Better an egg today than a chicken next year.

MAN OF SHALA   Better a nightingale once than the blackbird every day.

SLINKING FIGURE   Every sheep hangs by his own leg.

MAN OF SHALA   Squipetars speak Squip.

(SLINKING FIGURE *speaks some Albanian.*)

SLINKING FIGURE   *Kafa pa duhan si Turku pa iman.*

(*The* MAN OF SHALA *throws him to the ground.*)

MAN OF SHALA   *Pse!* So what?

(*He forgets the* WOMEN *and shoots the* SLINKING FIGURE *dead. Tosses
the empty cartridge on the corpse.*)

WOLFERT   What'd he say?

MAN OF SHALA   He said, coffee without tobacco is like a Turk without
belief. I know this man. From Iapetus. Killed a friend's
dog. Night is the dog's time. Part of an old blood. Only
I forgot you were women. I am dishonored.
(*A strange* MAN *approaches, looks at the white can, then at* FOX PER-
SON. *Meanwhile the* MAN OF SHALA *is distraught.*)

MAN   Now, say, waddaya want this what make,
see that what for? I guess, unnerstan?
What I mean, for what that you make, say?
You oil or what it do that you make here or
railway maybe sometime? I guess, right here,
what I want to know right now, John.

FOX PERSON   I don't understand.

MAN   Americans, hey?

FOX PERSON   Yes.

MAN   Don't understand American, hey?

FOX PERSON   Don't understand your American.

MAN   What that for? Railway?

FOX PERSON   No.

MAN   Oil, hey?

FOX PERSON   No. For Evil Eye.

MAN   Well, John, I don't see no use anyhow.
(*The* MAN *goes off. The* MAN OF SHALA *spits.*)

MAN OF SHALA   If this is what education makes of the Sons of Kombi,
the Squipetars, down with education. We are Sons of the
Eagle, a proud people. This man has spent too much time
in America. Because of you I am dishonored.
(*An* ALBANIAN WOMAN *enters and picks up the dead* SLINKING
FIGURE's *gun.*)

WOMAN   Rifles! They're taking Tirana! What has happened?

WOLFERT   WHAT THE FUCK DOES IT LOOK LIKE, STUPID?

WOMAN   Who can tell what is happening in Tirana! Is this a
               Moslem magician who has been conjuring devils to find
               our treasure?

MAN OF SHALA   He kill a dog. It is the Law of Lek.

WOMAN   Is this his gun?
       (*Picking it up.*)

MAN OF SHALA   Put it back.

WOLFERT   Why!? Good gun. Who cares?

MAN OF SHALA   Satan is afraid of rifles. He will not disturb the body
               if the rifle is there. It is a question of honor, and
               I have already dishonored myself. (*To* WOMAN.) Join us.

WOLFERT   You're a fucking barbarian is what you are.
               Fucking bojar walloon. Blow him away
               and then don't even steal his things.
               Monstrous! Where's your mercantile spirit!
               And how come we haven't found no Pancake? Huh?
               Answer me that! Maybe there's money on him.
               He brought money before. A gold half-Napoleon.
               Fucking bojar walloon. Look at you.
       (*Sits down.*)

MAN OF SHALA
       (*To* WOMAN.)
               Tell them the story of the Man of Pog.

WOMAN   A man from the old city of Pog once went to the mountains
               and found the golden image of a human being as large as
               himself. Alas, it was too heavy to carry. He broke off
               four fingers with a stone and put them in his pocket.
               Then he hid the golden man under some rocks. Next morn-
               ing when he returned with help there was nothing but the

rocks. The man went mad and lives in the mountains naked.
The gold was pure. It was beaten into ornaments.

(*The* MAN OF SHALA *arises.*)

MAN OF SHALA   I said to a magpie: let no one uncover this gold till two
gray mice have driven three times around this tree in a
carriage made of an acorn cup. With a small black mouse
riding inside. I believe a crafty neighbor must have heard
me. I am the Man of Shala and the Man of Pog.

(*Throws down ornaments.*)

You are *gogoli,* insane.
Human life means nothing to me.
I care only about gold and treasure and
the songs of the oras.
What good is my soul when my body
is dead! *Pse!*
Pancake would have given us gold, or if not
Pancake, then Ahmed Bey would have given us gold.

(*He looks around.*)

But you two, you see nothing and cause me only dishonor.
Find Pancake yourselves. I don't care if the Shoshi kill me.
Fools.

(*Stalks off. Pause.*)

WOMAN   Shall I wash your feet?

WOLFERT   Beat it. BEAT IT. Witch. Striga!
(*Blackout. Duck call. View of the A and B rings of Saturn as we slowly
sail above them.*)

FOX PERSON   Passed over the Encke division in the A ring. Roughly
82,890 miles up. The Encke division is a gap in the A
ring about 124 miles across. In the middle of it is the
Encke Doodle, a filamentary ringlet six to ten miles
across. Saw a man sitting in a chair torturing a cat.
Looked like a fucking Albanian. Threw a brick at him.
We were going too fast. It splattered through the A
ring. Missed by 1,200 miles. What's a man doing sitting

in a chair torturing a cat in the middle of the Encke
Doodle anyway? You tell me, I don't know, shitass no.
Door fell off the tub. Found a tuba. Can't play the
tuba, but kept it anyway. Parked the tub. Parked the
tuba. Caught some Zs. Set up the old card table on this
bodacious rock in the middle of the C ring.

(*View of* FOX PERSON *and* WOLFERT *playing cards on a boulder in the
C ring.*)

A little cramped. Nice view. No sign of Pancake. About
9,115 miles above the cloudtops. Winds of methane and ammonia smoking along at 650 miles per hour.

WOLFERT   Like waterskiing on frozen catpiss. Got to be more to life
than this.

FOX PERSON
(*Shuffles and deals.*)

From now on this is home. Trouble is, how we gonna find the
fastnesses at Tohu Bohu on Ann's Spot without the Man of
Shala? How we gonna get off this flying turd period?

WOLFERT   You got any chew?

FOX PERSON   Even supposing I did I wouldn't give it to you.

WOLFERT   So you won't give me no chew?

FOX PERSON   Wolfert. Have you ever considered the question:
where do we come from and where do we go?

WOLFERT   You can't get on base without you have no base
and no ball, and we don't have no bat neither.

FOX PERSON   I mean, you ever wonder where you go
when you croak?

WOLFERT   Ten of clubs.

FOX PERSON   Really! Where?

WOLFERT   Shit if I know.

FOX PERSON   Jack of hearts.

WOLFERT   You win. My deal.
     (*Shuffles.*)

FOX PERSON   What happens if we don't find Pancake?

WOLFERT
     (*Dealing*)
          We'll find Pancake.

FOX PERSON   What makes you so sure?

WOLFERT   He's gotta turn up somewhere. Three of spades.

FOX PERSON   Queen of hearts.

WOLFERT   Seven of diamonds.

FOX PERSON   Three of diamonds.

WOLFERT   Four of clubs.

FOX PERSON   Four of hearts.

WOLFERT   Ace of spades.

FOX PERSON   King of spades.

WOLFERT   Seven of hearts.

FOX PERSON   Nine of clubs.

WOLFERT   Jack of spades.

FOX PERSON   Queen of spades.

WOLFERT   You win. Your deal.
     (FOX PERSON *shuffles.*)
          What I am worried about is the cheese. I mean, are we
          looking for Pancake, or are we looking for the cheese?
          What if we find the cheese and no Pancake? Then we have
          two cheeses. A real one and a fake one. What do we do
          then? Worse yet, what if there is a fake Pancake just

as there is a fake cheese? How are we gonna tell the difference? It stands to reason if we can't tell no fake cheese from no real cheese how in the name of shit's creek are we gonna tell a real Pancake from a fake one? You tell me that.

FOX PERSON   We must be worldly, Wolfert. We must accept the worldliness of the world in the worlding of its worldyness.

WOLFERT   What the fuck is Ann's Spot anyhow?
(*Voice-over of* WINGFOOT. *A slow pan of the cloudtops of Saturn coming to rest on Ann's Spot.*)

WINGFOOT   Ann's Spot is a vast anticyclonic storm, emanating from thousands of miles below the surface of Saturn, flowing eastward in the South Temperate Zone at a speed of 25 miles per second. The storm is composed largely of a jet of frozen phosphorus welling to the surface in an intense low pressure system three thousand miles in diameter. The storm may be centuries old. The fastnesses at Tohu Bohu are hidden in the mists of Ann's Spot, and represent a final outpost of the Sanjak of Ops.
(*Eerie green light. Sparks and glimmers. Winds roaring overhead. Mists and indefinite cloud shapes. Soaring upward, the rings are faintly visible through the swirling translucency. Three objects are visible on stage. To the left, a round, flat shape. To the right a spindly, tall one. In the middle another, proportionately shaped as well as sized. Pause.* FOX PERSON *and* WOLFERT *step forward gingerly.* WINGFOOT *appears in a pool of light.*)
This am Wolfert, Fox Person. This am Pancake.
(*Points to the round, flat shape.*)

PANCAKE   Put forks under my eyelids.
(*The* MAN OF SHALA, *the second shape, takes his cloak and does this.*)

WINGFOOT   For do it all not now
At Cat, Pancake?

PANCAKE   So here is we all of a sunset up.

WINGFOOT   At Cat am?

PANCAKE   Great big bunch of us am.

WINGFOOT   For who was what did is the question.

PANCAKE   We all plod Yarth the same.

WINGFOOT   All kinds be, Pancake.
Furious lot shall have been. At Cat.

PANCAKE   X to X′ under the Crowe's eye.
X the Golden Theater am. Are am.

WINGFOOT   Whyso, Pancake?

PANCAKE   Whyso not, Wingfoot.

WINGFOOT   Perplexity am what.

PANCAKE   Perplexity am what jumped up and got back to where
it was when it all began so no one could accuse it
of not being just so.

WINGFOOT   Who it was was, Pancake.

PANCAKE   Mmmmmmmmmmmmmm . . .
(*Pause.*)
Be done shall is.
Are shall have did and shall be unto.
Are will be did too.
Are is and are is not.
Are have was will be too.
Are the mostleastbestest X be.
Did did too.

WINGFOOT   Who was as who do, kinda.

PANCAKE   "Kinda," Wingfoot?
(WINGFOOT *looks embarrassed.*)
Being did was as is and therefore should am.
Would be was too.

Would be much like should am.
Only it got bigger feets and got more hoohah and therefore
himher big feets all the same.

WINGFOOT   All smoke have to get did elsewhere if himher
want to get on base without no bat and no ball.

PANCAKE   Were will be.
Were was and is.
Were have done did.
Were the X shall be.
Were the who will be.
Were the elsewheres unless of be did am.

WINGFOOT   All the same but smoke, Pancake . . .

PANCAKE   All smoke too was did likeso
At Cat.

WINGFOOT   Without no base and no ball?

PANCAKE   X the moon through the C where they's O.
X the ink on the C to clear the are did.
X the huge freestanding be am.
X the whole shebang cross the blackdress.
But as everyone shehe know you don't get nobody
out without you have no base and no ball.

(WINGFOOT *looks chastened.*)

PANCAKE   Who the who there, all bunched up, the same?

WINGFOOT   Fox Person, the same. Wolfert, the same. And, ah . . . fake
cheese.

(*Ruminative pause.*)

PANCAKE   Pity, the fake cheese. Ahmed Bey sent you to me did he?
Why should I believe you? He is not even himself!
Assuming that you are who you say you are, as Wingfoot
has attested, why should I not put you to the sword?
Answer me that? Do you know who Ahmed Bey is? He is

Zogu and Zogu is King Zog. Zogu was under the delusion
that Mehmet Shehu who he surmised you murdered was a
counterrevolutionary agent burrowed into the flesh of
the Albanian Workers' Party presided over by the tyrant
Enver Hoxha. Even though King Zog was dead he continued
to be obsessed by these fantasies. Things have multiple
causes, as you will learn if you spend any time in Tohu
Bohu. What is up today is down tomorrow. Context is
everything. No man knows what he does, even the avatars
of the Drangoijt. Why did King Zog think you murdered
Mehmet Shehu? Beats me. But you and I know he was wrong.
We have fewer friends than we think and more than you
know. The Man of Shala arrived here before you, after in-
suring that Wingfoot would be able to find you and guide
you here. I would not have shown such generosity in view
of your pedestrian tastes and questionable morals. The Man
of Shala calls you Dumbbell and Shit-for-Brains. I am over
nine hundred years old and I know many things. You see,
another reason Ahmed Bey sent you to me was that he was
not Ahmed Bey but a false Ahmed Bey and he imagined I
would kill you. The relation between the real and the false
Ahmed Bey is not clear. If the false is but a factotum for the
real Ahmed Bey my argument stands as presented thus far.
If, however, he was a counter-agent for the Albanian Workers' Party then his motive would be vengeance, for Mehmet
Shehu was not an agent of King Zog, but the evil genius behind Enver Hoxha himself. In either case, an iron logic
holds: you see, I am to be your executioner.

(*Clears his throat.*)

To insure both that the murder of Mehmet Shehu is never
detected, and to avenge it. Again there is a complication,
for *I* am the murderer of Mehmet Shehu, therefore this
story has a happy ending for you, and therefore I am the best
friend you ever had. Shehu was a dragon; I am a drangue.
That is the simplest explanation of the event, and in Tohu
Bohu there are explanations so bizarre, so recondite no

human mind can fathom them. I have been blasted by the cold winds of Saturn for so long, and flattened by her enormous gravitational pull, that I am scarcely human. But I am a great hero of our people, in the tradition of our greatest warrior, Skanderbeg, who defeated the Turks in twenty-two consecutive battles, who vanquished even Sultan Murad and also Sultan Fitaj Mehmet, the conqueror of Constantinople. A moment of silence for Skanderbeg.

(*A moment of silence.*)

So, not only am I going to spare your lives, for you have traveled a great distance, but I am going to tell you a story about the oras. You will listen carefully. For this story also has a happy ending. Of sorts. If any story has a happy ending. By Zaa, by E Thana, by the power of the sun and the moon, all these things are true—remember.

FOX PERSON   What about the Man of Shala.* Will you protect him from the Shoshi?

WOLFERT   Shit on him.

(*The* MAN OF SHALA *grimaces at* WOLFERT.)

PANCAKE   I shall grant him a *besa,* a pass of safe conduct, through the Shoshi lands.

FOX PERSON   Glory to your eyes.

PANCAKE   Wingfoot tells me you know about the oras. I will
tell you about the man who married one of them.
Will someone prop up my eyelids for they have
fallen down over my eyes.

(SHALA *does this.*)

There was a man who lived alone. His wife had died. He was thirty-seven years old and did not want another wife. One night the ora appeared at his door. She sat down. He offered her coffee. They sat by the fire for a long time without speaking.

(The scene is enacted by FOX PERSON (ORA) *and* WOLFERT (MAN).
Long pauses.)

ORA   Long life to you.

MAN   Long life to you.

ORA   Glory to your eyes.

MAN   Glory to your eyes.

ORA   Have you ever seen a woman more beautiful?

MAN   No.

ORA   Will you marry me?

MAN   No.

     (Pause.)

ORA   Will you marry me?

MAN   No.

PANCAKE   She went away. But a year later she returned, and appeared just as before. Just as before she sat by the fire, and he gave her coffee.

ORA   Long life to you.

MAN   Long life to you.

ORA   Glory to your eyes.

MAN   Glory to your eyes.

ORA   Have you ever seen a woman more beautiful?

MAN   No.

ORA   Will you marry me?

MAN   No.

ORA   Will you marry me?

MAN   No.

PANCAKE   She arose and gave him her hand.

ORA   Come with me.

PANCAKE   He did as she bade.
(*They walk about till they come to the third shape, the tall and spindly one. He uncloaks himself. It is her* FATHER. *He wears antlers and his face is hidden. Strange, sounds, trees, lights.*)
They went to a place, a strange place and strange mountains. A place in our mountains, but a place no one had ever seen.

MAN   THE TREES WERE ALIVE!
(*Falls to his knees.*)

PANCAKE   . . . was all my friend could say. Her father spoke to him.

FATHER   Have you ever seen a woman more beautiful?

MAN   No.

FATHER   Will you marry her?

MAN   No.

FATHER   Will you marry her?

MAN   No.
(*Pause. The* ORA'S FATHER *stands.*)

FATHER   You *will* marry her.

MAN   Yes.

MAN OF SHALA   A goat is tied by his horns, a man by his word. But the things that a man knows because he has seen them, the things he considers while he walks on the trails and while he sits by the fire, are not many. All these things are very old, and none of them are written in books, therefore, they are true.
(*The* ORA *and the* MAN *sit and drink coffee.*)

PANCAKE   He built her a beautiful house. Rugs and tables of carved woods, bowls of copper and silver. Cigarette holders of amber and silver with jeweled bowls, sashes and turbans of silks, cushions and water jars, great quantities of rich and delicate foods. No one but him ever saw her. They were very happy.

Slow blackout.

End of play.

ANTHEM

(Chorus/Ensemble from *Albanian Softshoe*)

Music by Michael Roth

Back where to - mor-row the quick may be dead, with a hole in the heart or a ball in the head. Back where the pas-sions are ra - pid and red. Oh we're back! Oh we're back! Oh we're back to the Bal - kans a - gain! Back to the Bal - kans a - gain!

Methane Cliffs

(Fox Person, Wolfert, & 2 Women,
from *Albanian Softshoe*)

Music by Michael Roth

Moderate/songlike

Mister
Original Bugg

H. L. Mencken's *The American Language*
is one of the most amazing documents this civilization has produced,
a treasure trove of obscure learning,
lunatic particulars, and wonderful
folklore. Somewhere in it I came
across a list of unusual, but real,
American names, both first and last.
Later I found some others and began
to collect them. So *Mister Original Bugg*
came out of this interest, as a miniature drama on the original act of
naming. Kim Sherman wrote some
music for the piece, now lost. Someone was going to do the play in a
roller rink in Los Angeles, but the production fell through at the last moment. So the play remains unproduced. I cannot imagine why.

PERFORMANCE NOTE
The three women are in their twenties and take on each of their varying roles with great seriousness.
A straight deadpan delivery is called for throughout. Physical action must be sharp, fast, and acrobati-
cally precise.

Scene. Three straight-back chairs upstage. A doorway. Downstage a small table.
Vase of strange flowers and next to it on the table a small tray. FIRST WOMAN
enters. Pauses. She wears a scarlet derby. Big grin on her face. She produces a
visiting card from her vest pocket and deposits it on the tray.

FIRST WOMAN My name is Mister Original Bugg.
> (*She bows and exits.* SECOND WOMAN *appears. She wears a black*
> *broad-brimmed hat and sports a drooping moustache.*

SECOND WOMAN My name is Fly-Fornication Smith.
> (*She deposits her card and exits. The* THIRD WOMAN *appears. She*
> *wears a bow tie studded with flashing lights.*)

THIRD WOMAN My name is E Pluribus Unum Husted.
> (*She deposits her card and exits. The* FIRST *reappears. She wears big*
> *shoes.*)

FIRST My name is Willie 3/8 Smith. No relation.
> (*Deposits card and exits.* SECOND *reappears. She wears a top hat and a*
> *long white beard.*)

SECOND My name is . . .
> (*She goes blank. Looks at card.*)
> > My name is Loyal Lodge No. 296 Knights of Pythias Ponca
> > City Oklahoma Smith. No relation.
> (*Deposits card and exits.* THIRD *reappears. She wears big green tennis*
> *shoes and a green beanie.*)

THIRD My name is Doodlebug Hightower.
> (*Deposits card and starts to exit. The* FIRST *enters dressed exactly the*
> *same as* THIRD, *whom she trips on the latter's way out.*)

FIRST   I'm called Monkeydo Moffatt.

(*Deposits card and exits.* SECOND *rushes in wearing absurd dark glasses.*)

SECOND   Frog Robbins . . .

(*Rushes out. Rushes back in and leaves her card.* THIRD *enters with a black top hat and fluffy pink slippers. Huge card. Pince nez. She reads slowly.*)

THIRD   I'm known as Daniel's Wisdom May I Know Stephen's Faith and Spirit Choose John's Divine Communion Seal Moses Meekness Joshua's Zeal Win the Day and Conquer All Murphy, junior.

(*Creeps out stealthily, looking all around.* FIRST *enters wearing a bizarre hat with blinking lights, ringing bells, and a spinning windmill.*)

FIRST   Sal Hepatica Palmer.

(*Deposits card and goes out.* SECOND *enters with a black veil draped over her head, and wire antennae.*)

SECOND   My name is I Will Arise and Go Unto My Father Jones.

(*Feels her way out, and is again tripped by the* FIRST *as the* THIRD *enters on all fours. Animal ears and whiskers. Card in mouth. Deposits it in tray. Sits up on haunches animal fashion.*)

THIRD   My name is Pictorial Review Hardpan.

(*Sits panting until the* FIRST *appears with dogcatcher hat.* THIRD *rushes out.* FIRST *takes off hat, finds card in hat, replaces hat, puts on strangle goggly eyeglasses.*)

FIRST   People call me Kansas Nebraska Bill Clinton.

(*Deposits card and goes out as* SECOND *rolls quickly in on skates, deposits card, and shouts on her way out:*)

SECOND   Byzantine Botts!

(*Pause.* THIRD *enters wearing enormous feather boa. Black lipstick.*)

THIRD   They call me Polly Body.

(*Grins. Pause. Goes out. Returns. Deposits card, goes out and while doing so is tripped by the* FIRST, *who enters wearing a dunce hat and huge hairy gloves.*)

FIRST   My name is Mister Christian Girl.
(*Looks around and seeing no one scoops up and pockets all the cards. The* SECOND, *meanwhile, appears at the door wearing a hat that is too large to fit through. After several attempts to squeeze through, she gives up and tosses her card at the tray.*)

SECOND   Alligator Dingbat sends his regrets.
(*She disappears. Pause.* THIRD *enters wearing a huge suit and huge necktie. She looks very stupid.*)

THIRD   I'm called Dubois Clock.
(*Goes out and is routinely tripped by the* FIRST, *who is dressed as in her initial appearance. Leaves card. Demurely announces her name.*)

FIRST   Call me Dumbbell Barf.
(SECOND *appears in her first costume. She carries a music stand and she bows. Looks suspiciously at* FIRST.)

SECOND   I'm Called Glorious Illumination Burp.
(*Deposits card and stands next to* FIRST. *Pause.* SECOND *whistles. Pause. The* THIRD *enters, hunched over, wrapped in a strange cloak. Speaks in a hundred-year-old voice.*)

THIRD   My name is . . . Midwinter Hush.
(*All three bow and take their seats. Music begins. Pause.* SECOND *arranges music on the stand. The song begins.*)

FIRST   I am.

SECOND   You are not.

FIRST   I am too.

THIRD   She is too.

SECOND   Who are you? Go away.

FIRST   All I know is I am here.

SECOND Presently you will say
      we are voices.

THIRD   We ride the air.

SECOND When I am around
      you are not.

FIRST and THIRD How metaphysical!
        How angelical!

THIRD   I am skidding along
      a banner of light.

FIRST and SECOND Delight! Delight!

SECOND To be and then to not.

FIRST   To vanish in the silence.

THIRD   The silence after.

SECOND I am. You are not.

FIRST, SECOND and THIRD What is clear is
      what we hear and how
      it's etched out of time
      by what is not. If
      all the names the gods have given things
      were changed all would be changed.
      The same. The end. The sky is full
      of junk. The stars are very far away.
      Only what we hear is near.

Cleveland

After I wrote *Albanian Softshoe* and
began to show it around, through the
usual and inevitable means of public
reading, I began to hear people say
that I should write an entire play in
the vein of the more accessible first
act. Now, this had been conceived,
initially at least, as a parody of soap
opera. But parody considered not
simply as a negation, but almost as
an homage; so that a new, unforeseen
kind of drama might come into
being. So I made up *Cleveland*, specifically for my friend Anne Bogart.
Her production at BACA Downtown
was the first time I got to see a script
of mine really come alive.

PERFORMANCE NOTES

The appearance of an asterisk within a speech indicates that the next speech begins to overlap at that point.

Mirandan whispertalk consists of consonants only, except for an occasional ending. Mainly sibilants and fricatives. Vowels are free. C is pronounced like "ch" in church.

PRODUCTION NOTE

At the BACA production (1986) a narrator (the strange man of Scene Seven) introduced all the scenes and gave most of the stage directions. Anne Bogart's direction involved, therefore, a thorough and ongoing response to these introductions as an integral part of the author's text. Therefore, for the adventurous, these introductory scenic texts are given, in order, below. The narrator's text in Scene Seven is identical in both versions. For those who prefer a more conventional staging, the original configuration of the play is reproduced as a basic text.

NARRATOR   Scene one. Welcome to the theater. X all the way to X', a whole hell of a way. You ever wonder what the world'd be like if a circle were defined as a round straight line with a hole in the middle? Joan and her mother live in Cleveland. Joan writes in her diary. Later her mother sneaks a look at what her daughter has written. Far away in the land of Tlpccc, it is said there are no secrets between mother and daughter. Music plays. It is "nice" music.

NARRATOR   Scene two. The kitchen. The mother is trying to unclog the sink with a plunger. The sink makes strange noises. Joan is trying to do her homework at the kitchen table. More nice music. Far away, the Plain of Qqqsmsmccctu is littered with little stone jars filled with light.

NARRATOR   Scene three. The same as before. The kitchen. The man is using the plunger now. The mother looks on philosophically. More nice music. Joan is daydreaming. A long pause.

As heavy with meaning as a herd of grazing rhinodraconopeds.

NARRATOR Scene four. The mother is back at the sink, with the plunger. Joan enters, singing a bit of her strange song.

NARRATOR Scene five. Darkness. A wind of other worlds. Far away and far ago. Joan's dream. She is dressed as a Trotskyite Anti-pope. Losin' Susan, a blue Anti-pope, lies in an open coffin. The other Anti-popes are, respectively: Marta, black; Griselda, white; Bertha, green; Kate, yellow. Mister Barfly is now Joan's Swiss Guard. He carries a halberd. The room is full of lethal whispers.

NARRATOR Scene six. Next day. Again the kitchen. The mother is seated at the table reading a college catalogue. Joan is preparing an after-school snack. The snack is an unusually grotesque sandwich. On the wall there is a picture of the Massacre of Innocents. Perhaps at Skyeyesqll. The picture is tilted. How odd!

JOAN, a high school girl with a secret;
HER MOTHER, with a secret of her own;
a MAN, a neighborly Trotskyite;
SUSAN, losin' Susan and
   JOAN's other pals:
MARTA,
KATE,
BERTHA,
and GRISELDA;
RICHARD, alias PANDA HANDS, JOAN's date to the prom;
MISTER BARFLY, a teacher at a fashionable boys' school in Cleveland;
the MAYOR OF CLEVELAND, a man in a difficult fix;
and a strange MAN with a wand.

The play takes place in Cleveland during the prom season and in the dream-time of Joan.

Scene one. JOAN *in a pool of light. Writing in her diary. Her* MOTHER *reading it aloud, simultaneously, in another pool of light. Nice music plays.*

MOTHER   Dear Diary. I feel like I'm losing
my mind. Like Losin' Susan.
I feel sure Johnny will ask me
to the Prom. Johnny on the Spot.
If not him, then Panda Hands.
I will end it all if he does.
I do not wish to go to the Prom
because since we have lost all
our money we are no longer
fashionable. As we once were.
Ahead lies a life of meaningless
drudgery and not the glitter and
champagne of high society. Sigh.
I do not love Johnny. But I do
love Jimmy. In my secret heart
of hearts. Sigh. Jimmy the door.
Way to my dreams. I'm not sure
I want that. My dreams scare me . . .
Jimmy goes to the Boys Prep School
and I go to the Catholic Girls School.
Our Lady of the Bleeding Knuckle.
Our Lady of the Runny Nose.
A chasm of religion divides us.
And he will not ask me to the
Prom. Yes, because I am not
fashionable. If Mother could read

this she would know, yes, all
my unclean thoughts. To tell
the truth, dear diary, I feel
quite fed up with life since Dad
died and did not go to Heaven.
Strange things are afoot in the heavens . . .
(MOTHER *looks puzzled.* JOAN *whistles her song from Scene Seven.*)
I dreamed last night I was
Pope Joan. And a Trotskyite, like Dad.

Scene two. The kitchen. MOTHER *is trying to unclog the sink with a plunger. The sink makes strange noises.* JOAN *is trying to do her homework at the kitchen table.* More *nice music.*

JOAN   Mother, how can I concentrate on my homework
with you making that noise?

MOTHER   I'm sorry dear. It doesn't drain.
Mr. Barfly the plumber was supposed
to come fix it, but he never did.

JOAN   But I'm trying to do my homework.

MOTHER   Joanie, there's nothing I can do.
(*Pause.*)

JOAN   Mother, what's the largest moon in the
solar system?

NARRATOR   Why, Triton, dear. A moon of Neptune.
Not a very hospitable place. My, this
sink is hopeless. Miranda's much prettier.

JOAN   Thanks. Mr. Delaplane's science class is
really hard.
(*Loud crash outside.*)
What's that noise?

MOTHER
(*Going to look.*)
Just some commotion in the street.

JOAN Who is Pope Joan? Bet you don't know.

MOTHER Haven't the faintest, dear.
  (*Phone rings.*)

JOAN Oh, God, what if it's Panda Hands asking
    me to the prom.
  (*Rings.*)

MOTHER I thought we weren't fashionable enough
    to be invited.
  (*Rings.*)

JOAN Well, I still want to go. It depends. You
    get it.

MOTHER Silly girl.
  (*She gets the phone.*)
    Hello? No, he's dead. That's right. Dead. No,
    we don't need any. Thank you. Good bye.
  (*Hangs up. Pause.*)
    Well, it wasn't Panda Hands.
  (*Knock at the door.*)
    Who could that be?

JOAN If it's Panda Hands I'm not here.

MOTHER
  (*At door*)
    Yes? Can I help you?
  (*A* MAN *enters.*)

MAN Lady. Your front porch. It ah. Fell into the
    street. Somebody's underneath. In a car. One
    of those imports. Squashed flat.

MOTHER Oh, how terrible. Well, come in.

MAN Thanks. All you can see is the hubcap.

MOTHER The phone's right there.

JOAN   Mother?

MOTHER It's all right, Joanie. The front porch fell into the street and it seems there's a car underneath.

MOTHER What's the police number?

MOTHER Haven't the faintest.
  (*He reads it off the phone and dials.*)

JOAN   Mother, what if Jimmy asks me and not Panda Hands?

MOTHER Then I expect you should go. Even if we're not fashionable.

MOTHER No one answers at the police. Strange.
  (*Hangs up.*)

MOTHER That is strange.

JOAN   Very strange. Hey, can I go look?

MOTHER If you're very careful.
  (JOAN *skips out.*)

MAN   I'll call the wrecking company. You got a Yellow Pages?

MOTHER Sure, right here.
  (*Shows him. She goes to the sink and plunger.*)
   You know, I think I want to go back to school. Learn a skill. I'm tired of being a drudge. And since my husband died. It's rough being alone.

MAN   You're young to be a widow.

MOTHER He was a Trotskyist.

MAN
  (*On phone*)
   Acme Wrecking? Yeah, part of a house's fallen

across River Road near Willoughby. Traffic's
already backed up pretty far. And I think
there's someone trapped underneath. Yeah,
in a car.
(*Hangs up.*)

MOTHER He was a Trotskyist.

MAN So am I. Thanks, lady.
(*He goes out. She goes back to the sink.* JOAN *enters.*)

JOAN Oh, you should see it. Everything's all
smashed. It's really neat. Say, do you
suppose someone's dead under all that
pile of rubble?

MOTHER Could be, darling. Could be. Wash up, it's
dinner time.

JOAN If Jimmy calls I'm here. If Johnny calls
I'm not. If Panda Hands calls I'm dead.

MOTHER Yes, dear.
(*Pause.*)
You know, Joanie. I think I want to go back to school.

JOAN You'd be a great student. And I'll do the
grocery shopping. We'll trade.
(*They giggle.*)

MOTHER So. What's the biggest moon in the solar
system?

JOAN Miranda.

MOTHER Miranda's the prettiest. Triton's the biggest.

JOAN Darn. Well you tell me who is Pope Joan.

MOTHER Never heard of her.
(*They giggle.*)

JOAN   I want to be like Pope Joan. Only I want
to be a Trotskyist.

MOTHER   This sink is disgusting.
(*The* MAN *enters again.*)

MAN   Lady, can I use the phone again.

MOTHER   Sure.
(*He dials. Pause.*)

JOAN   If he's on the phone all the time
how's Jimmy going to call me?

MOTHER   Ever think it might be Panda Hands?
(*They giggle.*)

Blackout.

Scene three. The same. The MAN *is using the plunger now.* MOTHER *looks on philosophically. More nice music.* JOAN's *daydreaming. A lengthy pause.*

MAN   Jesus, lady, what'd you put down here, cement?

MOTHER   I'm afraid some bones got stuck. Last week.
Rather large game fowl.
(*Five of* JOAN's *friends enter. The* MAN *continues plunging.*)

MARTA   Guess who lucked out and got Jimmy?

SUSAN   Jimmy the Door!

KATE   Losin' Susan here.

SUSAN   It's on account of I can cha cha.
(*They laugh.*)

BERTHA   I got Jewel Rude Dude. He's such an elegant
dresser.

GRISELDA Very neat.

MARTA   What about you, Joan?

JOAN   No one's called yet.

SUSAN   You end up with Johnny on the Spot.

JOAN   No way, Santa Fe.

KATE   Oh, yes. I foresee it. Written in the sky.

GRISELDA   Sorry, he asked me.* I thought you knew.

MARTA   Sneaky. Sneaky* secret keeper.

KATE   Well that leaves me and you and*
you know who invited me? Guess!

MARTA   I shall be out of town. Thank God.

JOAN   Fiji Three Eyes.

KATE   Who's that?

MARTA   I'm really not interested.* I'm going away
for a college weekend. At Denison. Party school.

KATE   You shouldn't call him that.

BERTHA   But he's so cute.

GRISELDA   The name's not cute.

SUSAN   Last prom before I move* to Albuquerque.

JOAN   Who cares?

MARTA   That leaves you.
    (*To* JOAN.)

KATE   Guess!

GRISELDA   That leaves only* Panda Hands.

SUSAN   Oh, Jimmy and I shall bop the night away.

MARTA   Groan.

JOAN   Groan indeed.

GRISELDA   Coming to cheerleader practice?

JOAN   No, our porch fell off.

KATE   I wondered what all that garbage was
in the street.

BERTHA   Come on. Let's get going.

GRISELDA   Okay. Okay. If it's got to be it's got to be.
Johnny on the Spot.* Yech.

KATE   So. No one wants to know* who invited me?

BERTHA
(*To* GRISELDA.)
     You got any gum?

MARTA   If I had any gum I wouldn't give it to you.

SUSAN   That leaves only* Panda Hands.

JOAN   That leaves only Panda Hands. Yech.

SUSAN   Too gross for words.
(*They laugh. The* MAN *stops plunging.*)

MAN   Well it's pretty much cleared. I guess.
(*The* GIRLS *trail out.* JOAN *with them.*)

SUSAN   So long, Mrs. P.

MOTHER   Bye bye, Susie. Have fun. Don't be too late,
Joanie.
(*He sits wearily.*)

MAN   Howzabout you and me go down to
party headquarters and lift a few?

MOTHER   What about the front porch?

MAN   It's not going anywhere. Say, what's
your name?

MOTHER   You wouldn't believe if I told you.

MAN   Try me.

    (*They laugh. She approaches.*)

Scene four. MOTHER *is back at the sink with the plunger.* JOAN *enters whistling a bit of her song. The* MOTHER *suddenly stops plunging.*

JOAN   I thought that guy fixed the sink.

MOTHER   He did. For a while. It's the thing in there that
       that grinds stuff up. It's strange.

JOAN   At least most of the wreckage is gone from
       the street.

MOTHER   How was practice?

JOAN   Nifty. Anyone call?

MOTHER   Nope. No one ever calls anymore.
    (*Pause.*)

       Why is it so dark out today?

JOAN   That time of year, Mom. Honestly . . .
    (*Pause.*)

       Mom, why don't you ever talk about it?

MOTHER   About what?

JOAN   You know. Dad. All that stuff.

    (*Her* MOTHER *goes back to the plunger.*)
       I know we're not fashionable.
       Okay, Mom, but. But Christ. There's
       a limit. You could talk.
    (*Pause.*)

       I mean it looks as though I'll be going
       to the prom with old Panda Hands himself,
       but I'll go. I don't hold it all inside.

    (*Her* MOTHER *stops plunging. Pause.*)

MOTHER   I would like just once to do some-
       thing original. Just once is all

	I ask. Even if we're not fashionable anymore.
JOAN	Mom, don't talk like that.
MOTHER	Maybe go back to school. Earn valuable career credits. An exciting career in robotics may await me.
JOAN	Mom, please talk to me.
MOTHER	That nice man who fixed the drainpipe was a Trotskyist like your father. It makes me nervous . . .
JOAN	Mom, I don't care if we're not fashionable. I love you.

(*Pause. Her* MOTHER *sits.*)

| MOTHER | Well. All right. We were in New York for the party congress. We had just met the Mayor of Cleveland. Of course he wasn't a Trotskyist. He was far too fashionable for that. A fine, big man he was, with a fine, big, round head. He said to your father: "Fine work. That report on solid waste." Then he introduced himself to me. It was an awkward moment because, of course, your father had no idea what the mayor was talking about. It seems he was at the wrong hotel. "We're Trotskyists." We said. "My apologies." He said. "May I buy you a drink?" And he did. One of those elegant little sidewalk cafés. Lovely. |

(*A sad moment.*)

We were sitting on the sidewalk. Or,

rather, at a table on the sidewalk. And
your father leaned over to make a point
and spilled his espresso. As he moved
forward with the saucer in his other
hand the heel snapped off his shoe and
well he slid back into the chair. Of
course the coffee got over everyone.
And the chair leg broke and, it was
quite remarkable, he did a nice,
little, wholly unintentional back-
flip into the street. I shall never
forget the sight of his shoes, the
soles of them, as they lifted high
into the air. He was trying to save
the cup, poor dear. But it shattered
in the street, and then the first car
ran over it. And the saucer which had
been undamaged miraculously up to that
point. He was a quite fastidious man.
The second car ran over your father.
Quite a large car. A limo, I think.
"My word." Said the mayor. What a
strange thing to say. Of course he was
dead. Your father, I mean. That's about it.
More coffee.

JOAN   At least now I know. The truth.

MOTHER   Yes. That's the least of it. Now you know.
      (*She goes back to the plunger. The phone rings.* JOAN *gets it.*)
      Panda Hands.

JOAN   Oh. Hi. Sure. I guess.
      (*She grimaces to her* MOTHER.)

Black.

Scene five. JOAN's *dream. Dressed in red as a Trotskyist Anti-pope.* LOSIN'
SUSAN, *a blue Anti-pope, lies in an open coffin. The others are, respectively:*

MARTA, *black;* GRISELDA, *white;* BERTHA, *green;* KATE, *yellow.* BARFLY *is* JOAN's *Swiss Guard. He carries a halberd.*

JOAN	Are we prepared, Barfly?
BARFLY	Yes, excellency.
JOAN	Bring them in.
BARFLY	Singly. Or together? Excellency?
JOAN	En masse. We might as well deal with them all at once.

(BARFLY *goes. Returns with the others. They arrange themselves about the room. Pause.*)

	Bertha, you look well.
MARTA	No need for small talk, Joan.
KATE	What are the conditions you propose?
JOAN	Ah, Griselda, I hear you are fully recovered.
GRISELDA	Tolerably.
BERTHA	What is to be the final disposition of the Matriarchate of Cordoba? Merged with Cadiz?
JOAN	Not quite.
KATE	And Tunis, Carthago, Malta?
JOAN	That depends on your decision, my dear.
KATE	My decision! It is not apparent from my information that your decision to summon this conclave, this silence of Anti-popes, has been informed to the minutest degree by a regard for my opinion.
MARTA	Be still, Kate.
GRISELDA	Hibernia? What of Hibernia?

BERTHA	Macedonia. The Sanjak of Novi Bazaar?
MARTA	And what of the Eastern Matriarchates? We who provide a buffer between you all and the Turks? Have you considered the possible consequences?
JOAN	Of course, Marta. Of course.
MARTA	Now that Diotima has passed on . . .
JOAN	You are referring to Losin' Susan . . .

(*Who sits up in her coffin.*)

SUSAN	I don't want to move to Albuquerque.

(*Lies down.*)

KATE	That isn't Latin. Is it Ladino?
BERTHA	Be still, dear.
JOAN	I have called this silence of Anti-popes because there is a traitor in our midst.
BERTHA	Explain yourself.
JOAN	If you allow* me.
MARTA	Preposterous.
GRISELDA	Let Joan speak. (*Pause.*) There. Go on.
BERTHA	All this beating around the bush is tiresome.
JOAN	I suspect one of you of fomenting an antireformation.
KATE	No!
BERTHA	Impossible.
GRISELDA	How can this be?
JOAN	It is true. These (*She shows the document.*) are a set of 496 antitheses concerning our

canons of heteroclite unorthodoxy. Found nailed
to the door by one of my Swiss Guards, Jimmy.
Some one of you has sought a codification of the
undreamed of, the unspoken, and the unthinkable.
It is signed with a crow's feather. Thus.

MARTA   It's a hoax.

KATE   Yes. Joan, it must be?
    (*Weeps.*)

GRISELDA   Griselda, please.

KATE   No, you're Griselda. I'm Kate.

GRISELDA   Sorry.

BERTHA   So emotional . . .

MARTA   I don't trust you, Joan. Are you accusing
one of us, and if so, which? If you have
charges, present them. I have my Nuncios
and Legates with me. In the antechamber . . .

JOAN   That will not be necessary, Marta.

MARTA   I knew it was a mistake to come.
This is a trap.

JOAN   Be quiet.
    (*Pause.*)

In at least 98 of the aforementioned 496 antitheses
there is incontrovertible evidence of the Mirandan
heresy.
    (*Gasps.*)

KATE   Impossible.

GRISELDA   That was stamped out centuries ago.

KATE   How can you be so sure?

JOAN   There are numerous quotations in the

             demotic script of whispertalk, the Mirandan
             cipher.

BERTHA   If that is true, then perhaps you are the author
             of these documents. You are, after all, the
             world's leading expert on whispertalk . . .

GRISELDA   Be still, let her speak.

JOAN   I cannot tell who it is.

MARTA   Of course not.

JOAN   Therefore I have taken steps, with sadness,
             but also with a firm sense of determination
             and duty, to abolish all of your matriarchates.
             From now on there is only one Anti-pope,
             and I am she.

      (BARFLY *bars door.*)

MARTA   I knew it.

GRISELDA   But Joan, how can you be capable of this?

MARTA   Damn you, Griselda, for ever talking me
             into attending this silence. I was foolish
             ever to trust a Trotskyist Anti-pope. My
             fastness at Antioch could have held out
             forever against her rhinodraconopeds.

KATE   Will you ransom us?

BERTHA   Sorry, Joan. A legion of my best fusiliers
             are deployed in the Great Hall, just beyond
             those doors. If I blow on this Anti-papal
             secret clerical dog whistle they will rush
             to our defense.

JOAN   Two legions of my Swiss Guard surround
             the palace grounds, Bertha. You have no
             choice but to renounce your powers and
             accept me as the supreme Anti-pontiff.

(*Pause.*)

You see, Bertha, all your fusiliers are dead.

BERTHA   I don't believe you.

(JOAN *snaps her fingers.* BARFLY *opens the doors to the Great Hall.*
JOAN *points down the corridor.*)

BERTHA   I still don't believe you.

JOAN   You are aware, I presume, of the symptoms
           of ergotic poisoning?

(*All look down the corridor and gasp.*)

MARTA   Demon.

JOAN   Twitching and quaking.

SUSAN   (*Sitting up in her coffin.*)
           I don't want to move to Albuquerque.

KATE   Be quiet, fool. Your character would never say
           that.

(SUSAN *lies down.*)

JOAN   Diotima here was the guardian of the Glassy
           Sphere. With her voices at my command
           I do not need your approval. My word is
           law. Whichever one of you is the Mirandan
           agent I don't know. It hardly matters.
           The ransom will be a million obuluses. Each.

GRISELDA   Each?

KATE   Each! But that's absurd.

MARTA   You'll never get away with this, Joan.

JOAN   Except for you, Marta. You will remain here
           till the next intersection of the Seven Cosmic
           Circles. Then Diotima's disembodied voice
           will tell us who is behind all this heretical
           whispertalk. It may be a long time.

KATE   But we trusted you, Joan.

BERTHA   I never trusted her.

MARTA   Oh, what a fool I am.

Blackout.

Scene six. The next day. The kitchen again. MOTHER *at the table intently reading a college catalogue.* JOAN *preparing herself an after-school snack.*

JOAN   The prom's tomorrow.

MOTHER   You must be very excited.

JOAN   What's that?

MOTHER   Catalogue for Polytechnical College.

JOAN
      (Reading over her shoulder)
      "Human Body Fluid and Advanced Polymerization."
      Golly, Mom.

MOTHER   Just looking at what courses are
            available.

JOAN   Gee, when you said you wanted to go
            back to school I thought you meant
            something like. Business I or Creative Writing.

MOTHER   How was cheerleader practice today?

JOAN   Fine. Learned some new tricks.
    (Pause.)

            Only. Mom.

MOTHER   Yes, dear.

JOAN   I had a kind of bad dream last night.

MOTHER   I shouldn't have told you. So explicitly.

JOAN   No, it wasn't about Dad. It was something
              else.

MOTHER   The sink is fixed again. There's fresh coffee.

JOAN   It was all kinda confused. All about Pope
              Joan and stuff.

MOTHER   I have to mend your dress for the prom.
              Why don't you try it on?
          (*She goes out for the dress.*)

JOAN
          (*Off.*)
              Mr. Delaplane said you know a lot about
              astronomy but that nobody knows the
              orbital eccentricity of Triton. It's
              too far away.

MOTHER   I knew it. I should never have told you the
              details. About your father's death.

JOAN   Was it ever fashionable to be a
              Trotskyist?

MOTHER   Yes, dear. Once it was very fashionable.
          (*She enters in a bright red prom dress. Her* MOTHER *sets about mending
          a hem. Pause.*)

JOAN   How come you know so much about astronomy?

MOTHER   And we were personal acquaintances of the
              mayor. If things had only worked out a
              little differently. We might still be
              fashionable.

JOAN   Mom, would you tell me something?

MOTHER   Our kitchen sink might not have been stopped up.
              Our front porch might not have . . . fallen into the
              street. Poor dear, you know they haven't tccmbbd
              the body yet.

JOAN   What? What did you say?

MOTHER   Slip of the tongue. They haven't identified his body yet.

(*Pause.*)

JOAN   Have you seen that man? Again?

MOTHER   What man?

JOAN   The man that fixed the sink.

MOTHER   Once. Briefly. But it won't happen again.

(*Pause.* MOTHER *finishes her mending.*)

JOAN   Did you sleep with him?

MOTHER   What do you want from me? Do I tell you how to live your life? No, damn it. Is that how they teach you to think at that fancy Catholic school? Just because we're Trotskyists and you feel socially embarrassed. Just because we were once fashionable but aren't anymore. Just because I want so desperately, once in my life, to do something, anything, original . . .

JOAN   Okay. Okay. Just curious.

(*Pause.*)

MOTHER   He's had an accident. Very serious one. He won't be back.

(*Pause.*)

JOAN   Mother, who are you?

MOTHER   Another cup of coffee?

JOAN   Really.

(*Pause.*)

MOTHER   Since you ask. My name is Bqbqpstu,
Emissary of Larav, Empress of the Sshhs,
who live on the world you call Miranda,
a moon of Uranus. Very, very far away.
I'm here on a secret mission.

(*Her aspect becomes strange and unearthly.*)
My world, Miranda, is in danger.
Triton sleepstickers and stickwalkers.
Hammer-headed and creased foot splutch.
The rain skies up and the suns dump on
fells. That and the rats. They sqssqu
and shake. Badass hocus pocus. Snsps. Pssps.
Qvspt. Xxp. Tsspppcqtsm! Sks. Polymers.
Xxxxxs. Plplp. Qsssp. Sskllpc. Hssssssp.
O. Ppbbppsspc.

JOAN   I knew it, pure whispertalk.
You should know. I am immune to the
subtle poison of whispertalk.

MOTHER   What, who are you, to know our way?

JOAN   What did you do with father?

MOTHER

(*Holding up a clear glass vial*)
Only the purest spinal fluid for the wind
machines of Larav. Empress Larav.

JOAN   Dad? And Mr. Barfly too? You fiend.

MOTHER   Mr. Barfly. And the man who fixed the sink.
And Mr. Delaplane next. And then the Mayor
of Cleveland. And soon you, my dear.
Qssssmsssssplxmnsxsxsxssssxku!

JOAN

(*Squaring off*)
Xtr. Tr. Rqnrhrdtt. C!

MOTHER   Tritonian? I suspected. Show your glide
wave number and fight.

JOAN   I am Becky Brighteye, girl space cop, and
I'm taking you back to Triton, world that
you and your kind have despoiled. With
your wind machines and inverted energy
schemes. All of it Xxqmmmntnp, as you
say it in your dialect.

MOTHER   Once I get your time feather, you're finished.

JOAN   Try and get it.
    (*They fight.*)
    Qqkwvll. Llllgpppvmvptzc.

MOTHER   Hsstu. Psspmpsstmpt. Ptzc.

JOAN   Bhtsspssbh.

MOTHER   Filthy girl. I should've scwwpsst you in
your sleep. Sleep hsp.

JOAN   Tsstssttp to you. What's your real name
before I take your feather.
    (*She defeats her* MOTHER.)

MOTHER   Inglefinger. Fourth Dyad. Tenth moeity.

JOAN   One of the unclean ones? That's how desperate
you are.

MOTHER   Wolfling, we'll destroy you yet.

JOAN   I've got a hot pllptpccclpu waiting for me.
In a small apple grove in Indiana. Then it's
clear sailing back home. With your time feather.
You'll be out cold for a week.

MOTHER   No, no. (*Faints.*)
    (JOAN *drags her halfway off. Her feet remain visible. Doorbell rings.*

RICHARD [PANDA HANDS] *enters, dressed formally. He wears panda gloves and carries her corsage.)*

PANDA HANDS   Hi, Joanie. I heard someone whispering. So
I didn't come in. So I just stood outside.
Here's your corsage.

JOAN   Oh, that's beautiful, Richard. But the prom's
tomorrow night.

PANDA HANDS   The fifteenth. That's what it says on the
card. That's tonight. Gee, what's wrong
with your mother?

JOAN   One of her fainting spells. Don't worry.
Let me just get my coat.

PANDA   Like my gloves?
(She puts on her coat.)
Shouldn't we, like, call the doctor?

JOAN   You warm up the car. I'll be right out. It's all right.

PANDA HANDS   I'll go warm up the car. Okay?
(He goes. Pause.)

JOAN   Fthr. Fthr. Qskmpplptu. Pxp.

MOTHER
(Groaning)
Glpglpmpa. Gld. Dddd.
(She holds up a strange feather. JOAN *snatches it in triumph.* PANDA HANDS *re-enters.)*

JOAN   Shall we go.

PANDA HANDS   Golly. Sure. What's that?
(Points to the feather. She puts it in her purse.)

JOAN   Skip it.

Blackout.

Scene seven. The prom. In the men's room. Nice prom music in the background. The MAYOR OF CLEVELAND, *a chaperone, stands to one side. His head is wedged in the towel machine. He is formally attired. A strange* MAN *enters with a wand.*

MAN   I am the Imperial Fsqqtu for Becky Brighteye.
I think I deserve better than this. Plopped
down on a contemptible third-rate planet.
Populated by third-string coat hangers and
hat racks. When I talk to one of you
you say many things, but all you ever
mean is "I believe in pop music. I believe
everything I hear on the radio." In my earthly
aspect I perform a boring and meaningless
task over and over. All your solutions to
problems are simpleminded. You want to
look inside things, but the insides
of most things are the same. One, two.
On, off. Boy, girl. Cat, dog. All
the same and very boring. Pleasure is
on the surface. Pleasure is not boring.
On my world people go mad from excessive
happiness, which you would never understand.
Nor would you ever understand what a Fsqqtu
is, which is why I am not going to explain.
When the screws from the big bank come to
close this circus down they'll show fire
and say: "we've come. We're taking everything
you've got." I wanted to build a system,
to perfect an art. And look what I've got.
Out of control *stuff*, a rat shoot at the
county dump, an endless prospect of indigest-
ible cheese.
(He shudders.)
On this world one can deduce nothing
on the basis of looking at the sky.
That is not so where I come from.

Everything depends upon the sky.
I would like, yes, I would very much
like to talk about the sky. But you
would not understand. So . . .

(*Pause.*)

I glide the way and skin the smooth, in case
any more Mirandans show up. This is the men's
room of Panda Prep. The prom, remember? If you
listen carefully you can hear music in the
background. Cheesy band. Golden oldies, in
the local argot.

   That's the Mayor of Cleveland. A chaperone.
He's drunk. Looks like he got his head caught
in the towel machine. How'd he manage that?
I haven't a clue. Sh. I hear people coming.
Sh.

(*Backs into a stall and disappears.* LOSIN' SUSAN *enters. Realizes her mistake and exits.* PANDA HANDS *enters. Urinates. Washes hands. Exits. Returns. Does a doubletake. Re-exits. Pause. Re-enters with* JOAN.)

PANDA HANDS   Will you get a load of that?

JOAN   What's wrong with him?

PANDA HANDS   It's the mayor. Looks like he's had an accident.
   (*A teacher,* MR. BARFLY, *enters.*)

BARFLY   Pardon me.
   (*He exits hurriedly. Re-enters.*)
   Hey. What's going on here?

PANDA HANDS   Sorry, Mr. Barfly. Sir. It's the mayor.

BARFLY   The mayor. Why so it is.

JOAN   He's stuck.

BARFLY   How the devil'd he do that?

JOAN   Beats me.

BARFLY What are you doing in here young lady?

JOAN We were looking for him. He got drunk and threw up in the punch bowl.

BARFLY The mayor?

JOAN Sad to say.

BARFLY Tony, what are you doing in there?
(*Muffled noises from the* MAYOR.)

PANDA HANDS What do we do Mr. Barfly?

BARFLY This has to be done discreetly. A lot of fashionable people are out there.

JOAN It sure calls for discretion. Maybe we can find a crowbar in the custodian's room.

PANDA HANDS This is too much.
(*He exits.*)

BARFLY Young lady what are you staring at?

JOAN It's pretty amazing if you think about it.

BARFLY Watch the door. No one must know.

JOAN Discretion. Right.
(*Someone tries to enter. She blocks the door.*)
You can't come in.

BARFLY No, no, no. Don't do that.

JOAN You said I should watch the door.

BARFLY Where's Richard?

JOAN Went for a crowbar. Or a more appropriate tool. A Phillips screwdriver perhaps.

BARFLY This is ridiculous.

JOAN I find it very interesting.

BARFLY	Could be the ruin of a fine public figure.
JOAN	Never been in the men's room before.
BARFLY	Tony, are you all right? For Christ's sake what happened?
JOAN	This sure is a fashionable school. I go to Our Lady of the Bleeding Knuckle.
BARFLY	Why don't you be quiet?
JOAN	Just trying to lighten the mood. Sorry.
BARFLY	Where'd he go?
JOAN	You mean Panda Hands.
BARFLY	Richard.
JOAN	Beats me. Maybe he went home. We call him Panda Hands because he paws all the girls.
BARFLY	Tony, help is coming.
JOAN	That band sure sucks, doesn't it?
BARFLY	Why don't you go away?
JOAN	This is a fascinating experience. Wouldn't miss it for the world.

(PANDA HANDS *enters with the rest of the girls.*)

GRISELDA	Oh, look!
KATE	Wow!
SUSAN	What's wrong with him?
PANDA HANDS	Everybody's looking for you, Mr. Barfly.
BERTHA	I've never been in the men's room before.

(*The door opens.*)

A MALE VOICE

> (*Off.*)
>> Sorry.
> (*Closes. Reopens.*)
>> Hey, what's going on here?
> (*The girls hold the door shut.*)

BARFLY

> (*To* RICHARD.)
>> Would you get them out of here?
>> Did you bring a screwdriver?

PANDA HANDS   This was all I could find.
> (*It's a hammer.*)

BARFLY   What good is that? Go find a screwdriver.
A Phillips screwdriver.

PANDA HANDS   But where?

BARFLY   Look. Use your imagination, Richard.
> (PANDA HANDS *exits.*)

JOAN   Quite remarkable, isn't it.

KATE   Very.

SUSAN   Never seen anything like it.

KATE   That band's lousy, isn't it.

BERTHA   The pits.

GRISELDA   This sure is a fashionable place. Did
you see all the ivy outside?

SUSAN   He threw up all over everything. Really gross.

BARFLY   He's the mayor. Remember. Show some respect.

SUSAN

> (*To* MAYOR.)
>> Sorry, sir.

BARFLY
    (*To* JOAN.)
        And you. Keep an eye on that door.

KATE   Want some gum?

JOAN   Sure.

BERTHA   Is there a party after the prom?

GRISELDA   Who knows?

SUSAN   Jimmy the Door's such a good dancer.

GRISELDA   Johnny on the Spot's stepped all over
        my feet. See.

KATE   Wow. That's awful.

BERTHA   Can I have a stick of gum?
    (KATE *doesn't reply.*)

JOAN   Mr. Barfly, sir, do you have a relative
        who's a plumber?

BARFLY   Why, yes, do you know him?

JOAN   We had some trouble with our kitchen sink.
    (*Muffled sounds from the* MAYOR.)

BARFLY   Easy now, Tony, we'll have you out of there
        in a jiffy.

JOAN   Sir, Mr. Barfly, what if we greased his head
        with a stick of butter? I'm sure we could
        find a stick of butter.

BARFLY   Very funny.

BERTHA   I'm bored.
    (*She goes out.*)

KATE   Let's go back to the dance.

BARFLY   Not a word of this to anyone. Promise.

GRISELDA   Sure.

BARFLY   I mean it.

KATE   Mum's the word.

SUSAN   I've never met a real mayor before.

GRISELDA   Good night. Mr. Mayor. Good luck!

SUSAN   Goodbye, Joan. See you soon.

JOAN   Bye.
             (*They troop out except for* JOAN, MR. BARFLY, *and of course the*
             MAYOR.)

BARFLY   What are you staring at young lady?

JOAN   (*In a strange voice*)
             Maybe you should go help Richard and
             the others find an appropriate tool.

BARFLY   Yes, maybe you're right, young lady.
             (*He gets up to go. Pause.*)
             Oh would you do me a favor and don't mention
             my cousin the plumber? Around here. That's
             not a very fashionable profession.
             (*He goes. Long pause.*)

JOAN   Don't worry
             Mister Mayor. I'll stand watch over you.
             You had a kind word for my father
             even though he was a Trotskyist
             and you being a fashionable mayor
             and public figure and all in all
             quite the thing. Everyday despair
             gets to a person when they're trapped
             by the limits of their ecosystems . . .
             Back home in Skyeyesqll the air's

so thick you could stir it with
a spoon. My real father's an Xylmn.
they don't have Xylmns here, and I
guess it would take too long to explain
what that is and you've got problems
of your own. Enemies of our Way
have tried to force the issue.
Inglefinger, my fake mother, got
more than she bargained for. We're
a tough people. We never look back
and when we do a thing we do it right.
Still, Triton's not much to look at.
Old Queen Larav needs the spinal fluid
for her wind machines. Out that far
if you don't keep the air in motion
it freezes up. And that's a sticky
situation. I can tell you. I know.
Isn't this corsage nice? Richard's
a nice boy. Panda Hands. Not a bad
dancer. There are more of them
around here. Mirandans, I mean. I'll
be one of the missing. Others will take
my place. Uranus, our sister planet,
has a pretty, velvet ring, black as coal.
It glitters in the night sky like black
pearls. I sing and dance a lot. On my
days off. Would you believe I'm nearly
five hundred thousand years old. A Pisces.
Mr. Mayor, I like Cleveland and well
I'll miss school. Our Lady of the
Bleeding Knuckle. Our Lady of the
Runny Nose. There aren't any Catholics
on Triton. No Trotskyists either.
We have a different way of doing things.
We keep whatever daylight reaches us in
these little stone jars. Sometimes the

whole Plain of Qqqsmsmccctu is covered
with them. Our enemies on Miranda are
pretty dumb. We've almost got them beat.
Another few centuries at most they say.
I'll miss my girlfriends, especially
Losin' Susan. She's a riot. I think
she's still a virgin. Who knows?
But Inglefinger's right. Miranda's
a prettier place than Triton. That's
why we want it. Our rhinodraconopeds
need it for grazing. Tough shit, you
Mirandans! I figured out my Pope
Joan dream. It was about how worried
I was about the prom and feeling bad
because I got stuck with old Panda Hands.
You want to hear some whispertalk?
"Skrxxsx. Kxrs. Bkssxx. Xs. Bkxxxllxxxllmnnmcc . . ."
That's the first line of a poem about the Sea
of Kxrs. Frozen methane. Looks a little like
Lake Erie. Panda hands will want to go and
make out behind the shopping center.
But I'm gonna tell him I want to go to
Indiana. Will he ever be excited! A
pllptptcccplpu's there waiting to take me
home. You ever seen a time feather. This (*Holds it up.*)
is one. Pretty isn't it? I'll tell you a secret.
I don't love Jimmy the Door anymore. Want to
hear one of our songs?
(*She sings a strange song.*)

In the land of Tlpccc the trees grow upside down,
    but Nobody knows they do.

(*Pause.*)
Tlpccc, that's like China. On the other side
of the world. Get it?
(*She whistles a refrain.* PANDA HANDS *enters.*)

PANDA HANDS   Was that you singing?

I didn't know you could sing.

I got a screwdriver, a Phillips screwdriver.

JOAN   Richard, I've got a great idea.

You want to go for a drive?

Blackout.

Bad Penny

A Play at Bow Bridge

Anne Hamburger of En Garde Arts
commissioned me to write a site-
specific theater piece for Bow Bridge
in Central Park. At the time, I wasn't
convinced site-specific theater was
much more than a gimmick (as many
still do think); how wrong I was. Public parks, like all sites of ostensible re-
laxation, have always seemed ambiguous. Indeed, both Bow Bridge's
architect, Calvert Vaux, and Frederick
Law Olmsted, the park's designer,
died raving maniacs. So I decided I
would make a play that would explore
the wonderful but dangerous
(meta)physical openness of the place.
Also, I endeavored to create a play
that would merge seamlessly with the
landscape and culture of Central Park.
Bad Penny, given its small scale, was a
great success, and I think I learned

PERFORMANCE NOTE
The appearance of an asterisk within a speech indicates that the next speech begins to overlap at that point.
A double asterisk indicates that the next subsequent speech begins to overlap at that point.

more from the experience than from any other working experience, especially about the much undervalued realm of public speech and its relation to the spiritual and the political. The terrific cast, led by Stephen Mellor and Jan Leslie Harding, was directed by Jim Simpson.

PERSONS OF THE PLAY

FIRST WOMAN

FIRST MAN

SECOND MAN

THIRD MAN

SECOND WOMAN

BOATMAN

CHORUS

Scene. Near a large rock on the shore of the lake fifty yards northeast of the bridge. A MAN *and* WOMAN *talk. A* SECOND MAN *stands on the far shore about twenty-five yards to the south; a* SECOND WOMAN *stands on the bridge, facing them. A* THIRD MAN, *with a bullhorn, sits in a chair on a small rock in the lake some twenty-five yards due east of the first. A* CHORUS *of twelve is hidden amongst the bushes and reeds on the southern shore of the lake, near the* SECOND MAN. *Pause. The two on the bridge appear to be a couple but aren't.*

FIRST WOMAN   I come here every day, every
                single day. I come here, to this
                spot, every single day and
                every single day, every single

goddamn day, it's the same or
it's different or it rains or it's
clear or it snows or it's bright
and beautiful or it's dark, rainy,
and kinda foul. Or it's like it
is now, kinda strange. Sometimes
the sky reminds me of home and sometimes the sky reminds me of the
sea, or sometimes it doesn't remind
me of anything at all, much, and
I pay no attention and sometimes
the sky looks like its own reflection
in an oily puddle of rain water, like
nothing, like nothing at all. Sometimes
I think the sky is only pretending to
be the sky, or that it's a fake image of
the true image of the sky, like what you
see in a puddle, and that in fact there's
no true sky at all. I mean, anywhere. But
I realize there probably is a true sky
somewhere since if there's an image of
something there's bound to be an object,
somewhere, an object corresponding to that
image, don't you think, somewhere? Maybe.
I dunno. Do you realize that we probably
look like a couple, but aren't. Do you
realize that? I think the true sky must
be a wonderful, wonderful place where
all the lost things of the world assemble,
are discovered, and are kept in safe-keeping.
Forever. Safe forever. Lost hats, socks,
thumbtacks; I think there is a separate place
for solitary shoes and socks and other stuff,
solitary stuff. I think there is a separate
place for twisted paperclips, and too-short

pencil stubs, and old newspapers, like big,
dumb birds with broken wings, skittering
across the pavement, the pavement of the sky;
I think there is place for bent coathangers.
These places must be located up there, in the
sky, because there is no other place available,
no other place that empty, no other place that
someone hasn't laid claim to, and filled up
with some kind of perfectly ordinary junk,
whatever kind of junk there is that is
appropriate to that kind of place, because
you never know, given the people who live
there, wherever, and what they look like,
and what kinds of junk they like, and who
they are. All that stuff. Other times
I think, no, all that's a crock, and the
whole damn sky is just a big, fat illusion.
You want to know why I think that?*
I mean *when* I do think that because**
I don't think that all the time, I only
think that some of the time.

FIRST MAN   No.
    (*Pause.*)

    Go away or I'll call the police.

FIRST WOMAN   Well, the way I see it, all those stars
up there, out there, all those millions
upon millions of stars; which obviously
we can't see new because it's day,
but there're still there, as we all
know or think we know because all we
actually see at night are the *images*
of stars, not the starts themselves;
all of which means that during the
daytime what we are not seeing is

the image of a star—or stars—
maybe even thousands of them. How
can you say you're missing much of
anything if all you can be sure of
is that during the daylight hours
you cannot see the stars because the
image of something else blocks out
the image of the stars? Especially
when you consider that all you see
at night is the image of stars, not the
stars themselves, which are far too far
away for anyone ever to see them. The
actual stars, I mean. It's totally
ridiculous. So, in fact, if that's all
we see, if that's truly the case, then the
whole damn sky is one big fake, one great
big, vast, optical illusion. I mean, really!

(*She looks at his tire.*)

FIRST MAN   I had a flat tire, over there.

FIRST WOMAN   Then what are you doing here, in the park?

FIRST MAN   What do you think? I'm going to change my
goddamn tire. There's no goddamn gas station
over there (*Points east.*), so I figure, what
the hell, I walk across the park,
maybe there's a gas station over there (*Points west.*). Besides,
my jack is busted. I know, I know. You're
going to ask how did I get the wheel off if my
jack was busted. I LIFTED UP THE CAR WITH ONE
HAND AND TORE THE WHEEL OFF WITH THE OTHER
OKAY?

FIRST WOMAN   I don't get it.

FIRST MAN   Neither do I, so can we just forget it?

FIRST WOMAN   Fine with me.

FIRST MAN   Okay.

FIRST WOMAN   Okay.

FIRST MAN   Okay

FIRST WOMAN   Okay.

SECOND MAN   What kind of a car was it?

FIRST MAN   What business is it of yours anyway?

SECOND MAN   Just curious, that's all. I mean, I didn't
mean to be nosy.* I wasn't trying to intrude.
Jesus, it's a public park, you know. I mean,
you don't have no monopoly on finer feelings,
buddy. I was just trying to be neighborly,
so don't mind me. I'm just another human being,
you are familiar with the species? Just another
rational biped, demonstrating a little natural
human curiosity. Natural human concern. But
I know, it's too much to expect. Fellow-feeling.
A little normal human empathy. No. Nope. So,
just go and feel paranoid. Fine with me.
I don't give a crap.

FIRST MAN   It's a Ford Fairlane 500. Candy apple red. Two
four-barrel carburetors. Four on the floor.
Montana plates. Three hundred pounds of rock
salt in the trunk. Parked on 69th between Lex
and Park. Parked illegally. I hate parks.
I'm a freelance memory fabulist and metaphysician
and card player. Failed card player. Can't ever
go back to Atlantic City. I have a cat named Myth*
and I don't need a passport.

FIRST WOMAN   What a coincidence! My hobby is myth, and my name
is Kat.* Only I spell Kat with a *k* . . .

SECOND MAN   Who're you trying to fool? Ford stopped making the
Ford Fairlane 500 years and years ago, and if you
really had one, it'd be a collector's item and you'd
have to be crazy to park it on the street. Are
you crazy? Hey, that guy's crazy! Either that or
he's a liar. Or both. Look, buster, I know what
I'm talking about. I know cars. Aside from which,
what's this stuff about there being no gas stations
on the East Side? There're plenty of gas stations
on the East Side.* I've seen 'em. I know. Oh,
for crying out loud, what do you want me to do,
give you the fucking street number, the color
of the toilet seat in the men's room? As a general
rule I can make the absolute statement: there are
gas stations aplenty in the area immediately East
of Central Park, even if it is hoity-toity, even
if they are hoity-toity, for gas stations, I mean.
I have seen them. I have walked by them. I don't
know where they are, but wherever they are, I know
they are there. I do not know when or where the sun
is when it comes up, nor where it has come up from,
but I do not doubt it. I know for a fact the sun
will come up. It's a fact of nature. Only a nut-
case would give me an argument on that score. So
you just go and shove it up your tailpipe, buddy.

THIRD MAN   He don't have no car, and he don't got no
flat tire. Nobody who didn't have no flat
tire wouldn't go and tear the wheel off'n
his car without he had no jack and no
wrench and no tire iron, I don't care how
strong he is, without his being a monster
like some monster football player, some
gigantic goon, and even if he were some
fucking monster goon, why would he
go and do a thing like that in the first

place because it's his car, isn't it?
And it wouldn't make no sense, and for
that reason I do not believe his story.
No, I do not. It smells fishy foul to me.
No, I surmise this guy is in the park
because he is out of work and is, in
general, up to no good. This park is
full of people, these days, who are out
of work and up to no good and you know
what I would do with all these people
who are up to no good in the park? I
would say, politely, why don't you get
your collective ass out of the park
and get a job or join the armed forces*
or at least do something that will be a
service to your country and not just be
a lazy good-for-nothing who doesn't contribute
to society and don't got no job of real work
as we folks who are responsible must do. I
mean look at that look on his face.

SECOND WOMAN
(*To the* THIRD MAN.)

Who the fuck are you talking about, you,
if you're such a high-and-mighty, big type,
American person how come you ain't at your
job, working away? What the hell are you
doing lounging around in the park, spying
on people who are minding their own beeswax?
I mean, you got one helluva lot of nerve
if you ask me. The man is standing there
next to his girlfriend,* with a flat tire—
show Mr. Minder-of-Other-People's-Beeswax
the tire . . .

(FIRST MAN *does so.*)

. . . he's minding his own business, and he's

from out of state, and therefore should be
shown some courtesy as a tourist,** and
some aggressive, hostile goon like you
has to show up and spoil everything. Did it
not occur to you maybe he was only postponing
the inevitable task of changing the tire to
take advantage of the great outdoors and
the splendid weather we are having, finally,
after the usual awful cold and shitty and
rainy weather that in this miserable nut-
house of a city passes for Spring?

FIRST WOMAN   I am not his girlfriend.

FIRST MAN   I am not a tourist.
  (*Pause.*)

FIRST WOMAN   Why don't you need a passport?

FIRST MAN   Because I never leave the country.
  (*Pause.*)

FIRST WOMAN   I knew it, I just knew it.

FIRST MAN   What did you just know?

FIRST WOMAN   I knew I shouldn't've picked up
      that goddamn bad penny I found
      on the path, over there, near the
      big fountain. I knew it would turn
      out this way: bad. BAD. Bad bad. But
      Kat goes and does it, goes and picks up
      the goddamn bad penny, which I know for a
      fact is a bad penny because it's tails,
      and when it's tails it's a bad penny and
      he who touches it is in for a bunch of
      bad luck, and will be eaten by trolls, or
      suffer the pharaoh's curse, or be killed
      by the Boatman of Bow Bridge, and no good

will ever come of it, that's what I've heard.

THIRD MAN   Then what the hell's a *good* penny? I mean,
how can you tell the difference? A penny's
a penny.* I don't get it.

SECOND MAN   She's trying to explain, Meathead. Why
don't you shut up.

FIRST WOMAN

(*To the* THIRD MAN.)

A good penny is one you find heads up. A bad
penny is tails up. The one you pick up and
pocket, the other you don't. It's a rule.
I violated the rule by picking up the bad penny.

SECOND MAN   Easy enough for you, Meathead?

THIRD MAN   I will not respond to that sarcasm.

SECOND WOMAN

(*To the* FIRST WOMAN.)

There's something the matter with you.
Normal people don't talk like you.
Normal people don't talk about the sky.
Normal people don't act crazy.* Normal
people act normal, and don't go around
thinking about the curse of the pharaohs
and if they do they don't talk about it,
they don't talk about it with anyone else
because they know it is shameful and a
bad thought and one likely to get them
in trouble with the boss, their family,
and arouse suspicion in the minds of the
authorities, who have better things to do
with their time, better things than this.

FIRST WOMAN   There is not a thing wrong with me.
I am a perfectly normal human being

with perfectly normal hopes and wishes
and aspirations and dreams and ideals.
Perfectly normal in all respects. I
possess a job, an apartment, the normal type
clothes and shoes you would expect of
one such as me. Normal. A cat, a dog, a
parakeet. I have no unusual interests,
except the one I mentioned before, the
interest in myth. I have no abnormal
desires and cravings. I believe everything
I see on television and never doubt the
authorities, even when others less prudent
push the panic button, raise the alarm,
sound the tocsin. All of it, futile.
Futile. I do not believe in werewolves
and vampires. I believe neither that
there are alligators in the subways, nor
that there are trolls in Central Park, yes,
trolls, among them the hideous Boatman of
Bow Bridge, hidden within culverts, thatched
over by bosky thorns and briars in regions
inaccessible to normal human trespass.
I believe in the future of the American
dollar, Wall Street, and that—
(*She has a private moment of the visionary kind.*)
        . . . a new kind of cheese . . .
will be discovered . . . a cheese capable . . .
yes, quite capable . . . of curing cancer . . .
It will be called Wonder Cheese, and it
will be miraculous; and whence it cometh
and whither it goeth, no man can say, and
the doings of this cheese shall be called
wondrous and inscrutable and its name
shall be chanted by the multitudes, all
over, everywhere, even in the park, even at

night, when unholy things are done, are
done by those who possess not the secret of
Wonder Cheese and . . . babble . . . babble . . .
no man can say . . . no man can say . . .

(*She recovers.*)

My name is Kat. I was having a basically okay
day until I picked up that bad penny. Now
it's ruined. Now I don't even know what I'm
saying. Weird. This is really weird.

CHORUS

(*Chants.*)

Let the world be covered with cobwebs.
Let the world be covered with shadows.
Let the world be covered with dead leaves.
Let the world be covered with rat fur.

(*Repeat.*)

FIRST MAN   My name is Ray. Never mind the last
name. Call me Ray X. I grew up in
Big Ugly, Montana. That's the name of
the town. Big Ugly Montana.
I went to Big Ugly High School and
played end on the Big Ugly football
team, which was called the Big Ugly
Metacomets. The Big Ugly Metacomets
were the best football team in the
state, only they were defeated in the
state championship game by the team
from Why Not. Why Not, Montana.
They were named the Why Not Downwind
Scars, and they were a wicked awful
bunch, even more wicked awful than us.
They stomped us good, and after that
they kidnapped our mascot, a bulldog
named Meathead. We all loved Meathead

because he was the mascot of the Big
Ugly Metacomets. And those damn Downwind Scars from Why Not went and took
him off. Meathead was heard from no
more. It was the saddest day of my life.

(*Pause.*)

Used to be my day job was at this site,
this nuclear toxic-waste site. Facility.
But this facility was actually a dump,
a dump located near the town of Futile.
Futile, Montana. Mainly I checked dials
and stuff. A little glove-box work.
A little light contamination. Routine.
Nothing to worry about much, if you bear
the mark of Cain on your forehead. Nah.
Time to play cards in the detox chamber.
Time to think about things. Big things
like Time and God and Destiny and so forth.
Big, mythic things. My night job was, ah,
unspeakable. Days and nights in Futile
made me think how happy I'd been before,
back in Big Ugly, with Meathead. Strange.

FIRST WOMAN   Wow! I can't believe it. You won't believe
this, but I had a bulldog when I was growing
up and guess what his name was was,* just guess!
Go ahead! Guess!

FIRST MAN   I know, I know. Meathead.* Right? Right.

(*The dialogue continues as the* CHORUS *chants.*)

CHORUS   Let the world be covered with cobwebs.
Let the world be covered with shadows.
Let the world be covered with dead leaves.
Let the world be covered with rat fur.
The Dead Boatman of Bow Bridge

is coming, he is coming to take the thief,
take the thief in his boat to Hell, he is
coming to ferry the criminal to Hell, the
one who stole his penny, the one who thieved
his bad penny,* the one who thoughtlessly
took what did not belong to him; that one
is going down to Hell . . .

(*Repeat.*)

FIRST MAN   Takes all kinds, I guess.

FIRST WOMAN   My name is Kat, and I grew up
in a remote part of the city, a part
of the city considered unfashionable
by those people who were our social
betters, and who continually reminded
us, the entire family, of this fact.
This was because our family business
would be incomprehensible to most
well-bred people, and therefore our
neighborhood was called the Place of
Solitary Shoes or the Place of Twisted
Coathangers or the Place of Gruesome
Doilies and no one would ever come
to visit us because we gave off a
strange odor that everyone found
somewhat disgusting even though we
washed and bathed regularly still we
gave everyone who came into contact
with us the creeps. So, all in all,
I guess you could say I had a
fairly disgusting childhood, a
fairly gruesome childhood, and labored
in dark spooky places assembling robot
vermin and big spools of lethal twine
and gruesome cheese, fake cheese, made

out of spoiled vegetables and petroleum
byproducts.

(*Pause.*)

In short, I came from a gruesome family.
Everyone looked at everything too closely,
and that's why I went mad. Gruesome mom,
gruesome pop, gruesome cat, gruesome dog
[FM: Named Meathead.] Precisely: named
Meathead; a gruesome house, gruesome sofa,
gruesome TV, gruesome radio, gruesome kitchen,
gruesome car, gruesome backyard, gruesome
gazebo, gruesome mailbox, gruesome garden
hose, gruesome carpet, gruesome back porch,
gruesome front porch, gruesome vegetable
garden, gruesome doilies . . . all of it
gruesome, all of it the work of gruesome
adults who look at you too closely, and
find fault with all you do. So, like I
say, I went crazy, then I got sane, then
I went crazy, then I got sane again, then
I got crazy again and got well once more
then I moved out, to a more respectable
part of town, learned to talk like normal
people and not like someone from the
gruesome neighborhood where I grew up,
acquired a few skills, the kind you need
to make your way through the world, as
it is understood by respectable people,
people who have no reason to be ashamed
by the facts of their origin, where they
grew up, what food they eat, the size and
shape and color of their shoes, and such
bad habits they might have acquired by
hanging out with the wrong type of people,
people not used to acting normal, people
who act strange.

(The choral chant stops. A long pause.)

FIRST MAN   What kind of a fool do you take me for?

SECOND WOMAN   I really don't know what you see in her.
You can tell just by looking at her that
she is a floozy, or homeless, or damaged goods,
or at the very least a very insincere person,
a person with no scruples; and just between you
and me, if I were you I would watch out she
don't lift a wallet or wristwatch or some
other valuable from off of you. Maybe even
that tire you got there; she looks like the
kind that would stoop to a thing like that.
Vicious. Antisocial. Avaricious. Maladjusted.
Possibly a drunk. Probably a loony tunes.
Human garbage. Schemer. Tramp. Weirdo.
Fake. I wouldn't be surprised if she hadn't
already planted a tiny, inconspicuous electrode
to your head, so she can monitor your thoughts,
find out what your dark, little secrets are
so her associates may be able to blackmail you
or involve you in bizarre conspiracies, where
your life may be at risk, or unwittingly you
may play a part, albeit a small part, the part
of a geek or bagman, in some incredibly wild,
dangerous and byzantine, clandestine operation
involving drugs, the mafia, the CIA, terrorists
of several rival Palestinian factions, and
covert actions against the civilian population
of at least five separate Latin American banana
republics. You are in danger, in danger of
death by deadly force is what I am trying to
get through your thick skull. Others may
tell you this is not so, but I am a friend,
even though we are not personally acquainted,
and yes, I am aware that my concern may strike

you as a bit peculiar; nevertheless, it is true;
in fact, I am your *only* friend* and I have documents
to prove this, documents which reveal a vast conspiracy
against you, a conspiracy organized by ones close to
you, family, friends, colleagues at your place of
work; all their schemes center on the total destruction
of you, your happiness, sanity, the health of your cat
and dog and houseplants; the destruction of your credit,
reputation, your morale, your good standing in the community,
and even your self-identity and your faith in God who is over
all, and who ordains all things, even vast conspiracies such
as this. Do I make myself clear? Be warned.

FIRST MAN

(*To the* SECOND WOMAN.)

I am telling you once and for all:
we only *appear* to be a couple. We are
emphatically *not* a couple now, nor
have we ever been a couple, nor will
we ever be a couple. So please keep
your advice to yourself, I don't need
it, I don't want it, I can't stand
it, and to tell you the truth it's driving
me crazy so shut up and go away or I'll
call the police and have them issue a
warrant for your arrest and you'll be
put away for good. Good riddance.

SECOND MAN What did you mean by all that stuff,
that stuff about the sky? You, Kat.
I am asking you a question, because
it's all set me thinking,* because
something about what you said,
something made me feel like a big,
dumb bug creeping over a sheet of
plate glass, looking through the
glass to an infinity of sky and more

sky, and allatime I was unaware of the
larger implications of this stuff. I
mean, I like to know where I am going,
and what I am doing and that whatever I
am here for, it's not just like some bad
joke, something to do with the zoo
at night or some deeply twisted nightmare,
I mean I am no mere insect; I am a
deeply caring individual with special skills
and habits, and a fondness for things like
Cuban cigars, Hawaiian shirts, and French
brandy. I have always striven to be more
or less honest, more or less courteous,
even to my social inferiors, even when
driven nearly out of my mind with an
insane desire to run amok and tear down
whatever small portions of the civilized
world I can lay my hands upon, without risking
my job or getting hurt on dangerous machinery,
or injecting some lethal substance into
my veins, while all the time knowing that
the moon and stars are whirling senselessly,
mindlessly overhead at speeds I can't even
imagine, much less make any sense of. It
scares me, it scares the shit out of me.
It scares me, and it scares me even more
that what I see when I look up there, at
the sky, isn't a picture of anything—it
isn't any *thing* at all. And yet it *is,* it
is everything there is—all jumbled up,
all jumbled together in a mad merry-go-round
of comings and goings, of appearing and dis-
appearing, and none of it strictly speaking,
means *anything* at all. Except to us down
here, in our littleness and stupidity and bitterness and rage and greed. And you know what

bugs the hell out of me even more than that?
Do you? I mean, really, DO YOU!? because I
don't mind telling you I don't get excited
by things like this every day, and if you think
I'm enjoying this you are sadly mistaken and
the thing is, nothing up there in the sky
has changed a bit since the time I was seven
years old and first got interested in things
like that. Nothing has changed. NOTHING!
Nothing up there has changed since the time
of Christ, the time of the Incas, the time
of the pharaohs. Nothing very much has changed
for a very long time, except us. Only us!
Crummy, little, cheesy, lousy liars and
con artists that we are. With our cheesy,
lousy deals and bad debts and addictions and
pathetic bad faith and cigarettes and childish
obsession with the flag and baseball and comic
books and grotesque things like getting rich
when this whole, damn city is filling up with
people so fucked up you can't even look one
in the eye without being ashamed of being . . .
of being . . . of being anything but a snake coiled
up under a rock, over there, in the reeds, over
there, by the boathouse, or there across the
lake, where people go wading, even though you're
not allowed to, on account of all the shit and
broken glass on the bottom. You follow what
I'm saying, Kat, because I'm talking to you,
Kat.

    (*The dialogue continues as the* CHORUS *chants.*)

CHORUS   Incomprehensible, the bridge.
                Incomprehensible, the puddles.
                Incomprehensible, the sky.

Incomprehensible, the hats.

Incomprehensible, the thumbtacks.

Incomprehensible, the shoes.

Incomprehensible, the socks.

Incomprehensible, the stars.

Incomprehensible, the Great Nebula in Andromeda.

Incomprehensible, the flat tire.

Incomprehensible, the Ford.

Incomprehensible, the East Side.

Incomprehensible, the West Side.

Incomprehensible, the bad penny.

Incomprehensible, the dog.

Incomprehensible, the trolls.

Incomprehensible, the cheese.

Incomprehensible, the Big Ugly Metacomets.

Incomprehensible, the coat hangers.

Incomprehensible, the paper clips.

Incomprehensible, the all things gruesome.

Incomprehensible, Santa Claus.

Incomprehensible, the Easter Bunny.

Incomprehensible, the Tooth Fairy.

Incomprehensible, the plutonium.

Incomprehensible, Bow Bridge.

Incomprehensible, the Boatman of Bow Bridge.

(*Repeat.*)

FIRST WOMAN

(*To* SECOND MAN.)

Kiss my behind, you moron.

(*Pause. Turns to* FIRST MAN. *Hands him a penny. He pockets it.*)

FIRST WOMAN   Penny for your thoughts.

FIRST MAN   You don't understand. All I want
is to get my flat tire across this
damn park to a service station,

over there, where someone can
help me fix it. That's all I want.
I don't need any sermon or lectures
or advice, because like I say I'm
nobody special, but I'm me, just an
ordinary hard-working Joe, out of
Big Ugly, Montana, with the curse
of Cain on my forehead and a flat
tire, and no place to live, and no
prospects, and no future, and no
hope and nothing, nothing but rancor
in my heart. [FW: Despite even Meathead?]
Yes, despite even Meathead, because what
could be more useless than a goddamn dog?
A bulldog at that, ugliest creature
ever thought up, even in places
like Big Ugly, Montana, for Pete's sake.
Whose idea was this stupid monster
of a park anyhow, I could've had my tire
changed eons ago if not for this insane,
little blip of enforced rusticity, set
down in the howling wilds of the city!?
At least in the city the killers know
they are killers, and why they are killers,
and who the other killers are, and who they
kill and how and why and for how much money,
and what they must pay for their crimes, how
many weeks on Rikers Island, the slap on the
wrist, how many weeks their library card will
be suspended, maybe even revoked. Here all the
killers are sentimental killers, outdoorsy killers.
And you know what? I don't believe in myth
neither,

(*The* CHORUS *stops as the* BOATMAN's *rowboat heaves into view, far off,
behind the* FIRST MAN, *who does not see it. The* FIRST WOMAN *does.*

The BOATMAN *is shrouded in black and carries an oily torch.)*
   . . . even though I have a cat named Myth. No,
to me myth means "bullshit," and I hate cats and
dogs and parakeets and I especially hate my car,
even if it is a Ford Fairlane 500, because what
can you do with a car when you got a flat tire,
and no will help you, and I am sick of this
damn fruit-basket turn-over we call New York City,
the only god there is in New York City is this.
(He holds up a dollar bill.)
   So I don't want to hear any stuff about the sky,
the earth, the trolls or the Boatman of Bow Bridge
because it's all a bunch of malarkey, you can
take from me, sure, shitass no, and I'll tell
you one more thing, I think truth and beauty and
love bite the big hairy banana, and that nobody
but fools believes in anything but power, money,
muscle and good old-fashioned American cheese;
and I'll tell you one more thing: there ain't
no Santa Claus, there ain't no Tooth Fairy, there
ain't no Easter Bunny, there ain't no wonder cheese;
there ain't no Heaven and Hell; there ain't no
such thing as right and wrong; there ain't no such
thing as no human soul; and our lives mean absolutely
nothing, and we would be better off had we never climbed
up out of the muck from whence we began, out of that
primordial slime, spawned out of what unimaginable,
putrid sludge and goop, because human existence is just
one, big, awful hoax and shitwagon; and if it were up
to me I would go and fill this whole damn park with leaky
drums of plutonium wastes and by-products, acids, and
oxides. That would fix this place for good, and you know
why, baby, because plutonium has a half-life of 24,161 years,
baby,* and that's a long, long time. So: I say, to hell with
your Boatman of Bow Bridge. I don't believe in him. I don't

believe in nothing but lies and deceit and mayhem and
vileness and corruption and curses and may all my curses
come down, like a ton of bricks, on the mythical head of
the Boatman of Bow Bridge, and if he hears me let him
come and drag me down to Hell, because I do not believe
in him;

(*The* CHORUS *begins* "Incomprehensible bridge," *etc., louder than before. The* BOATMAN *nears.*)

for I *do* believe only in cheese . . . crud . . . power . . .
bad shoes . . . insects . . . goop . . . gunnysacks . . . tar . . .
furballs . . . cardboard . . . ooze . . . bad fruit . . . pitch . . .
mold . . . cinders . . . oily rags . . . asbestos . . . all of it,
buckets full of it, heaps of it, nothing, nothingness. So kiss
my ass, Mr. Boatman of Bow Bridge, come on and kiss it, I
dare you, wherever you are, show me your stuff because I
don't believe in you. So there.

FIRST WOMAN   Don't call me "baby;" Kat's the name, and I wouldn't talk
that way if I were you because that penny I gave you was
the baddest of bad pennies, and there is a Boatman of Bow
Bridge, a truly wicked awful troll, and he's going to come
for you, believe you me, and you're just asking for it,
buddy, whoever you are. Ray X from Big Ugly, Montana.
Because there are some things people don't understand.
There are some things people only screw up when
they mess with them.

(*The* CHORUS *stops as the* BOATMAN *arrives and summons the* FIRST
MAN. *After a blank moment of horror, the* FIRST MAN *climbs into the*
BOATMAN'S *rowboat, and they depart. Pause. The* FIRST WOMAN *continues quietly, with conviction.*)

Just because we think we know everything
doesn't mean we do. Some things escape us
and drive us slowly mad. People come to the
lunacy of places like parks to escape the
even more terrible lunacy of their lives
in the city, lives lived without love in

many cases, lives of terrible, meaningless
work, lives of torment, addictions to
strange and disgusting substances, lives
devoted to insane passions, obscenity
piled upon obscenity, lives rendered un-
endurable by long incurable wasting diseases,
diseases that could have been avoided had we
taken our medicine as the doctor warned us,
or not been who we are, damned by ignorance
and bad luck and by our own servility and avarice
and lack of cunning to a life of crime and useless
boneheaded self-abuse and substance abuse and other,
stranger kinds of abuse we know not the names
of, and pains, night fevers, retching and public
vomiting and the dry heaves, the bellowing and
howling, crying and weeping as we yearn for more
of whatever it is we think we lack; as the Boatman
of Bow Bridge completes the ring and circles the
square of his infernal destiny and rubs out the one
who would not believe, the one whose name was Ray X
where X stands for the nothingness of the unknown, X the
nothingness of infinity. Ray, that hopeless loser,
that goon.

(*Pause. The "proverb" chorus begins, chanted by the* SECOND MAN
and WOMAN, *the* CHORUS, *and the* THIRD MAN.)

CHORUS AND OTHERS   What you don't know can't hurt
       you; make hay while the sun
       shines; soon ripe, soon rotten;
       if every man would sweep his
       own doorstep the city would
       soon be clean; the dog returns
       to his own vomit; the exception
       proves the rule; do as I say,
       not as I do; dead men tell no

tales; call no man happy
till he dies;* facts are stubborn
things; practice makes perfect;
a little pot is soon hot; honey
catches more flies than vinegar;
you can lead a horse to water
but you can't make him drink;
judge not, lest ye be judged;
as you sow, so shall ye reap; a
bad penny always turns up;
nature abhors a vacuum;
thought is free; the squeaking
wheel gets the grease; today you,
tomorrow me; there are more
ways of killing a dog than
choking it with butter; curses
like chickens come home to roost;
wonders never cease; blood
will tell; if you're born to be
hanged then you'll never be drowned.

FIRST WOMAN   For all things beneath the sky are
lovely, except those which
are ugly; and these are odious
and reprehensible and must be
destroyed, must be torn limb from limb, howling,
to prepare the ritual banquet, the
ritual of the Slaughter of Innocents.
For they all must be slaughtered
to pave the road of illusion.
(*She puts on a strange hat, as do the others. The* BOATMAN'*s craft
gradually pulls out of sight.*)
For the Way is ever difficult to discover
in the wilderness of thorns and mirrors
and the ways of the righteous are full

strange and possess strange hats and
feet. For the Way leads over from the
Fountains of Bethesda, where the Lord
performed certain acts, acts unknown to
us, across the Bow Bridge of our human
unknowability, pigheadedness, and the
wisenheimer attitude problem of our
undeserving, slimeball cheesiness; and
scuttles into the Ramble, there, of
utterly craven, totally lost, desperate
and driven incomprehensibility—friend
neither to fin, to feather, nor tusk
of bat, bird, weasel, porcupine, nor gnat.
And we who are not who we are must forever
bury the toxic waste of our hidden hates
in the dark, plutonic abysm of our human
hearts, and be always blessed in the empty promise
of the sky that looks down upon us with
a smile, a divine smile, even as she
crushes us all beneath her silver foot.

End of play.

Cellophane

Sometime in 1984 I decided to make a language experiment, using as a basis, some aberrant verb forms I had come across, once again, in H. L. Mencken's *The American Language.* For a long time these bothered me, got under my skin. I found myself shuffling phrases around, making new, even awfuller combinations: "If I hadda been, I mighta could." Terrible, terrible, terrible. This was based on slang, or on some debased idea of slang, but wasn't really slang at all. No one ever talked like that. And yet, the more I considered the matter, the more it seemed that the phrase comprised a very exact statement, both philosophically and emotionally, of an idea very difficult to express in any other way. Eureka!

This was the undiscovered continent of bad writing, and so I set out to explore the place. For two and a half years I wrote a page or two every day, pages full of clumsy constructions, double (and triple) negatives, demented neologisms, and every conceivable combination of out of fashion, dated, or wholly artificial slang. Not to mention argot, cant, the tortured language of the workplace and the pitchman. I explored verbal detritus of every kind. I found to my great surprise that the stuff possessed great expressive power, was usually about important ideas, and almost always was far more speakable than the better class of American language.

Out of this original text (itself called *Cellophane*), I made two plays: *Cellophane* based roughly on the first half of the manuscript, and *Terminal Hip*, from the second. *Cellophane* can be done with almost any number of performers (and has been); *Terminal Hip* generally by one. Among the many delights of the actual rehearsal process was the discovery that a ghostly narrative would invariably emerge. Faint, to be sure, but very real. Certainly as obvious as the narrative to be observed in unmediated historical data (and I *do* believe this matter can be unmediated).

I like to think of *Cellophane*, and have described it as such on many occasions, as a spectral portrait and chronicle of America through the medium of bad language.

True ignorance approaches the infinite more
nearly than any amount of knowledge can do.
—HENRY ADAMS

The sun is the breadth of a man's foot
—HERACLITUS

From *Mad Potatoes*

1

AIN'T I SOCIETY, YOU SAY.
You ain't seen nothing yet hardly.
Not nobody don't chew no tobacco nomore nowheres here.
You can't get nobody out nowhere around no base without
    no ball.
Nobody who done that's brother don't know from nothing
    nowhere, you can take it from me sure.
You gotta have done to
    not know it mighta could if we all hadda been
    of one mind.
For we all among us both we and them it had only
    one idea between.
It was someplace else.
We was not at that place else.
We all was
At cat.
It was the tore-downest place ever.
You gotta have seed it to not never nohow have no idea
    what it am else.
So it was
At cat.
All day
At cat am.
Like that.

Most bestmost.
All day among what where they are not at's plumb
   worstmost's noplace to get a load of what we mighta
   did if we hadda could only am done did.
All
At cat.
Not once at dog am.
You aks how it be, all that, well it just am, amn't it?
More beautifuller than all other what whosoever we were
   so them says who knows.

2
Brang dog to what is to who.
Now for instance can you see the whichway likemost?
Noway.
Nope flits and ain't no yup.
It got the beautifullest ears.
It got near to what was practically impossible.
Call it who do am.
Call it for what are.
Call it special time for
   which was is and shall perhaps as otherwise
   flop down from having been did to as it long time
   had done and had been doing without no nevermind.
It growed nope on it
   like feets.
It growed yup on it
   like feets
At cat.
All this was which am.
All this were who to who.
All this were who to not who
   cause of being elsewhere
   as for instance
At cat.
Cat and not dog were both am.

They were both am if they mighta could but
    you gotta get no base withouten no ball if
    you got no ball no matter whether you chew or not
    nowhere in no wise.
It don't matter.
Mostlike it stay the same up down.
Mostlike it anyhow was till it growed
    different and that's a fact.
Don't matter what you brang long as it is what you
    brang truly and not some other like as how you go
    and chew bothersome or else it ain't no way allowed to.

3

For it behind the great labernath am.
Of the school of mad potatoes.
Just when you think it hadda been shall have done
    could it be
At cat.
It hardly were else otherwhere.
If it were not it mighta have did
    was in some place other
    as for instance Y to Y'.
Like as how
    twixt it and he and she are
    between his self the same and an X be.
Like the crowe.
Like the other side
    done up most whatfer most beautifullest.
Why the
At cat's
    X to X' all the way crisscross am?
It cross the blackdress.
Why the not
    amn't it ever
At cat?
The labernath be am

there else and allatime us'ns and your'ns
  mighta did and therefore was done.
You hafta done did no base withouten
  no ball and if'n you chew
At cat
  you out am withouten no hadda what am else.
What was at the
  labernath had he done else and so be the C to C.
The C is in.
It ain't all
At cat
  but mostbest it are and shall have been did unto so
  you who were as what it was was am.

4

Whyfor was it this and that?
Simple time was am twixt before.
It growed on them.
It growed on them till it drop otherhow
  smack dab up and down as can did.
It piled up and am are
  clear from X to X′ like as how you have seen from
  watchifying what hadda been had had it been done
  to elseways.
Whyfor was it then this and that?
You go aks at him labernath.
They tell you some crowe.
They tell you there some indeed crowe.
All manner of fat X and heretofore so whichways
  anyhow maybe.
It am called Y in the night.
Yeah! It go do and misdo!
Yeah! He have did a name upon it else it mighta
  hadda not been so were it
At cat.
Same stuff are.

Same as round O and O and O both C′ to C back
 near to where it was when it was done to in the
 name of what gone did what was done and else not.
All that O at midnight walking are.
Simple time it takes to.
Simple time curled up
At cat.
It ain't all what him do but she is close.
You can hear him and her both the same are.
For all night long one big hullaballoo is.

5

Fortune's basket case.
Like to as am.
Bird do.
What am are.
Thing who.
All whatsa matter was did.
X amn't.
Nope.
Y amn't but elsewheres sure.
Sure it was do.
Sure it were
 did am.
Allatime so.
Buncha us'ns mighta.
Buncha their'ns hadda been too.
All the same.
Go up, go down.
Cross the C.
Cross the crowe's eye.
Cross the blackdress.
Cross the moon to the.
Cross the whole shebang to who do.
Cross to who in the name of what.
Cross to who is am did in the name of what will be.

There it is.

There it is am.

All in a row them.

Justa laying there doing nothing.

Just heapa being elsewheres no way doing did am.

Were it always so you aks.

?

Who knows? Who

?

Who for golly sake do know what else

??

Who done what as akses.

All I say are you don't never get no base on balls
    without you got a base and a ball among.

6

Say them potatoes been longtime round say

At cat.

Whyfor not?

Allatime did.

Once the dog are you got pearly X.

Place upon a put why.

Globs of it.

Dumps full.

Whole sorta where am.

The X's.

The Y's.

Came across in and out.

All

At cat like they knew.

But they are did not knowed cause if they hadda been
    it could be told afore from how they was doing to
    what they been up to up to then while all the rest
    was going back and forth saying "yup" and "nope" and
    all suchlike no nevermind don't you know sure as hell
    or it do else.

Cause unless of it you fall the labernath.

Who as has the labernath him do all.

Who has was something else.

Who the X was too.

Lastmost seen among the sky did were and am.

Wow that labernath!

Suchlike as you never seed no.

Who am Y.

Skyfull up to what am.

All in betwixt the X and him and she and me and those
    it are both the same.

Who the difference are is both the it what who did what.

A cat.

Longtime looksee allatime at zero am.

From *Hollowness*

1

Two hollow eyes follow a cat's crie.

Night sticks to the windows at dawn.

A tree hangs from a cliff, upside down.

The helping hand of the law falters.

A sound in the street, in the street, in the.

The forge closes down.

The wheat, the barn, the sweet.

The empire of beggary, the blue doom.

The cross has melted like cheese across the
    stone.

A ponderous kind of it.

Beleaguered hoohah.

Nighthawk hoohah.

The correct guess flies out the window.

The imp of it.

The goblin X.

The gremlin Y.

The sky fills up so fast with invisible objects
    each one weighing more than a ton.

The people the.

Ten of them inhabit a storm.

Cloak the.

Oh, says the vendor, where is the.

The hat scuttles across the pavement.

It clears up, it darkens, it rains.

Someone has to brush.

Someone has to.

People fry food.

Gunk swells up.

A shout wanders aimlessly about the bunker.

Went, was.

Were, sit.

Grave mention is make of light wit.

Acuity. Tergiversation, lust.

Boredom, really. Heartache, really.

Something rests on its side, crushing that.

2

Vacuaria. Dolt's Hill. Glunk.

All kinda whole lotta of.

All is as am.

Big hole of monster abstract donut.

So much too is, such a derrick.

Such an hoohah knocked-over chimney.

Down by where him rat waltzes.

Bountiful plump one.

It go out by back way in.

It shall did sure, suspanthers.

All the way to the bank was am.

Cellophane warpers all the way to the bank.

Scrunched-up hoohah all the way.

Mile-o-jello-wiggle, all the way.

Heaps of industrial hoohah all the way,
 yeah! To the bank. Yeah!
Big mother and tilted.
Gorgeous living 3D one and smashed one
 and chicken-wire one and melted one
 and tuberose one and declawed
 and defanged one and one on fire
 and one on stilts and zonked-out one
 gone bananas on bad juice.
All the same.
All the same on fire shall have did am.
By the dump all the way to the bank.
By the creeping haystack.
Up there up in the sky all the way.
Down there beneath the potholes.
Over there twixt Dolt's Hill and him
 godforgotten boneyard be am.
Where owls and cats and mice.
Where oldentime him burning rubber innertube.
Where things rest.
Where all kind is as am.
Where the sign says nothing
 and the sky stand straight up
 in mute astonishment at the land.

3

Fire trash causes fire tracks.
Track fires stop fire trains.
Throw your trash up in the air.
X . . . (Y) . . .
Place where gas.
Sheer drop.
Blue wall, bent.
Airbrush the heaven globe.
Shade the seat on top of the locomotive.
Hedge, privet.

Why the moustaches, monsieur?
Why the grotesque shoes?
Why the galoshes?
Why the so many lawyers?
Why the shade between?
Prez needs it so bad.
X all the way to Crazy Day on Power Corn.
So bad the big blue X am.
So bad the sniffles him got at where it was.
Hairball the.
China freeze the.
Mexico uncorked the.
Wait till you see what him ice do at the
    back door near the labernath.
Switch the candlepower of bats.
Crazy bats, big ones with blue eyes.
So bad, they come running.
Stomping down the boulevard.
This, that.
Boolean number system uncorked in blue widget.
An L eats up an O.
Clear to hubba hubba mostlike him switchblade.
Prez needs it so bad it eats at him chewy-like.
Gum. Squire's Castle. Waterfilled balloon.
So long the dist, quite the apple jar.
Lost foam, singing wires ing.
Come to dust.

4

No to moon no.
Y to Y′ and still the night, and still the night.
Bittersweet yes and no, twice, the same.
Snow, falling.
Things happening in threes.
Silence, noise, what's far away
    close up.

Broken clutch.

Spent, the.

Cursed with strange weight.

The rock split, shattered.

No to moon no.

S the old rock on a fling, rose, white, dead.

The old matter, dragon matter.

Remember me to as it shall will have been
   done to as it was did done.

All in a line, on fire.

W in a wheelbarrow full of winterstars.

X the creaking axle of this.

X the face of the frozen lake, staring,
   staring straight up at.

Bogus, hoohah.

Lights out, the.

The dance of trash high in the.

Globe.

Fear machine.

Quiver music on top of old flat earth the.

Dancing bears. Magic squares. Snow.

Less than most leastwise am.

Through the music of March's insanity.

Beautiful moon creeping overhead on the.

Careless. Garlic. Smoke. Shoes.

Scribbled out.

Wax, wax paper. Inflammable substance.

Mexican food.

Hatted clocks, hats, clocks.

5

Tremendum. A close place. In one ear
   and out the other.

List who was me, on the outs.

Crow capable, crow inextricable, crow why.

Were, will be.

Heather, winter grasses.
Catch, toss, swing, dart, slide, out.
Where the garden was.
Where the.
Air on the outs.
Water on the outs.
Bowling with ghosts in a Dutch legend.
All of it, crumpled up, on the outs.
The pledge of allegiance to the flag,
    in one ear and out the other.
You can count on me,
    in one ear and out the other.
Mismatched socks.
Empty flapdoodle, dancing a jig
    among tombstones, whiskey bottle
    balanced on himher head.
Because of hats, all hats
At Cat.
Farewell the pomegranate.
Enter the closed door at full stride,
    in one ear and out the other.
Slambang.
Bury the hatchet twixt X and Y and the skye.
Cause of ready who.
Turned-over mat of perfect lilac-purple sunset.
Perpetual sunset on dammed canal, on risers,
    in one ear and out the other.
Concrete, sand elevator, water towers
    cut of an antique pattern, wood.
Wooden floor.
Wooden tabletop.
Wood the mad the.
Swing my things in a high ghostly parabola, all
    of princely cellophane, in one ear and out the other.

6

X was tossing hats and sailing paper plates.
The dog came home on fire and so on.
Grabity discovered the loftiest of high ideals.
Corn discovered grabity could have did
    if it mighta could.
Oldtime grabity the thinker.
Tusk now and tusk not.
Monster bojar am in the shape of a whatsis.
Fine-looking big hairy one, god.
Wind in the world doing nothing, doing nothing,
    doing nothing.
Badass footstomper was am.
Been waiting to shall have been gone done
    while going up to bat cleanup.
Switch-hitting monster am.
Grabity don't will am there.
Us'ns and Your'ns maybe but never not
    there no way nope.
What would you do without no someplace?
What would you do without no chew?
What would you do without
    no maniac Prez doing the bottle jig
    out by where the wind machine plumb
    went and broke down you tell me that?
What would you do without no wind and
    nothing standing there?
At cat.
Strike three and no base on balls be.
Corn in Carolina am.
Heaps.
square empties filled with stuff.
Shall, hit.
All the way to the way to the bank.

Singing: "Hooha, blankety-blank the hoohah!"
Beer engine slides into Coke machine on second.
A well-oiled insoluable conundrum transfixes X
 in the name of Y while down the road some a
 man is trying to find Y′ in the crowe's eye
 strange.

7

Strange the Y all bent up and dented.
Blew the who to tragic eightball.
Eightball trumpet earwax and so forth.
Pure chew, loud thump and release pin.
Grabity gotta nail him too sure.
You don't not have no super shoes when as how
 you don't need not to never.
Ask for the labernath it's all over sure.
They got music there as do the
 shame-ball double-up and fall-over
 three times running while it drills
 corrosive z's on that there river bottom.
Technology comes here too am.
Cause if'n it less were it on stilts am too
 to buy air for the burning.
It makes hot tires and grabass thorns.
Sure you got to know winter hush slopes
 clear down the wedge till it topples
 on somebody else's property line.
Call that a question of cards.
Had to had sort of.
Allatime the nightless rider had to had sure.
All time sorta sank down on top of him,
 deserted loot, stuff, that and bad vegetables.
Ship the clandestine.
Open the what, wash the whole hog.
They got food as defies all measure.
The whole shebang rings a bell.

It flies up the chumney and comes out
    smelling like roses.
Meat course. Strange salad. Stranger wine.
Given in trust to whatsisname's acquaintance.
For the sky dreams of other empties than those.
For it has eyes for you and me and the crowe even.
For it are hongry.
And, face it, we are a darn pretty bunch.

From 'S Sake

1

Crisp winter day like a crumpled dollar
    billed unfolded and ironed out flat.
The day they scorned shall come to haunt and
    roost and haunt and grow mad things all about the.
All around the.
On top of that there drum.
A gorgon fishhead made of stone.
Sakes alive! It's a
    bucket full of blood. It's a two-headed
    shoehorn. It's an
O on wheels, heat-seeking an X,
    in the furry incunabulum of night.
The bag is dropped.
The hook-up fried the apparatus wrong
    so that it thinking fakes on the fire-bowl gets.
Shaboom the Room.
Ycelpt Nordgar the Envious
    first among thorns, our
    ancient expedentitious axe
Blade.
Bloodroom, welcome to the!
Cast they net upon the.

Come up with snake eyes and the
    music of strange birds.
Caterpillar on the clavicord, dust on
    the plucked heartstring.
Nolo contendere.
Munch, ford, drown, bloat, break, rise,
    rain till X and Y debright the C beam.
Upright, worldwrecker.
Gotta chain. Gotta thump.
Spike the ointment with lye.
Don't mess with me or my materials.
Bottled gasp
    of utter disbelief in anything but gas or
At cat.
All the same, bald hill in azure strife with a
    bad god whose name had nothing to do with.

2

Seacoast evening, dead drunk on a thimbleful of eyesight.
You ask, are there truly alligators in the subways?
I am the way, Jesus said, and the light and the life.
There is no way through to the father except around me.
Sign up now for a promising career in robotic
    technology and a half gallon of alcohol . . .
Haste and opposing it, furies of important verbs.
Love's dialectic, the series of exploding rooms, each
    full of the wrath of the former.
Corner dweller, bright red, the unbeliever's
    swizzle.
Flumpus. Dormant. The old story with big shoes
    reduced to a pile of old postcards.
Geiger count of day, day locked up, locked up war too
    outside.
Crush, splat, dump, dream, desire, disappear.
A load of lisp.

A pound of praying substance, precious ounces
    of purity reality.
The shadow of solitary things, each one
    at odds, askew.
I don't know who I am.
I don't have change for the bus.
My shoes change color in the snow, they
    grow wings in the opera house.
I am thoroughly at sea in the weariness
    of prolonged political emptiness.
Political emptiness steals my food, sleeps with
    my wife, rides the subway in my shoes, writes
    these words with them thorn.
Thorn name box bow wow ox am up did.
Upchuck thorns red light baloney.
Red light baloney don't never not do the whole
    hog and chew too because of uncoordination.
Uncordinatedness hump the Beaver Dam box
    top with a flush in hearts.
Ringo guards the quit offense, seeks work elsewhere.
Where a man can hang and chew both sometimes ditto.

3
Zsst the rotating title to wrongdoing Z.
Corn upon the wing, duped into am did was how.
Polestar spun.
The arcane X.
Both was.
Was be did up to, like a cow.
Hiding in the gravel, butt up.
For those sake the moustaches?
For whose sake them monster shoes?
For whose sake the O
    in search of quiet?
For whose sake the pliable
    K factor, unchronicled as yet?

For whose sake all that gambols, trots,
    heaves, chews, and sighs?
For X belongs.
Down there scrunched up is toad.
Dry season chiselled.
Movable mohawk.
Drizzle.
Huge useless hands.
The humble globe.
Space for nothing.
Sheets of flame advancing cross time and
    memory am.
Waxen shapes.
Frozen drink, rotten stone.
Low-flying mammoth bugs.
Glue, frame, chop, blast, sweep up.
Curious about the.
Scatters.
X to Y.
X′ to somewheres they told of once in error.
Places shift, rushing by.
The mad girl's lust for solitariness,
    and honor, in the arab lands.
X upon the uncharted road.
X on the move forever the blue the gasp the.

4

Even to the.
Even that.
Even to the place of pointed toes.
Even theye.
Even the curious fractal, the sham
    imagery of the real world.
Even at the bottom of the sea.
Even in the French language.

Bags of hot shoes, door gone wet and soot
   astray in the white noise.
Flower, conch, strange wind from the
   pretty times done did.
Monster goofus ointment.
Pterodactyl man in himher crips jeans
   prying open the future's head.
Egg, can. Recalcitrant.
Cannister. Pandas. Broke. Cheese. Wired. Nuts.
In the tractor hall girls of cement
   gloat shall to other strange stone am.
Pandemonium of red flags.
Earthquake in neon went.
In neon went the crowe's eye downtown too.
Too aero the neon sweeping right.
Far, too far aero the neon even pissed the fumble hey.
Too are the aero even did.
Clean, crisp multiple-organed freestanding
   hoohah killer clown lateral to.
At cat.
At cat the cat attack.
Gorgeous cloud of vent stream, aero by
   suffocation hat, covered with.
All aero covered with dead bluejays up to
   X all over unbeknownst to aero neon person
   with foot on corn pedal to power itch.
Black-hatted groovy dead knowing not even.
Even to the end of the.
Even to theye.

5

I am dreaming of a time where a table and a chair
   are floating across a river on aer are.
I am dreaming of a time where.
I am dreaming of a table and a chair
   floating across a river.

I am dreaming
    all the same hoohah curled up so fine at
    pressurized brick chomp go do it jump.
P and non-P broken bells at
    home plate full of steam gears and all
At cat.
Electronic machine for deciphering code
    where none intended.
Bad heap excoriating past doings of bad
    mound of heavy scrap O.
Tilted, been.
Gunmetal, bluing.
All held together on principle of interlocking
    latch and doodad, no screws, even in the
    grip, nosiree.
Get used to the noise of use, the suicides,
    the blimp, the fires.
Haymaker. Frozen monster in big cheese
    bucket. Follow the tracks across.
Clear the night air cellophane all the way
    to X and back in a whiff of an O and Y.
Time with locked antlers, and half the alcohol.
Mexico on stilts, and half the alcohol.
X and Y in pearl flight, sad bats and
    ruminants, clear eyed, wet nosed.
Been as did was, shall be.
Been too up to say stay down X be did.
Been misspelled to wing the aegis cry too far to.
Been a case of seeing clear to yell as if the empty.
Who the yell.

From *Cellophane*

1

Flight. Path by the hedge. The unities.
Belltone. Oxide dusting the upside did.
Curving slow, Time's amber bucket drop.
Slide, splook, splash.
Bubble, gateway to spleen wire.
Fix the net.
Craze the priest class. Drugged. On fire.
Gotcha, moonman.
Hot time in the foreknown, O.
Where are the gentle ways, where are
    they now, lost among the.
Crane the neck, see.
See the tall prevailing ones, the.
Set down the spade, come on over to.
Room for shall did and hatching plots am.
Coat on the famous floor, fury.
Dust in the eyes, too late for tears, too late.
Utter corroboration of tedium, whisk.
Blitz the wet ones.
Frost on open eye, glazed over, no need
    now to harbor a grudge.
The burned city, still now, freezes over
    like a cup of coffee at the North Pole.

2

Frosted festival world, spiked with dazzles,
    and topped with painted sparrows.
Dead corn clean whiffed and say what.
Box on top of another box and froze clear
    through.
Basket type jive and clean as a whistle.
Boast was for nothing wrapped up and did,
    and clean as a whistle.

Bangle ing who about the frost see, clean
  as a whistle.
Quartz fire wrought shall in mid chamber
  lock jammed with light left on till the
  X bulb burn out in such like fashion.
Quartz style X am did bag.
Quartz style X and bended light on stilts
  'twill.
All manner of bagged light shuttles.
Bangle corn god who chews.
O the quartz beam on X the pure hectic track.
Bad O the quartz glow of frosted over
  world afore X.
X the O a bangle title shall have did am,
  without no base and no ball neither.
Clean whiffed the cornstalk crowe why'd.
X as an oxide clear if wolf dust are imbibed.
Quartz all one kinda chew if X and Y be done.

3

Stump the master, master the stump
  X on off the wignut so so.
An huge, futile irreversible of cheese.
Tango the ripcard tear-away boats it shoe.
Tango the whole damn busload am.
Tango the rifle without no kill ratio.
Tango the heartbeat quite the hazard hup
  master X stumped by a corpse ugh.
Illness naming pour of did was it.
Tango illness gone big on boxes.
Such a bogo-bogo up and dumped be did.
Such a quite as was did bogo.
Hemp on chew bussed on porky powerdrive.
Amiable chew thing switched on tango.
Tango bogo irreversible cheese slop.
Goon tango on stilts stars, O.

Goon break to slide of reptile
   chair in orbit grass.
Bogo bogo moon drift till the poison drum.
Song up on golden slivers the shoes.
Tango on slide to trombone blackdress.
Near the corner where naming pours off it
   what tango with tear-away cheese.
Near the full horror with tear-away cheese.
Near the amiable cheese with tear away
   wingnut on permanent G stripe.
Near the whole shebang with tear-away
   glassy envelope full of tango stardust.

4

Classical shoplift chairs the bean stop.
Who the French doors?
Who the wild boats it blue?
Who the ambidextrous candelabra?
Who the king pretzel?
Who them alltime lowdown hunch scattershot boys?
Who would ought to have done did?
Quite the showboat.
Quite the who was.
Classic pocketmodel flipside trouble-shooter
   on mission by a clean shot on rubberneck C.
Broom the quite the classical top inch peristyle.
Classical the broom closet rubbernecks and
   hang out if sand was.
Boom to under the rug factor lift aloft on beggar C.
Quite the azure pot-bellied lowdown on humdrum.
Pork pie hat on pork pie on fire on on in classical
   shoplift scene with seasonal frightwig if.
Consternation of constellations in golden parking
   lot.
Milk truck on lost journey to whose French doors.
Classical curve of quartz bogo to whose French doors.

Splendor of broom closet found on spilled secret
    gas stored in semi-indestructible tanks O.
Spilled pork pie under fuming lift on way to
    where the French doors aer are.
Crane, jar. Seek, rubberneck.
Thumbs down, wash the strange fruit.
Who the French doors in what whose names aer are.
Classical highball in special tizzy through whose
    emblematic French doors.
Whose cool wood on wheels quite.
Whose cool style flapping this way and that up to
    and including whose French doors.
Square windows where was why a French door necessary.
Classical cool wood, quite the skye's theye's in that
    oldentime golden parking lot aer are.

5

Who the Americans are, bring my pants and
    no thistle.
Who the Americans are, the Americans find
    and the first to the moon cuts cheese.
Spoon X the ladle Y crash course in the sea breeze
    bum side up, scoop that slop O.
Golf the wig, gravel up and bat dive
    for broom whack one day too was.
Scaly mountain bojar thing.
Him on wheels, she with cellophane parasol
    warped on fluid drive for whose namesake.
Cats cut cheese on moon, look back in
    warped indifference.
Blue the moon gilts up cockeye, so they say.
Who as gets holds on for sure, contradiction
    city.
Who as has, flowers, repossessing deep dark
    nether-wood, stone chalice, drink blood

and cut cheese, holy condo man, it's all
    whangdoodle and contradiction city.
Clockwise and sky dumb, blue bells and
    mineral garden shack press eject button
    and contradiction city.
Got no Mickey Mouse logo for at was and did
    no chew without no base on balls.
Had some, but no Mickey Mouse, boats it on
    zero mind puzzles it through to contradiction city.
Who the Americans are, all on contradiction city.

6

Corn of my condition: the whisp of letter:
    the ink of dream: the loss of ink:
Pure heavy water tuba floats as Z was
    cute the amber's mainframe shall.
X the till waters pill out and pearl
    blows the horn clear to C bright so.
Blow the X horn, cross the blackdress so.
Bad feet of saurian bojar inflict the O,
    they top the quite high, they dead the charge.
Cause of fruit, knife, jammed doors on
    X patterning Y doom, a silver tassel.
Santas. A swarm of him. Song
    dead weight Ohios the dread lack of green.
Green the advent this blue day is,
    boasts of, and would box in and hold.
Dire hats boat the sleaze of drifting under
    will have should and so forth's aren't.
Dire hats and warped peccadillos of armadillos
    deaf to noon and common sense.
First, second, third, seventh, all skies of it
    had the dust up as the rails sung.
Not to be a night unveils no arc of
    self nor definition of the halfmost as moon.

Not a quest, a curious eye for recovery
   of stolen cars, prints, old masters, all.
And O the labernath that blues speak of blat.
Pure bat and so if until all's still aer are.

7

Off the door. X upon J no sightline clips, clops.
Noire, Noirer. Noirest.
Golly fruit done up in wonder cheese
   waxes up to O and not till water's hoar
   in flakes of emerald rotates.
Dolly up, ride the red caboose, split, smash, gut.
Train the night cheese how to dolly up air cake.
Aero cement all dollied up.
Quite the noire.
Quite the florid Santa cheese.
Quite the vile sawdust factory hoohah.
Sonar wingtip lubes the celestial Santa.
Terribleize that azure asking how to of
   sky's 's 's noire the quite.
Flatten the rug butt so noire the quite
   dollies up *ho ho ho.*
Mad golly fruit grasping Y in the name
   of X for human blood.
What do you want for most of it?
What are them as do circles of heaven point?
What squeeze may approximate Santa's chair?
Float that green apple system load.
Pork the quietness.
Pork the mad golly fruit so aer are.
Pork the gleaming green fungo fly hoarfrost
   X bite to chomp wishbone slimes it too.
Pork the slime.
Pork the noire as it cheese X. Please keep hands.

8

Cosmic cyclone mystery tent empties.
All scratched out.
No chocks. Billions of
Barking dogs are called with
   inaudible cosmic food.
Until donut wars.
Gravel the pave.
Grave man thinks links'll sell empties.
Time traveler with warped needs speak
   to intern Santas.
Intern toes hold X book on up to suitable
   other than mystery tents O.
Nun's breath corrects dog's breath.
Intern quacks solicit suitable duck for
   seasonal plays with Santas.
Santas from hell.
Why the red zoot suit?
Why the fake beard?
Why the ridiculous hat?
Why the cheesy demeanor?
Why the badass attitude?
Intern Santas howl at moondust.
Lethal stardust infect lunar cheese.
Green lunar cheese is until off the wall
   dream of sponge earthly dream yes.
Waddles across the blackdress to here.
Wakes us up, O plenty what.
Intern cheese receives the cosmic message.

9

My learning's lamp done washed up look-see.
My learning's pipe is all smacked and
   so much crossed over pop shebang.

My dayglo dream rides shotgun over
    all so much creaked air and pop shebang.
Intimidation rolls a cake.
Intrepid loons founder suchlike and
    mosthow crye at crazy.
Tinted folio, angles's intact, gold and azure
    and violet features on antique vellum.
Angel ringlets I never X once dreamt of.
My learning's heart a sour apple's pith.
My pitch and pull, a reasoned jest.
My sole lament, a winter's night's air aer.
Two times the frost, a man on skates.
A child almost drowned, a tent erected,
    a bridge remembered, a dent un hammered
    out and so variously troubled by dented
    shadow and doubled light.
You, floating on your mystic ocean, forty-five
    minutes in the air.
Time's corrugation.
Breath on glass, frosting it.
Time to get, the soul's slow motion, the red
    earth dip's ledge.
Blacken the face, show your eye's you, find
    gold into a cat's cradle song on to what, what.
Crocus ups, purple valiant, spring's up screw.

10

He hears voices saying "You blew it."
The voices are located square on the glass
    torque slide and it fractures.
Nothing seems to hold up their noises.
Sun pops up, which star can't drop the
    blue note.
Dip for charity's, apple the birdsong.
Dip the cry for apparent and current dust.

The voices march in ain'ts' bags and
   swear by failure.
Heel and toe, succession's Sasquatch.
Rain of mad hail upon the antique
   breastplate rattles the cat.
Some Santas barf in the creeping alleyways
   alongside real Americans till up trot
   a screwball and Martian screwed up.
Have you hat enough for this, or canst?
How does the bean super do which was
   as will be?
Done pipe-flitters' axiom, screw.
"You blew it," screwed tight.
Shake the flour can, get the particles.
You lift the rod one inch too far, and
   the core's crazy, you're plastered
   on account of the ceiling.
A lead coffin, your head thrown away.
Clicking away, the counter's counting.
All of a blue day, portending nothing.

11

The chosen few is a horny bastard, and
About the only thing it won't get you
   is a seat on this bus or train.
Or that bus or train.
Or any train or Bugs Bunny on X aer are.
For the skye's T is an X in transit.
For the skye's Y is not done in by
   about the only thing anybody done did.
Who fews the ink with fire?
Who drills the sainted cheese?
Who golfs the square balloon?
Pals, tabled.
Square hole, round eye.

Bump that polecat, hinge that
    oyster bed.
Amalgamated sawhorse tool and die.
Born-again amalgamated saw horse.
Super glue born-again tool and die
    robs a bank and glues everyone's
    hand to the floor on purpose fire.
So to escape strange destiny with stranger
    nest egg, glyphs, soot, a row of calendars.
Laws and torts push dummy buttons.
Laws and no base on balls, and if one
    is chosen it is few and it says to its
    stranger antagonist "about the only thing
    in the jungle you don't look like is
    the hunter."
All on the same sightline am did.
Aer, are.

12

He hears more voices "You blew it."
Rocks am built the high fastness at Bogo Bogo
As if X on fire kilt the bar.
Won't, bore, detonate, cream in one's pants,
    offer chew to mysterious stranger.
Go on being as if you didn't blow it.
Go on thinking on how the rocks am
    done built was.
Careen into the soft shoulder, yelling
    at the kid, who tries to open the door,
    reach over, try to pull her back, she
    grabs the wheel, headlong into the
    oncoming traffic, cut cheese and
    croak.
Go on being as did if you didn't know.
Blue sky, all that jazz.

Feeling the shock waves meet at the
   other end of the world.
Can't, hope, drop dead.
Blue sky, all that standard jazz.
Coeval, mummified rat meat four
   thousand years old.
Melted, splattered all over the ceiling
   of the X the Y the cooling unit.
No retirement, no geranium in the men's
   room, no base on balls, no chew.
At the other end of the word there must be
   some place far other than this one too.

13

Global power breakfast feet meet at X
   the precious limo cheese at sunset did.
Global power cheese wolfs it down and
   upchucks huge blocks of rear entry
   back door weasel craft.
Straw hat and sunspots, unnoticed.
Immobile limo dreams.
Breadline antimatter squats on top
   the square feet.
Fake rebop bounces around the head
   of global power breakfast and at
   six AM forgets that brown shoes and
   blue pinstripe suits barfs and boats it,
   cuts cheese and croak.
Wolfs it down, barfs it back up.
Business, Popes, real Estates.
Meet at sunset, wolfs it down then
   find inscrutable beetles in Wheaties.
Sell, buys, barf it back up, wonder why
   it's nightfall forever when it's Power
   Breakfast Time and X and Y and the

pumpkin there I can't see my eggs
the cheese covers everything shall have
done too and what am unspeakable.
Limos in limo heaven, with little limo wings.
Burning limos, in limo holocaust O aer.
Dreaming limos at the bottom of the sea.

Three
Americanisms

After my extended language experiments *Cellophane* (1986) and *Terminal Hip* (1990), I made the conscious decision to forego this drastic direction lest it become a manner of its own, a mere style. Indeed, the whole point of the approach had been, in the words of poet Mark Weiss "to break the teeth" of a false eloquence, the ceaselessly edifying, dreadful wreck of the American theater—even at that time sliding into the lifeless, joyless bog of Anglophile inanition where it largely remains to this day. A theater of the clueless, the hopeless dull. Politically smug, complacent, and self-congratulatory.

But in 1990, or a little later, I had occasion to write three more pieces, not entirely in the earlier vein, but similar. Like *Cellophane* they were originally written as poems. However, I quickly broke off the project, fearing the work had lost the urgency any true experimental work must possess. A few years later, looking around for some solo pieces for a late night show at Soho Rep, I took another glace at these, decided they were better than I had thought, bundled them, and gave them the title *Three Americanisms*.

As with *Cellophane* and *Terminal Hip*, a ghostly narrative runs through the series. Mark Margolis was sublime in the first, but got a movie after just three performances (we put him on a monitor). Jan Harding and Ron Faber were equally fabulous, but given the odd schedule, few people ever saw the show. It is one of my best.

Three Americanisms opened on May 22, 1993 at Soho Repertory Theater with the following cast: Mark Margolis, Ran Faber, and Jan Leslie Harding. Direction: Jim Simpson; music: Mike Nolan; design: Kyle Chepulis.

nota bene: These three pieces were originally entitled: *An Elegy on the Invisibility of Richard Stans, A Screeched Elegy [with Furballs]*, and *Multitudinous Roadkill*. They are excerpts from an ongoing series of *Strange Elegies*.

Re Sierpinski carpet and Menger sponge:
. . . mathematicians in the early twentieth century conceived monstrous seeming objects made by the technique of adding or removing infinitely many parts. One such shape is the Sierpinski carpet, constructed by cutting the center one-ninth of a square; then cutting out the centers of the eight smaller squares that remain; and so on. The three dimensional analogue is the Menger sponge, a solid-looking lattice that has an infinite surface area, yet zero volume. . . .
   One cylinder rotated inside the other, pulling the liquid with it. The system enclosed its flow between surfaces. Thus it restricted the possible motion of the liquid in space, unlike jets and wakes in open water. The rotating cylinders produced what was known as Couette-Taylor flow.
—JAMES GLEICK, CHAOS

I'm throwing twice as hard, only the ball's going half as fast.
—LEFTY GROVE

PERSONS OF THE PLAY

FIRST MAN

SECOND MAN

FIRST WOMAN

Scene: A dark, wide, open place. A strange MAN *appears. Pause. He smiles, begins talking to us.*

FIRST MAN   I am running on empty in a region infinitely
                       sparse, infinitely many.
                Those there who are who do not donut
                       as good as we used to was.
                We trample them down and yell
                       in place of bellringing sure.
                We get up on our hindparts, hey,
                       and exchange wigglies.
                We party monster-like till the
                       moon fries our velvet shadows.
                Patience we do not much care for.
                We are of that other kind, the self-similar
                       mailbox-mouthed.
                To prong donuts excited our wiggly
                       forks.
                Why, you inquire, meaning no gas.
                Because the big end belongs to the
                       North, and we are not nosey, nope.
                Because our breath is of stone, yup.

Because we collect no dust on our
    hindparts by error's somersault.
We are both beastly and robust,
    upon the horned plains of the earth.
Robust we are, and widely distributed,
    infinitely sparse, infinitely many.
Our wigglies astound the friends of Ralph
    with terminal pissed-offedness.
Our brambles are full of poisoned wigglies.
Our minds move slow, but in wide
    circles.
Nothing much hinders the sky thought
    on its lark, on its random lasso.
So as far as we go, still
    we stop.
As for stop a mop will do.
Kill it and grow wigglies, especially
    the abject kind.
Pray to the moose for restoration
    of hindpart sensation.
Pray to the moose for mops, and stop
    signs to deter foreigners,
    fork lifts to deter grabity, storks
    to deter chimneys, stillness to
    deter noise, and noise to deter
    mooses, in particular the abject
    kind, sure.
Things tend to stop.
Things tend to start up, likeso.
They tend to bend light
    till we who dwell in bent halls
    of bent mirrors get the bent message
    likeso and fall over, all bamboozled.
The stop people have the start button
    to do the work of bottleneck.
The other way works the same, except

for being otherwise contagious with
feathers of false starts, bent wigglies,
extraneous moose noise and the whole
damned abject monsterosity of killed
feet, empty hearts and done-in brain
power, railing against the whole darn
whitewash of amateur washouts by
professional doorstops, yesmen and
loose women, yeah.
I am galloping through a region of rusted
jumbos, atomic glimmer glass, archaic
rosebuds, mystic armadillos and
borderline hayrakes looking for a
few good men to catch them porkypines.
I am walking slow through a world
of glass gone haywire.
I am walking slow on the sticky stuff
of another man's cellophane, sure.
I am walking slow without no more
bad thoughts than you would expect
of one such as me, gone bananas
on mystic glimmer gas, and
whoop-de-doo!
For he who thinks otherwise I have
prepared the cauldron of hot,
boiling oil, just in case he don't
back off and not look at me right,
him being a monster weirdo, or a
social undesirable, or basket case,
or one of them as wears jewelry,
or a bone through the nose or a gold
pin screwed through the nipple like
I seen at the gym giving me the abject
willies, so that I grew full strange,
and wiggly.

World's full of people stuck on someone
    else's cellophane.
World's full of places where your feet clink
    off the glimmer glass, where once long ago
    the earth hotted up ten million degrees,
    no shit, sure.
As I am trudging through a Menger sponge, a
    solid black block of basaltic lord-knows-
    what, I find X in the name of Y and
    grow doilies.
These are not the doilies I have a hankering
    for, therefore I do not like them, yup.
Upon the oath I confirm box lunches.
Upon both the oath and the breaking of it
    I implement oases and office checks.
I seek out Chubby for bollide sneakers.
I sneak out the same door Chubby uses,
    with both his oaths and tools, lie in
    wait humming the credo shit floats,
    boat my blues, dig up my old book
    of fake dreams, and think much upon
    the invisibility of Richard Stans, yup.
I fear I am a black sheep barging through
    the back door, braying, into a blind
    alley leading to a black Ka'abah, where
    I'm not supposed to go.
I fear Ralph, even though he's dead.
I fear all the doilies, who are strange
    to me.
Strange feet fear the same stuff, likeso.
I go great guns upon the hangnail sarcophagus.
Piles of spare wigglies arrive in mad crates
    infinitely sparse, looped and knotted.
Grace's a fear park of the rider people,
    and sheer destiny palls.

Grace's got the same strange feet I do,
    yet none fear her the way they do me.
Strange, Grace.
Strange to be an Ichabod Ka'abah.
I prefer this to that for no reason.
I prefer this to that cause of how I have
    done choosed this, and not that.
That one dwells in the forest of swill, all
    candles smeared with mystic nightshade ooze.
That one's a rider perilous, a double
    headed trouble-shooter, a ne'er-do-well
    who aced his fate and wears no icy halo.
That one heaps me hot so, yup.
This one bursts like grievous nightshade, opening.
OO cats' eyes glory in the opening up, yup.
They air out the terror of the night, yup.
But they irk me with their terrorist tendencies.
For strange people are moving around
    inside of my house.
Boing, they go. Boing.
And once they are done with the boings
    commence booing and the booings
    are as bad as the boings and the
    boings having driven me half off
    my nut I begin to boo too so my voice'll
    get lost in the booing and they will
    henceforth get lost and be gone and not
    notice I am here, alone, in my house
    and start all over again with the mad, mad
    business of boings, boings which I hate.
That is why I prefer this to that.
OO cats' eyes light up the fractal zone, sure.
I am trudging slow in a region of Couette-Taylor
    flow and perpetual turnstiles, sure.
Junk bats boat in the blue wind, ho.
Hovering in deepest glide.

Ralph there, dead.
Buoyed in dead hope, gone cat.
Dust in rills, another
    planet.
We shift our errors, compounding
    the wilderness.
Needlemen approach.
They signal, holding up
    painted wigglies.
Wind, wind and no water, yup.
Boulders bunched up, yup.
We consult the mystic oracle.
We offer up mystic glimmer gas.
We talk to our wide one, Chubby.
Chubby tells us plenty, yup.
We take their wigglies and kill
    the mothmen, sure.
Junk bats boat in the blue wind, ho.
We, we and them, them and the others, strange.
Seasons cooled, cooked.
I think about the whole damn enterprise.
I ornament the region with unholy images
    of the directory tree.
I put on someone's clothes, not mine.
The clothes cling to my human nakedness.
I am ashamed.

(*Pause.*)

Nothing of value inside, please.
Nothing of value please don't steal my stuff.
    My stuff is worthless, so please don't
    steal it, the car is a wreck, and
    a pox on all your houses if you do.
I am caught forever on a Sierpinski carpet
    in a region infinitely sparse, infinitely many.
Carbon copies of my previous lives
    afflict my hairy feet with scurf.

The pointed hat is my American destiny.
Stolen cars have held up nothing of value
    and you know what to do.
You know what to do lassoes X in the
    name of Y, stuffs shirts and says to
    Hadituptohere: Kwitcherbellyachin."
You know what to do fears not the
    ghost of Ralph, on account of him
    being a corpse, and therefore abstrack.
We all trudge through the howling
    badlands of prehistoric lawn furniture.
We all act as though we had met the first
    fur person in a back alley, bodacious.
We all act strange on account of our
    badass attitude problem.
We all bad on account of the Divine Will
    of Chubby, who likes not our American
    shoes on account of they being cheesy,
    so kwitcherbellyachin'.
You know what to do, just like me,
    that's why I am running as fast as I can,
    with all my stuff wrapped in a red bandanna.
(*Pause. He goes out. Another* man *appears, also strange. The* SECOND
is a bit more well-heeled than the FIRST. *He smiles and begins talking.*)

SECOND MAN   Strange stuff, stuff whining in the air door.
    Stuff people don't see.
    (Chubby, we gotta do somepin.)
    Thoroughly tough, though.
    Tough through and through.
    (Chubby, face it: we are the
        fly in God's ointment.)
    Strange stuff, all kinda
        gussied up likeso.
    X the mercantile whodunit.
    Stuff, gussied up with fatal bric-a-brac.

I am forging the whole damn Big Ugly.
I am driving through the Great Wahnanganewee,
    on all fours, Indian fashion, on the head
    of a pin, with no saintly nevermind.
Because the boiled cup of strange air flaked up
    and foamed, damped down, dried out
    and blew away, just below critical,
    all in a tatter.
Because of bears and air doors.
Because of boars and them men there, badass.
Because . . .
Strange stuff, and the wind upon the water
    like God in the hay.
X the frost on the dead man's open eye.
X the fever before the episode of bellowing.
X the rain upon the recent dead.
X the whodunit.
X the Y.
X the same, gussied over in fatal funeral weeds.
Robber shoots robber as victim ducks.
I am riding, all slipshod, through
    groves of sacred cauliflower.
I am riding, all sacred, through
    groves of slipshod funeral weeds.
I am honking turtle chairs.
Robber shoots rubber and the tisket's
    a tasket.
Duck shoots duck till the sky implies
    a further monad nomad.
    . . . ? . . .
For rain down as rain up was.
The whole ghastly glitter, whaled.
Gee and haw, hawsered.
I shoulda done rubber boat bloat.
I shoulda chair grease and hemlines
    creaked with bargain-basement

stress fractures, hula hoops,
   and whatnot bric-a-brac baloney.
You know why?
You know Y.
You know how the Y am did from its
   former days, hawking rubberbands
   in some grimy barbados, raincaked
   in a kitten's grave, under the floor
   moon, shank-shivered in ebony coal dust, sure.
You know Y for sure, hotcakes.
For I am learning the lingo of stretch
   disaster.
For none other of them rotates the glove box
   bankrupt.
For I too was, cuffed and bumped
   and all bobtailed.
For I clawed my hairy way
   to thisnthat.
It was not am likesome, for it war
   shoatly.
Chlorine boxes sprung leaks above
   so we smote the hexes and slew the shoats.
Fudges of unknown slime succumbded to their
   baser instincts and was did elected, among
   us, kits to cats of senatorial cabbagery, sure.
Sunken lore bellied up and dovetailed
   heartbreak.
The nightseed grew a directory tree.
Glimmers of gasses inflicted seismic
   opera upon the friends of good
   works who had gone belly up in fear
   of sunken lore and tragic glimmer gas.
Dogs learned a nether lingo
   and cussed the Y.
Dogs proclaimed Western Civilization
   a feeble fellow.

It was not am likesome.
For I was there, and saw it, and liked
    not what I saw and was saw-milled
    in hairy feather dust and buried living
    dead standing up in pure amazement.
Whining on the air door stuffed people are.
Whining dreadful, they cousin bunches
    and skin their flicks.
They revert pseudo-comic android retail.
They remind the producers of incurable
    bric-a-brac and cast skinks.
Grasses grow up and while away
    unexampled.
Folded up wigglies rant on glimmer gas,
    pop out, darken the light source, fur
    the bald part, slow the fulsome vat of
    superheated cheese, stuff the poor folk
    with jars of dry rot (furball puree),
    reverb the god woofer, bounce down the
    darkened staircase, turn over the cooling
    corpse to see if it's rigid, dry the eyes
    of mystic Ahab (Ahab, who shall return
    the third time as Richard Nixon), smother
    the last saint in the slashed featherbed,
    black out and be borned again in mythic bric-a-brac.
They, the ghostly android shuttle crew, emote on cue
    and smote shoats, half-crocked, and croak.
They, the cheerful quasi-human redundant,
    grow buds on they directory trees.
They take off glasses and see the mystic orgy
    of doomed impenitents, high on glimmer gas.
They pop the dead back, and abdicate the
    next life for fear of this one, strange.
They dark the deep of it, strange.
They hang the neap tide, hey.
They fashion devil grommets from demon

mice, magnify contagion, dive-bomb
the wicked in their old goon hotels,
black hubs of badass bubble.
They seek satiety, where I used to roam,
one lone blur, with all my thousand
furry feet, trailing my hideous gowns
of funeral weed and bric-a-brac, sure.
For I would investigate regions of niter
with my wimple woven of star's flesh
and spiderlegs, kinda strange.
And I would loosen the steel bands
of oblivion, cry out, stand on my
furry head to signify some horrid
bio-theological paragogical bear trap,
some ghastly parable implicating us all
to the Cosmic Upstart himself, who shall
rain down hot coals upon us, all in the
name of Impious Misrule, cheese, and the
cold mystic thrall of cosmic pitchblende.
For I too was done up likeso.
For I too roared and bellowed, rolled over
and possum played, all to escape the
horror, the horror of happening once
too often to consider the human mythos
ripe, as it truly is, in fairest form, all
of a fine autumn eve, on a full stomach.
I too was strong enough to run off, hiccoughing.
I too was strong enough to stay.
I too grew strange the more I thought upon it.
Junk bats boat in the blue wind, ho.
Hovering in deepest glide.
Ralph there, dead.
Buoyed in dead hope, gone cat.
Dust in rills, another
planet.

We shift our errors, compounding
    the wilderness.
Needlemen approach.
They signal, holding up
    painted wigglies.
Wind, wind and no water, yup.
Boulders bunched up, yup.
We consult the mystic oracle.
We offer up mystic glimmer gas.
We talk to our wide one, Chubby.
Chubby tells us plenty, yup.
We take their wigglies and kill
    the mothmen, sure.
Junk bats boat in the blue wind, ho.
We, we and them, them and the others, strange.
Seasons cooled, cooked.
I think about the whole damn enterprise.
I ornament the region with unholy images
    of the directory tree.
I put on someone's clothes, not mine.
The clothes cling to my human nakedness.
I am ashamed.

(*Pause.*)

Oort. Grommet. Gort. A pox on all their houses.
Ahab. Nightman. Weasel. A pox on all their houses.
We who are not them hoard our sacred bric-a-brac.
The anomaly has outlived them, God and Ralph, both, sure.
Why did the door person open the door for you? Why was
the door person friendly and courteous? Why did your
server acknowledge you within two minutes? Why did you
receive your drinks promptly? Why was your food served
promptly? Why was your hot food hot and your cold food
cold? Why did your food taste good? Why was the atmos-
phere enjoyable? Why was the restaurant clean? Why was
the restroom clean? Why, during the course of your meal,
did a manager visit your table? Why have you been here for

the first time, for a few times, or many times? Why do we
approve the cut and design of our server's costume? Why,
when we approve the uncut part of the U.S. Constitution,
do we not approve the cut part, the part about dancing—
drunk—in the forest at night, howling before strange gods,
all before sun-up, in strange hats, aglow?

. . . ? . . . (!) . . .

A pox on all your houses, you.

May the very floors renounce their wall-to-wall nativity
    and fold up, all furry, like a systematic ogive mare's-nest.

May the North become South, and so forth.

May the unfurry ones, far from God, become furry like us,
    except Ralph.

May Ralph stay dead, even if he gets ticklish down there,
    and kinda restless.

May he stay good and dead on account of how we don't care
    much about him ever since he done you know what
    to you know who and that's a fact no shit sure.

(*He smiles and goes off, as a* YOUNG WOMAN *enters, wearing dark
clothes, perhaps in mourning. She smiles and begins talking.*)

I have trouble with that, politically—
    on account of you and yours being
    a loathsome, misnormal dickhead.

For which was up and done be done did am.

Lotsa y'all got all pinched up, sure.

Lotsa us'ns have had it up to here
    on account of y'all, yup.

You go figure how it all came about, sure.

Banjo playing ain't no way allowed no more, here.

Gum chewing ain't neither here nope, sometimes,
    maybe.

You gotta behave if you wanna creep low
    under that there wall of flying debris.

He who stands up gets conked good.

He who gets conked good they lay out
    for the buzzards, no shit sure.

Howzabout you'd like to be an aminal omelet,
    huh?
Lay there for a long time, thinking.
Lay there for a long time, somewhere
    on that there Sierpinski carpet,
    in a region infinitely sparse and
    infinitely many, no shit, sure.
Being all pinched up ain't no fun.
Being the devil's doormat ain't
    my idea of Christmas and Easter
    on account of being plumb squoze
    till the lights go out and the cows
    come home and the whole ponderation
    of the whole damn land mass barks up
    the wrong tree, cuts cheese and croaks.
For I stood up and was am cutdown and kilt
    by flying trash, right here, you bet, sure.
For I am riding high in the tall grass,
    all greasy, of my catastrophe.
I am riding on what looks like a horse,
    but ain't not no horse.
We are loping through the high hay
    with men on fire behind us.
We are en route to the cubical empire,
    where the gum was sticky, the
    forest was dark, and the cats
    were the wisest creatures in the land.
Where we'd come from we'd rather not
    think about, being careless unredeemables.
What kind of horse this is, this
    strange black bucking beast, hell,
    I'd rather not think about, because
    the blast force of the Golden Haunting
    affects all who left the empty mansion
    having pocketed a fork, or knife, or a spoon.

For those there men behind us
    are of the tribe of Ichabod.
Flames consume them, like us, completely,
    again and again.
Flying bricks, stoves, car doors, bins, tray tables,
    hats, rotisseries, pots and pans, shoes and socks,
    coat hangers, typewriters and screen writers, waste
    paper baskets, all whistle about in the red clangor
    of the hot wind, no shit, sure.
I stand up, am cut down, again and again.

(*Pause.*)

Beyond snake is dog, beyond dog
    is all arcane cellos and watch out for
    them because they lost twenty-five
    pounds, quit drinking and have learned
    a thing or two since the Pretty Times
    Done Did and they have a thing or
    two they'd like to ask you, and just
    between you and me, it's not your name.
Beyond the cellos is broccoli, beyond
    broccoli is cabbage, beyond cabbage
    is cheese, and beyond cheese is the
    long, black barge, drifting there . . .
    all draped in black crepe . . .
    because . . .
Because, because ever wonder where your garbage
    really goes?
Because that black barge there which contains your
    you-know-what has come home at last, to roost.
Because that black barge would like
    to speak with you.
Because that black barge will find you out
    wherever you are, even on a remote,
    microscopic bud of an inconspicuous

island lost forever in a wild archipelago
of a minor Julia set, a Julia set floating
dizzily down through scale upon scale of the
whole damn jiggery-pokery of a full-blown
Mandlebrot Set.
For the mellow music of all these cellos
tiskets a tasket.
Cause of how you being a monster
dickhead and all, yup.
And Chubby himself in hot pursuit, yup.
And the sky full of empty stuff, yeah.
And the wind deprived of true motivation
for its visionary landscape project, hey.
And the world all woolly.
And the wool all worldy.
And the sheer unavoidability of it all,
including the "and" and the "the."
And the Way Out locked from the inside,
barred, barricaded with stacks of
cardboard boxes filled with oily
rags, powdered dioxin, and barrels
of plutonium oxide sludge that has
hotted up somewhat over the years so
we can't quite recall which of the
single-walled tanks are confirmed
leakers, and which contain the
ghost of Ahab waiting for the
last appearance of Richard Nixon,
dancing a jig in a graveyard
with a whiskey bottle balanced on his
head.
And all the teddy bears asleep.
And all those who want my things
prying open the locked windows.
And me slipping out in the night,
disguised as Napoleon Bonaparte.

And what I ride off upon, which
    looks like a horse, but isn't, strange.
Bledsoe's popeye bugs me so, so
    I do not care much for Bledsoe.
So the wheel turns and turns up
    a mythic rutabaga.
So I go to work happy,
    and work all happy and come
    home happy, proud of myself sure.
Because of being happy, and not
    like you, or him, or Bledsoe,
    a loathsome misnormal dickhead.
Being happy turns the wheel for me.
Being happy is my secret weapon
    in the war of all against all.
Being a warlock helps too.
Being a wheel turns my ticklebone's
    lights on and I confess to being
    possessed of lights, darks, and
    have got the map showing where
    the mystic potatoes are, the gourd
    of life, the mythic rutabaga, and
    know how to handle big wigglies.
Being a workaholic son-of-a-stiff
    greases the wheel in the warlock's
    oarlock, yup.
Because I knock on fate's false door.
Because I know where the warlocks
    buried Bledsoe's popeye, sure.
Because Bledsoe's eye is made of glass,
    so I go each and every day to work
    with my fist buried in the ham of life.
If the shoe wears, tear it, sure.
If the shoe fits, strike up the band
    cut cheese and croak.

If the shoe fits, there's something
    radically wrong with you, you
    loathsome, misnormal dickhead.
For I wouldn't want to tangle with me,
    on a dark night, in a blind alley, nope.
For I wear the shoe even when it
    don't fit, and if you don't
    like it, tough shit, because it
    takes two to tango, especially
    when it comes to tangle, no shit, sure.
For I am riding on a moonbeam
    in the tingle of a nightmare, yup.
And I know all things, all things
    fit to know, despite them shoes, sure.
And shoes be damned, if I get it into
    my head to go riding, in a region
    infinitely sparse, infinitely many, so
    then the shoe fits because I say it does.
And it gets kinda lonesome.
And it gets kinda darksome too.
And kinda weird, because of bad thoughts
    you shouldn't ought to've done had
    and better not talk about on account
    of they being strange, or on account
    of you being far from where you ought, yup.
All kinda such strangeness give you the blues.
And you are far from where it was you knew.
For the way is covered with gruesome doilies.
And where they come from no man knows.
No man knows . . .
   . . . ! . . .
  . . ! (?) . . .
Nor what good they are.
Nor what the hoar sock bended the
    bluebell to, to hoe the hell sock
    with rat cream till the sky shout,

    roll over, drop kick the heartache,
    roll over once more, pop up and sigh,
    wrap itself in the flag, and drop dead,
    a case of terminal burn out.
Cause that's the way it is.
And you who bite the beast may
    bite in vain.
May bite in vain because of devout concretions
    of fibrillated sharkhate having vented
    into the B chamber of the moose unit,
    even though the moose unit was sealed
    off years ago, sealed off with barking
    seals and sea lions, when some abject
    dickhead, some abject misnormal dickhead
    failed to duck when that monster flywheel
    leaped the track, and spun and spun all
    beastly blue-bright and shaggy, spun
    for a month of Sundays, strange.
No one likes to talk about
    that there incident.
No one much cares for them suchlike
    accidental incidents.
No one much likes to have they heart
    broke neither, nope, yup.
No one much has much to say about what
    stuff gets done roundabout here,
      nor why, I guess, maybe.
I put on someone's clothes, not mine.
The clothes cling to my human nakedness.
I am ashamed.

Slow blackout.
End of play.

Fnu Lnu

Originally entitled *Romantic Violence*,
Fnu Lnu was commissioned by the
Hillsborough Moving Company,
through Dancing in the Streets, as a
site-specific theater piece for the Italian Club in Ybor City, Florida. Ybor
was for many years a center for the
manufacture of hand-rolled cigars;
many of the diverse workers (from
Sicily, Galicia in northern Spain, and
Cuba) were anarchists, who built
their own schools, hospitals, and mu-
tual aid societies (like the Italian
Club). I tried to use local legend and
hearsay to create a new version of
Aeschylus's *Eumenides*, a strange and
wonderful drama about the origin of
the polis, and of political thinking as
such. The story of Fnu Lnu as a name
I found on the back page of the *Columbia Journalism Review*, a periodical I

PERFORMANCE NOTE
The appearance of an asterisk within a speech indicates that the next speech begins to overlap at that point.

love because of its careful, continual critique of the debacle of current American political journalism. The play went through many, many drafts before we arrived at the tiny, gemlike production version at Soho Rep. in 1997.

Let us therefore trust the eternal Spirit which destroys and annihilates only because it is the unfathomable and eternally creative source of all life. The passion for destruction is a creative passion too.
—MICHAEL BAKUNIN

PERSONS OF THE PLAY

DEEZO, a man looking for the answer to a strange question, and his gaggle of familiars:
    three ZOBOPS, sorceresses in Zobop society;
    three FIGURES, women, who also play a BUS DRIVER and two passengers;
    FIRST MAN;
    SECOND MAN;
    THIRD MAN, on the bus, has an abnormal faith in the power of prayer;
    the OLDEST ANARCHIST in Ybor City, Orestes diFanneli Flannagan;
    FLIM-FLAM MAN, the shade of Charlie Wall;
    a fortune teller lady, or mambo, later revealed to be the demon,
        MARINETTE BWA CHECH;
    a strange CHORUS, composed of three ALLIGATORS, two MORGUE
        PEOPLE, and CASTRO's fugitive BEARD.

In the Soho Rep. production (1997), the parts of DEEZO, the PERSON, the OLDEST ANARCHIST, the FIRST GATOR, and the FLIM-FLAM MAN were played by a single actor; all the rest by the three FIGURES we encounter at the top, who also sing all the songs.

Lights down. We hear a BUS TOUR GUIDE *give a potted, but very contemporary, description of Ybor City.*

TOUR GUIDE   On your left, Al Lopez Park. He had
              his best season in 1928 when as an
              outfielder for the Braves he batted an
              outstanding .337 in 612 at bats.
              On your right, the Afro-Cuban Club (La
              Union Marti-Maceo). José Marti organized the
              Revolutionary party here, and they say
              the message went out concealed in a
              Tampa Cigar. And there is José Marti
              Park with a statue of the dead Cuban
              martyr. They say Castro placed a
              wreath here, on his visit around the
              time of the murder of Charlie Wall,
              in 1956. On your left, the Italian
              Club. They say the place is haunted.

      Lights up, dimly, for the following.

Scene [poison ivy: **M**]. *In the ballroom of the Italian Club on Seventh Avenue in Ybor City, Florida. A strange man (*DEEZO*) at a table with micro- phone before him. He is our Master of Ceremonies. There is a battered suitcase by his side. Behind him, upstage right, three women (the* FIGURES*) are seated at another table, each with her own microphone before her. They sing.*

FIGURES   A man on fire
            A man on fire

knows what he is
trying to become.

A man on fire
A man on fire
has the special thought
he's on the run.

A man on fire
A man on fire
knows what he is
trying to become:

Smoke! The air
fills up with smoke;
it blots the sun

of who we are,
of what we known,
of what we come from,

Because a man
on fire know
he's on his own.

(*Lights come up on the man.*)

DEEZO   Call me "Deezo." Heck, you can call
me whatever you want. Doesn't matter
to me. Look around you and what do
you see? The Italian Club, right?
. . . wrong. For, tonight, this place
has been changed into a Museum of Mind.
Funny, the things you find in the
street.

(*He holds up a ball of hair.*)

Ladies and Gentleman, a Ball of Hairs.
No good for anything, but Deezo's Museum
of the Mind. Along with picture postcards

of the old days in Ybor City. Eyeglasses,
old rings, and false teeth. *Bolita* balls,
excavated bottles from the Florida Brewing
Company, and cigar boxes, bands, cigar
labels, and related ephemera.

Bolita is the numbers racket, see.
(*He puts the ball of hair back in the suitcase with the other stuff.*
Pause. Now he shows us something else: a strange tricorn hat. The
three F I G U R E S *behind him move about, and whisper.*)
And there is this funny . . . hat?
Looks like a hat.
(*He puts it down gingerly.*)
Creepy stuff.
(*Light vampiric laughter from the three* F I G U R E S .)
I'm the Master of Ceremonies. Just
for tonight, although this is the sort
of event that tends to repeat itself.
Like a tape loop, infinite regress, or
something nested in an image of itself.
So, things like this tend to go on forever,
just like tonight. But I'm getting ahead
of myself . . . guess I'm a little nervous.
(*Pause.*)
Sure . . . I can tell you *all* about Ybor.
Tell you what maybe you already know . . .
About the cigar factories. Stuff like
that. About how we all got along, ah . . .
despite coming from different places.
Places where life was so hard it barely
seemed worth the trouble. Places called . . .
(*A nervous pause.*)
Places named after saints and angels
of the Roman Catholic faith. Names like
San Stephano and Galicia. Beautiful
names like Gargantua, Pirandello,

Fellatio and . . .

(*Pause. Is he losing his mind?*)

Shit, I don't know. I don't know what the
hell I'm talking about. I can't stand
speaking before crowds.

(*One of the* FIGURES *stands up in the shadows behind him.*)

Because you see the stuff I know about
Ybor is all odd stuff. Castro's party at El
Boulevard Restaurant, the unsolved murder
of Tampa's numbers boss, Charlie Wall,
both in 1956, coincidentally. Or
the time Che Guevara leaped through
the window at Villa De Leon to escape
detection. All true. Scary stuff about
spiders and curses and blasted hopes.
The true stuff of the heart. Crime.
Loss. Public betrayal. Defection.
Cynicism. Bitterness. Greed. Stabs
in the back. Voodoo . . .

I mean, I don't want this to be a downer but
sometimes I get *really* anxious and upset and
stuff.

(*The standing* FIGURE *whistles to get* DEEZO*'s attention.*)

See that guy?

(*Points back at him.*)

He's been following me. Says I owe my
soul to the *bolita* man, his boss. Now,
naturally I have no idea what he's talking
about. But it spooks me. Weirds me out.
Heck, I don't believe in God or anything . . .
don't get me wrong: I'm not an atheist or
anything like that. I just don't believe in
anything, so . . . so I know, I know I shouldn't
be scared. But I AM. Like, like maybe in a
former life I was in love with a DEMON . . .

STANDING FIGURE   Deezo.

DEEZO   Say anybody got four quarters for a dollar?
             I want to call my sister out by . . .

STANDING FIGURE   Deezo, tell them what happened.

DEEZO   It wasn't me. I was someplace else,
             I swear.

STANDING FIGURE   Tell them what happened on the bus.

DEEZO   It was what happened *before* that. That's
             what weirds me out. I'm standing there
             waiting for the bus, looking at this weird
             hat, and this guy comes up, talking crazy.
       (*The* FIGURE *slowly sits down.* DEEZO *becomes a demented street
       person.*)
             You want to know why the "Y" in Ybor?
             Okay. Well I'll tell you then. People
             here don't listen to me, but when the
             glow comes they'll wish they had. They'll
             wish they had for sure. People talk about
             the old days like they knew what they were
             talking about, but they don't because of
             the destruction of Western Values; the
             destruction of Western Values has to do
             with why people come here to get drunk and
             go dancing. The cigar box of human history
             is full of pathetic losers, losers like you,
             losers like Mister Jesus Anybody, losers who
             don't appreciate the true cause of our human
             agony. Your role model, Mister Jesus
             Anybody, died for our sins and just look
             where it got him. What I'm saying is people
             talk like they left their mind in the microwave.
             Sure, I come down here myself every now and
             then, with my buddies, hoist a few, get shit-

faced and rowdy with the best of them, raise
a little hell, remove the occasional hood
ornament or aerial from tourist cars, tear the
whole car door off every so often when the
mood compels me . . . Hell, lost my new .357
Magnum in that alleyway over there just last
week. Cops were searching the trunk for
drugs and I just barely got rid of it—
unlicensed—before they frisked me. Gone,
when I came back for it. My luck the way I
figure, but, hell, I'm just as good as the next
man. I vote and pay my taxes, when I can
find the polling place. Because they keep
moving it around to confuse me. I heard that
story about Ronald Reagan and Charlie Wall
but I don't believe it. I don't believe my
mother either. Most of what she says is a
pure crock. And I don't believe what she has
to say about values and Western civilization
because it's like the good book says, HOW
WOULD SHE KNOW? That's right: how would
she know. And if she did, why didn't
she convey the fact to me? She sure had
plenty of opportunities before I up and got
hauled off to the State Farm. You tell me, I
don't know.

(*Looks hard at* DEEZO [*himself*].)

And another thing: that ain't the Italian Club,
it's the "Albanian" Club, as any fool can tell.
Just look at those shoes. Those are the shoes
of ethnic Albanians. Italians shipped out
after the war. Korean War. Moved their tents
up north, to the town of Schenectady.
Schenectady, New York, and the planet
Jupiter.

(*Pause. Gives* DEEZO *the once over.*)

As for you, Deezo, you couldn't find a license
plate in a cup of coffee.

And as for "Why the Y?", this is a spider-web
type of thing, infinitely extended in the realm
of the paranormal. In the Realm of the
Unreal. Because "Y" is a devil letter, 25th
of the alphabet. And 25 is truly 7, the
number of Old Horny.

(*Scowls and waves his hands. His voice becomes hieratic, and strange.*)
Irreversible Metallic Computer Virus
have already made you not existing
anymore.

(*He changes back to* DEEZO.)
So that's the gist of it. I turned into a
stranger. A man possessed. "Why the 'Y' in
Ybor"? That's all I could focus on. Lost
track of friends, family. Job. All of it. I'd
go tramping up and down Seventh Avenue.
Why the "Y" in Ybor? I became like a
metallized puppet in an imaginary opera by
the futurist Marinetti. People began to avoid
me. Because none of them had the answer.
They wouldn't look me in the eye. They'd
flinch and try to slide on by without
responding. Worse, some would get confused,
start babbling, babbling as weirdly as me,
now . . . It was as if my asking them "why the
'Y' in Ybor" was like tapping them on the old
brainpan with a stupid stick.

(*A strange* CHORUS. *The* CHORUS *sings very quietly underneath.*)

CHORUS   Why the Y in Ybor?
                Why the B in Bbor?
                Why the C in Cbor?
                Why the G in Gbor?

Why the K in Kbor?
Why the P in Pbor?
Why the Q in Qbor?
Why the T in Tbor?
Why the U in Ubor?
Why the V in Vbor?
Why the Z in Zbor? (*and repeats*)

(DEEZO *comes out of it, grins sheepishly behind his microphone. the seated* FIGURES *whisper something we cannot hear.*)

FIGURES   Heck, I don't know what I'm talking about.
Don't pay me any mind. Skip it. Really,
because you know I had to drop out of
junior college. This is true. Attention
disorder syndrome. Seems like I keep falling
into the hole of forgetting who I am . . .

FIGURE   Deezo.

DEEZO
(*To the* FIGURE, *sharply.*)
I know, I know. I was just trying to give an
example, okay? Jesus! I am just trying to
explain some things. How I had to drop
physics and accounting. Some kinds of weird
half-mad Diogenes. And all these numbers,
numbers with little pictures attached to them,
keep rolling through my head. Even at
night, when I go to sleep. That's right,
numbers. This "why the 'Y' in Ybor" is no
parlor game.

FIGURES   Deezo is a bad man.
Deezo is a dead man.
He left his hand
on the street.
He left his feet

on the moon.
Go ask Fnu Lnu
what to do.

DEEZO   Next thing I know I'm on this bus.
(*Realizing he has left something out.*)
            Jumped on the bus, see, to get away
            from this demented street person.

            The Seventh Avenue bus. Same bus
            I take every day to the Junior College,
            before I had to drop out on account
            of . . . skip it. And there are these
            guys.
(DEEZO *turns back to them. Lights up on the three* FIGURES, *our demonic Furies, smiling.*)
            They look like normal-type guys, only
            I know they're not. And they are talking:
(*We're aboard a bus. Rolling on its route through Ybor City. The three* FIGURES *become the* BUS DRIVER *and the other two passengers. One of them is talking to the other while the* DRIVER *describes the sights.* DEEZO *stares out, eavesdropping.*)

FIRST MAN   You know, they've done this thing. And
            what it is is this. They go and take plants
            you know, living things like plants and
            plant-like things. Like slime molds. Like . . .
            maybe fungus too.

SECOND MAN Funguses? Yeah? And so?

FIRST MAN   So they go and take these living things and
            pray over them. You know, like worship over
            the plants. Or nearby. In the vicinity. And
            over the seeds and things too.
(*Pause.*)

SECOND MAN They worshiped over the funguses?

FIRST MAN What they found out was that the things
that were worshiped over grew faster
than they would've without . . . without
being worshiped over and prayed upon.

SECOND MAN Even the funguses?

FIRST MAN Even the funguses. They grew faster
and bigger and more grotesque when people
prayed over them. No one can explain
it. So . . . It's a true scientific
mystery is what they say.
(*Pause.*)

SECOND MAN Sounds weird.

FIRST MAN No one knows why. No one knows why.
I kid you not. No one knows why.

ANOTHER MAN (AS CASTRO'S BEARD) I bet Fnu Lnu knows why.

DEEZO Who's Fnu Lnu?

Catastrophic change of light and sound as we enter the world of the Zobop society.

Scene [choke cherry: 🔉]. *All three* ZOBOPS *wear long, red gowns and red tricorn hats. They hold long silvery tin horns which they blow on from time to time. These are members of a cabal of sorceresses. As the scene begins we hear them sing.*

ZOBOPS Aye, aye, zobop.
Aye, aye, zobop.
(*Etc.*)

DEEZO And suddenly I was someplace else.
Someplace strange, and the three strangers
I'd met carried candles and sang strange songs.
(*An uncanny Zobopian pause.*)

Then they all spoke at the same time,
only I could hear each one distinctly.

FIRST ZOBOP   What nobody know about Ybor, Deezo,
is that there are two demon watching
over the place for all time. One is
Charlie Wall, the god of the game of
chance known as numbers. The other,
who we will now pass over in silence,
is Fnu Lnu.

(*Silence.*)

Charlie Wall possess this machine he make
long time since out of the tools of the cigar-
making trade, some few squeegees, recycled
bicycle parts. Not to mention certain
machinery left over from the building
of the famous Party Room at the Tampa
Bay Hotel in 1890. He call it "the
Seventeen Year Tampa Bay Clutch-Pod
Borer," because it look kinda like a
seventeen-year locust. This machine is an
annihilation machinator par excellence:
you point at the world and—poof!—the
world disappear. Now . . .

(*A hollow pause.*)

every day Charlie Wall is sitting somewhere,
somewhere in hell, I suppose and he point his
"Seventeen Year Tampa Bay Clutch-Pod Borer" at
Florida and poof! Florida vanish. Disappear.
Am disintegrated by foul rays of Evil. So:
first question you gonna wonder if this is so
why we have Tampa every day new, quite the
same? Well, it is because Fnu Lnu have
himself his own powerful machinator too. This
one made out of spare parts from old cigar box
machinery, box springs and some various

apparatus belonging to the *Piruli* man. This
machine Fnu Lnu denominate the "Ybor City
Scannable Boiler-Plate." Now every day Fnu
Lnu point his machinator at Florida and poof!
Florida created fresh, brand new. Where Fnu
Lnu is, no one can say. No man knows. But
every day the demon Charlie Wall point his
machine at Ybor City and destroy it, and
every day Fnu Lnu point his machine in the
same direction and bring back the whole
shebang. All this is a great mystery of cosmic
anarcho-syndicalism. All I don't know is
"why," Deezo. As for instance, "why the 'Y'
in Ybor?" That I do not know.* And you
better tell me. You better tell me.
You better had.

SECOND ZOBOP   You wanna know what I think? What I think
is that Deezo here is a phony imitation.
That's right, a fake. A walking, talking
mannikin who appears to be a viable entity but
is not. His believability is not believable. It
is suspect. I theorize he is a mere husk of
cigar wrapping stuffed with cigar ash and
leaflets from the days this was a red place.
All this engineered courtesy of you and me,
Mister John Q. United States Taxpayer and
orchestrated by, you guessed it, the CIA.
The CIA masterminded the 1902 strike at
Bustilo, when they insulted the *lector*
Francisco Milian, who resigned in outrage.
The CIA paid for the radical newspapers
La Gacetta and *El Despertar* (in Key West),
not to mention *The Daily Worker.* The CIA
was behind the big strike in 1920, after which
they began to install cigar-making machines,

displacing the workers. The CIA
sponsored the general strike on behalf of
Sacco and Vanzetti here, on the 27th of April,
1927. The CIA organized the 1931 strike
which resulted in the end of the *lectors*—no
more hearing books being read. Fine with me.
Everybody knows Cervantes was a communist
and Shakespeare too. What nobody knows is
that they both worked for the CIA.
Nobody that is, but Fnu Lnu. As for the rest
of them, you tell me: AL Lopez? A CIA
spook. Orestes Ferrara? A CIA double
agent. Tony Pizzo? A CIA stooge of the
first water. And Charlie Wall told Kefauver
the devil protected him, but everybody knows
it was the CIA; which is why this "Why the
'Y' in Ybor" thing puzzles me. Indeed it nags
at me, like an aching cavity. And I wish I
knew the 800 number for the flim-flam man,
even though I don't believe in him* any more
than I do in . . . the Marx Brothers.

THIRD ZOBOP   Sure, your name is "Deezo" and I'm
El Conde de mi Puchungo. But we both know
I'm not, and neither are you. And do you
know why I can say to your face that you are
not Deezo with such great authority that I
am like bedrock? Or a hill of granite? . . . Do
you, Deezo? Do you? Don't play stupid,
"Deezo." You know you don't belong. You
know you're not one of our people.

DEEZO   Why the hell would anyone want to be one of
your people?

THIRD ZOBOP   Deezo, look at your shoes. That's right.
Look down at your shoes. What do you see?

DEEZO   I see my shoes.

THIRD ZOBOP   No, Deezo, you see shoes. But they are not your shoes. Because you are not you. You are someone else.

You posed the question "why"? And I'll tell you why. The letter "Y" is the fork of time. Time and human choice. Y is the human question turned upside down. Turned upside down to ensure human freedom. So when you ask "Why the 'Y' in Ybor?" you steal breath out of my mouth and you blaspheme against the gods of this place.

DEEZO   Gods!? What gods of this place?

THIRD ZOBOP   Martinez Ybor, god of the cylindrical roll of tobacco, which when ignited issues forth inhalable smoke. And Charlie Wall, god of the game of chance known as numbers.* And of course, Fnu Lnu . . .

DEEZO
(*Out.*)

Do you see what I mean? This kind of thing happens to me ALL THE TIME. And what's this . . . this weird jive about me stealing the breath out of your mouth.

THIRD ZOBOP   You know as well as me. You've split off from someone else. And if you truly want to find out who, you got to first find out why, you dig?

And we of the Society of Zobop recommend, strongly recommend you search the entire neighborhood till you find someone who can answer the question "Why the Y?"

DEEZO   Thanks really. I think somebody lost a hat.
(*Holding it up.*)

(*Light vampiric laughter.*)

THIRD ZOBOP   You've split off from someone else, like . . .
like the short end of the human wishbone. Or
the imaginary left prong of the old existential
"Y." Deezo, you're a husk, a cipher, a wisp
of mere nothingness. You will do as you are
told.

(*The littlest* ZOBOP [*the* SECOND] *raises a gun.* DEEZO *first freezes,
then checks out the gun. It is the one the demented street person talked
about earlier.*)

SECOND ZOBOP   .357 Magnum. We found it in the same
alleyway where you found the hat.

FIRST ZOBOP   Why the Y, Deezo? You must find out
why, and only Fnu Lnu knows that.

SECOND ZOBOP   We'll take care of your hat till
you return.

THIRD ZOBOP   Return with the answer.

FIRST ZOBOP   Why the Y.

SECOND ZOBOP   Stay cool.

(*Lights change.* ZOBOPS *fade from view as we hear their song.*)

ZOBOPS   Aye, aye, Zobop.
Aye, aye, Zobop.
(*Etc.*)

DEEZO
(*Pause.*)
So folks, I changed clothes, polished my old
shoes and set off to find out the truth. The
truth regarding who I was, and the source of

the perpetual anguish that tore at my heart.
And the dance of numbers that dizzied me,
each night as I dozed off. Set off in the
glitter of the romantic Ybor night. I knew
where to find the old ones, the old ones with
the strange glow of wisdom in their eyes.

SECOND ZOBOP   Already my anxiety is at an end
Already I have what I desired
As I drink every day
As I drink every day
The ice-cream Tropical.

   (*Black out begins.*)

Scene [mescal: **〰**]. *One of the* ZOBOPS, *a strange woman, part fortuneteller, part mambo, appears downstage right but still behind* DEEZO, *who does not see her. She sings a song.*

ZOBOP   Moon, moon
light-witted.
Five little bulls
and one calf.
The moon
was eating a fig.
The sun
was eating a cabbage.
Throw me the lime.
Throw me the lemon.
Throw me the key
to your heart.

   (*She talks to him familiarly.*)
Sure . . . I can tell you all about the old days
in Ybor. Life was rough. But back in Sicily
it was even worse.
   (*She laughs a dry soundless laugh with her head flung back.*)
In those days in Tampa, anarchists and

socialists were many. "To you workers!
Italians, Spaniards, and Cubans: All to a
single man, keep firm and do not betray the
noble cause." And what did we ever get out
of it? Freeschoola and prejudice. One
newspaper said: "Only way to stop the flood
of spaghetti immigration is to prohibit
sidewalk fruitstands." Can you imagine?

(*Another soundless laugh.*)

One day I awoke with a magnificence on my
forehead, and discovered the spirit world, the
world of omens and signs. In this way I
became a true American. Americans all believe
in these things, because they are a
practical people and care only about
results. This is rational. Politics is not
rational because people cannot tell you what
they want. They simply don't know. They
simply don't know. They are not thinking
clearly . . . like me in the old days, before
I change my life . . .

(*Pause.*)

I think your problem, Deezo, is that there
is, somewhere, somewhere hidden in Ybor,
a ball of hairs. Yes, Deezo, a ball of hairs
willed by Evil Forces through
electropneumatic controller. These
controllers are located in the tufted part of
the hair. They float about, this way and
that, as the heat rises and lowers. It is a
common thing, and is both an omen and
—like the sign which appeared on my
forehead—a magnificence.

(*Pause.*)

This is why you have become obsessed with
this bad question of why the 'Y' in Ybor.

These balls of hair must be found out, locked
up in a devil's quarantine, because it is a
devil thing. It is a virus compared to which,
the Irreversible Metallic Computer Virus is
nothing, the sniffles. I am telling you the
truth, Deezo, because I can see you intend to
the good even though what is irrational have
you in its mouth, like food. Like Charlie Wall.
Like Charlie Wall and the devil. Charlie told
those people in Washington the devil protected
him, but the devil must have had a bad day
because Charlie got killed anyway. We used
to sing songs together, wonderful old songs.
But I forget the words.

Long time ago I knew another "Deezo." He
had a fight with Charlie Wall over a girl.
Tempestuous. Underage. She tore the heart
out of his chest. Yes, Deezo, the origin of
your anxiety is a ball of hairs located in a
secret place. Maybe it is the terrible flower
of blankness spawned by the cold, cold ones.
Spirits of Crocodillo and Old Moldy. The
reptile gods who slither about, unseen, in the
sewers and aquifer and hidden regions of the
underworld. Maybe so. Maybe.

(*Another laugh.*)

Go ask them. With Fnu Lnu gone they
are the only ones likely to know.

(*The* ZOBOPS *sing.*)

ZOBOPS   The devil has beautiful skin.
She ties her face in a bow.
She knots the bow to her knees.
Then she tears up the picture
    and paints her face again.

The devil has beautiful skin.
The devil has beautiful skin.
First she grows fat,
Then she grows thin.
Then she tears up the picture
and paints her face again.
The devil has beautiful skin.

(*All sing reprise.*)

Scene [henbane: **ᴍ**]. *Slowly, the tablecloth of* DEEZO's *table rises, revealing a miniature Gator Theater, within which are three* ALLIGATORS, *two adults and their child. [This is a live voice-over scene—three actors with live mikes speak. The* GATORS *respond to the speech, but do NOT mime it, nor even attempt a naturalistic playing out.]*

FIRST ALLIGATOR   So . . . Madame Marinette directed you
to us did she? Before you she has sent
a long line of wet and sugary people.
Some of these we have killed and eaten.
Some we have done otherwise with
because we are always forgetting
what to say and what to do.

SECOND ALLIGATOR   He wants to know why the "Y" in
Ybor.

THIRD ALLIGATOR   He has sharp, glowing, needle eyes.
Why is he looking at us that way?

SECOND ALLIGATOR   Hush, child, he is of the tribe of
Manatee and a terrible witch sent him
here. I don't know why.

FIRST ALLIGATOR   There's the word again. "Why."

SECOND ALLIGATOR   What were you saying?

FIRST ALLIGATOR   Beats me. Now you're doing it.

SECOND ALLIGATOR   What?

FIRST ALLIGATOR   Asking too many questions. All I know
                   about Ybor City is that at funerals they
                   used to lay out the corpses on big
                   blocks of ice. Like hors d'oeuvres.
                   Made my mouth water. They would drag
                   the ice up and down Seventh Avenue on
                   big wagons, making a terrible racket
                   with their infernal machinery. At the
                   house of the deceased they would
                   pause. I haven't a clue why they would
                   pause, but that's what they would do.

SECOND ALLIGATOR   Maybe they would pause because one of
                    them forgot what he was doing.

FIRST ALLIGATOR   What was I saying? Damn. Now you've
                   distracted me.

SECOND ALLIGATOR   The corpses. Like ripe canapés. On
                    ice.

FIRST ALLIGATOR   Oh yeah. And then after the strange
                   pause they would start up again, with
                   this terrific racket. Of beating on
                   drums and blowing on trumpets and
                   clarinets and bass bassoons.

SECOND ALLIGATOR   But what does that have to do with the
                    question "Why the 'Y' in Ybor?"

FIRST ALLIGATOR   You would have to bring that up. Ah
                       . . .

SECOND ALLIGATOR   What puzzles me is just two things this
                    Deezo fellow has said. One is: what's
                    an "Ybor"? and two: what's a "Y"?
                    Is it a question of mereology?

THIRD ALLIGATOR   Mom, what's "mereology"?

SECOND ALLIGATOR   Mereology is the study of the relation
                of the part to the whole . . . Ah, an
                insight! Maybe an "Ybor" is part of a
                "Y," or even maybe it's the other way
                around.

FIRST ALLIGATOR   How can one thing be part of another
                thing? That sounds ridiculous to me.
                The Rule of Blankness specifically
                forbids overlap of entity upon entity.
                That would entail an instance of
                complexity.
   (*All shudder in horror.*)
                And the Gospel of Crocodillo is pretty
                clear on the heretical nature of that.

SECOND ALLIGATOR   Whoa, we're getting ahead of ourselves.
                What exactly is a "Y"? Let's deal with
                the question of that first.

FIRST ALLIGATOR   Questions again!

THIRD ALLIGATOR   A Y is an ordinate in a rectilinear co-
                ordinate system. It is also used as a
                symbol to denote or indicate anything
                that is 24th or 25th in order or class of
                a collection of entities. It is also a noun
                suffix forming diminutives of affection
                such as:

FIRST and SECOND ALLIGATORS   . . . shitty . . . chewy . . . cheesy . . .

THIRD ALLIGATOR   It also denotes anything having the
                shape of a "Y," as for instance a Y-
                shaped piece of plumbing.

THIRD ALLIGATOR   Mother, now that we've figured out
                what a "Y" is, can we eat up this Deezo
                guy?

SECOND ALLIGATOR   No dear, he's a guest. and besides, he
was sent by a terrible mambo, and if we
cross her we'll all end up as belts, and
lady's handbags in Singapore. And
besides, he's not ripe.

SECOND ALLIGATOR   He's a green apple, with the terrible
light of the glow radiating from deep
within, just like Fnu Lnu used to . . .
do.

DEEZO
(*Out.*)
There's that name again: Fnu Lnu!

SECOND ALLIGATOR   Deezo, I am terribly sorry but we
reptilians of the Tribe of Crocodillo are
not giants in the intellect department.
You might want to try Orestes
diFannelli Flannagan, the oldest
anarchist in Ybor City. We do not
comprehend what an "anarchist" might
amount to, but you'll find him on
Seventh Avenue, in one of those
cafés, drinking the thick brew of
sedition from a quaint demitasse cup of
the kind favored by intellectuals
who are out of power.

THIRD ALLIGATOR   Madame Marinette forgot to tell you, you
owe her twenty-five dollars for the
character reading, plus tax. Basically,
Deezo, you're stuck in a hole, a hole
in a big cheese of a host, a host with no
glow. You dig?

(*Slowly the curtain of the Gator Theater lowers, revealing:*)

Scene: [loco weed: **CO**]. *Orestes DiFanelli Flannagan,* THE OLDEST AN-
ARCHIST *in Ybor City, sitting at a marble-topped table in a café somewhere
along Seventh Avenue.*

OLDEST ANARCHIST   Deezo, Deezo, Deezo. How you
                    disappoint me. Sure, I can tell you all
                    about Ybor, but Deezo, my friend, history is
                    no cigar box full of mere tricks. My friend,
                    Castro would never be caught dead without
                    his beard. His beard meant more to him than
                    his socialism. And look at the result. He
                    came here to Tampa, you know. Deezo, I'm
                    talking to you. That's right. He traveled
                    to Ybor City in November 1955. Just seven
                    months after Charlie Wall was murdered . . .
                    I remember the dinner for him at El Boulevard
                    Restaurant, which was then located at Palm
                    and Nebraska Avenues. He invoked the
                    spirit of José Marti, but even then I had
                    my doubts. I did manage to discuss a few
                    points of theory with him, before the
                    organizers of the event got worried and
                    ushered me out. Bakunin said that the idea
                    of the "dictatorship of the proletariat" was
                    only a mask for a new kind of tyranny.
(*Pause.*)
                    Even then Castro had it wrong. But the
                    young people had lost their idealism. Now it's
                    even worse—it's as if ideals mean nothing at
                    all, and those of us who remember the
                    passions of political engagement seem to many
                    like extinct reptiles. This is tragedy.
(*Pause.*)
                    Young people want to know such insane and
                    stupid things. It makes no sense to ask
                    why the "Y" in Ybor. People go crazy when

they don't recall the tragedies of the past,
and hold them in some respect. There is an
old Sicilian proverb: *Chi rispetta rispettato
sara.* He who respects will be respected.
All the rest is flim-flam.

(*Pause.*)

Why, yes, now, maybe. Now maybe when you
think about it, there is something to that . . .
to that question. Something big, with a big
idea nested inside. Like a cosmic cigar box.
And inside that another one. And so on. An
infinite regress of cigar boxes, each one with
the "Price of Gators" label glued inside the
lid . . .

(*A puzzled pause.*)

It's like Bakunin told me, before he lost his
teeth. All people, he said, and all men are
filled with a kind of premonition, and
everyone whose vital organs are not paralyzed
faces with shuddering expectation the
approaching future which will speak out the
redeeming word . . . Oh, the air is sultry and
filled with lightning.

(*Pause. Aware he's been a trifle larger than life.*)

A cigar after all may be a great cigar, but it
is only a cigar. And they don't let you smoke
them on the airplane. As for why the "Y" in
Ybor, I don't know. I really cannot say.

(*More personal now.*)

If I were you I'd go talk to the flim-flam man.
He knows everything. Picked up the pieces
after the death of Charlie Wall. Charlie Wall
told Kefauver the devil protected him, but
where was the devil that day?

(*He laughs wickedly.*)

Just look at you, Deezo. You couldn't find a
license plate in a Cuban sandwich. That's
because of the *glow*. The glow is so deep in
you, you look like you're almost radioactive.
Hot. Heat. Fun Lnu's not hot. He's as cold
as a cup of coffee at the North Pole. Go and
ask *il truffatore inglese*. The flim-flam man.
As for why the "Y," go and ask him that too,
but don't listen too hard. It's too hot today
to listen to anyone, or anything. I mean, it
is really hot in Ybor City. Go and ask the
flim-flam man. I have a suspicion he is
behind it all. I've always thought this heat
possessed a political dimension.

(*Pause.*)

The Museum of Mind is a terrible thing,
Deezo. A haunted house. I much prefer
the world, because there are different kinds
of people in it. Study (*To* DEEZO)
simple justice, Bakunin, and the rules
of baseball. Go talk to the flim-flam man.

(*Pause.*)

Tony Pizzo was a good man. He had a
wonderful collection of things: cigar
boxes, cigar labels, cigar bands, old
picture postcards of pretty girls. As
for Ybor City today, I tell you, too
many liquor licenses are gonna drown out
the violins.

(*Lights change as we see the trio of* FIGURES *again. They sing another
song. These are the* BUS DRIVER *and two passengers from the earlier
bus scene.*)

FIGURES   Frank Carranza
               killed his wife

with five little sticks
and a pin.

(*The song passes through the room like a rumor.*)

Scene [belladonna: 🔲]. *The* FLIM-FLAM MAN *sits in* DEEZO's *chair; he has been waiting for* DEEZO. *We hear a door open, the footsteps of our tortured protagonist.*

FLIM-FLAM MAN   Frank, I told you not to come here.

BUS DRIVER   We did what you said.

FLIM-FLAM MAN   Frank. Beat it.

BUS DRIVER   Pay me. We took him off the bus. Just like
you said. Put on the Zobop regalia, me
and Beano here. Isn't that right, Beano?

THIRD MAN   Sure, Frank. Put on the Zobop duds, just
like they was sharkskin suits. If you pray
over a ball of hair it'll grow up to be a . . . a
big man. Like with Stankus over in St. Pete.
The guy who can lift a car up. Lift a car
up off the ground.

BUS DRIVER   Shut up, Beano.

FLIM-FLAM MAN   Beat it, Frank.

BUS DRIVER   You owe me, man.

FLIM-FLAM MAN   You're a piece of shit, Frank. I don't owe
you anything. My silence regarding the
accidental death of your spouse is all the
payment you'll ever get out of me. Now
beat it. Beat it, Frank.
(*The shadowy* FIGURES *disappear back into the gloom.*)
What I have to give you, Deezo, is what can
only separate you from your former life. "Y" is
split right down the middle. "Y" implies choice,

responsibility, all that jive. Hard stuff for a
cat balanced on the edge of nonidentity. This
is your show, sure, your Museum of Mind, but
I, too, knew you in another life. But then I'm
getting ahead of myself.

What nobody realizes, Deezo, is that Fidel
Castro has flown to the North Pole, where
the Devil lives, like a great, creaking heron.
Flapped and wheezed invisibly overhead.
This is true. This happened a . . . a few days
ago. The Devil is having his tea party:
Ronald Reagan, Ross Perot, Frank Sinatra,
Kim Il Sung, and Charlie Wall and Fidel Castro.
The Evil One himself is a bright scarlet, with
crumpled horns. He bears a massive hump
upon his left shoulder, and a thing upon his
thing which causes him pain. They are all
seated at a long, black table carved out of
Mpingo wood, drinking a bitter tea made of
wormwood, lighter fluid, and Drano. Before
them are trays of cookies baked from
caterpillar wool, sawdust, sandpaper, and
invisible ink. Each speaks to the other in his
own language, often complicated by a code or
cipher, so no one has much of a grasp on the
gist of the conversation.

Castro's beard abandoned his boss just as he
soared over Tampa, in the middle of the
night. It floated down through the morning
mist, and landed on a trellis of white roses, just
around the corner.

(*Pause.*)

Fattened by the dew, and what he could steal
from spiders and lizards, Castro's Beard was
about to settle down and become quite the

model citizen, a man of apparent parts, fancy
clothes, a Bay Shore Drive address, a few
aliases, and a reputation to maintain. Not to
mention a profound grasp of the science of
mereology, as it pertains to the *bolita*.
But before he could complete his
transformation someone scooped him up, like
a common . . . well, like a ball of hairs, like a
. . . ball of hair the cat coughs up . . . And
locked him in a suitcase. A suitcase like
yours, Deezo.

So . . . Deezo, my friend. There is no such
thing as no "ball of hairs." Only Castro's
Beard, just another Cuban exile, in search
of freedom.

As for Marinette, the mambo you consulted,
you must remember her? She was my girl, you
know, till Fnu Lnu showed up. That's how
the rumors started. From Haiti she was, a
real hot little devil. I know, I know, she
claims to be Italian. From San Stephano. But
after the, ah, murder she revised her
pedigree. Why a man would do anything for
a taste of her. She
(*A strange music begins.*)
wanders through the woods alone
because she doesn't want to share her
food; she boasts how many she has
eaten.

Human flesh is frothy, and trembles
when you poke it with a fork.
She and I hang our skins in a closet
or roll them up in jars at night;
Then we blast through the roof

and sit on the branches of trees
and sing our songs. I forget the words,
but I have them at home.

Do you know now, Deezo, who I am?
I am the letter Y.
I am the question Y.
I am the answer Y.
I am the force that drives the winds;
   that gallops through the night,
   backasswards, on a blind cayuse;
   that can suck the soul out of
   your body through the keyhole
   in the front door.

I am Baron Samedi; I am Petro-e-Rouge,
et Ti-Jean Pied Sec; I am Prince Zandor
who hops about on one foot.
(*In his demon voice.*)
   Deezo is a bad man.
   Deezo is a dead man.
   He left his hand
   on the street.
   He left his feet
   on the moon.
   Go ask Fnu Lnu
   What to do.
(*He recovers.*)
   Fnu Lnu, you'll find at this address. That's
   where he works. In the Pathology
   Department. Now, beat it.

   You know every time I look at Tony Pizzo's
   collection—there's one photograph of her
   in it—I think of her. Marinette . . .
   She broke a lot of hearts, but she was worth
   it.

(Pause. A lovely cameo of the young MARINETTE. *Smiling fetchingly.)*
She was smiling, a white dress she wore.
Waving to the crowd from the Anti-Suffrage
float in the Panama Canal Celebration, back
in . . . was it 1912? Everytime, I think of
that picture I have to sit down, Deezo.

(We see the three ZOBOPS. *All sing a strange song.)*

ZOBOPS   Radegonde Baron Samedi
Guardian of the cemetery you
who have the power
of going into purgatory
give my enemies
something to do
so they may
leave me alone.

Scene [black nightshade 🏴]: *We're at the morgue. Two guys in lab coats
are talking with* DEEZO. *For a time we hear only him—their replies are inaudible until indicated in the test. They obviously think he's there to identify a
body, which he isn't.*

DEEZO   No, no, no. I'm not looking for a corpse.
The guy is alive, or at least that's what
I'm told. He works here. Must be Chinese
by his name. Or maybe from Persia,
someplace different. Someplace where the air
is fresh, cool, and subject to improbabilities.
He knew things. Fnu Lnu was his name.

FIRST MORGUE PERSON   Fnu Lnu is not a name.

DEEZO   You see I have a complex metaphysical
problem to unsort. A series of nested
paradoxes actually. My own believability is
at stake.

SECOND MORGUE PERSON   At present we have only one client . . . at
    present . . . in residence, ah, on the premises.
    You can take a look at him. Dead for a day
    or two.

DEEZO   Let me see. C'mon. Let me see.

(*They roll out the slab.*)

SECOND MORGUE PERSON   We found a suitcase.

FIRST MORGUE PERSON   It was all he owned.

SECOND MORGUE PERSON   Someone named Beano claimed it.

FIRST MORGUE PERSON   The luggage was delivered to the Italian
    Club.

SECOND MORGUE PERSON   Over in Ybor City. Up on the third floor.

FIRST MORGUE PERSON   It's spooky as hell up there.

SECOND MORGUE PERSON   What with all the renovation and
    redecoration.

FIRST MORGUE PERSON   I had better warn you. The body's been
    mutilated.

DEEZO   It's him.
    (DEEZO *takes a look at the card attached to the dead man's foot.*
    Wonder of wonders!)
    It's Fnu Lnu.

(*The two* MORGUE PEOPLE *exchange the classic glance of incredulity
and roll their eyes. Pause.*)

FIRST MORGUE PERSON   "Fnu Lnu" is not a name. It is a rubric.

DEEZO   What do you mean? It's him. It must be.
    Why, it says so on this tag. What could be
    clearer? Come on, come on. I want to see who
    he is.

(*Pause.*)

SECOND MORGUE PERSON   "Fnu" means first name unknown.

FIRST MORGUE PERSON   "Lnu" is short for last name unknown.
(*The two* MORGUE *workers undrape the dead man.*)
His heart's been . . . surgically removed.

SECOND MORGUE PERSON   (*To* FIRST)
Say, he bears an astonishing resemblance . . .
(*He turns to* DEEZO, *horrified.*)

FIRST MORGUE PERSON   (*To* SECOND)
Known on the street as "Deezo."

SECOND MORGUE PERSON   Jesus, Hank, it's him.
(*He turns also. The two exchange glances once more, for our* DEEZO *is gone. Pause. The* SECOND (*littlest*) ZOBOP *slowly comes downstage, and sings.*)

SECOND ZOBOP   The yard of my house
is very particular.
It rains and is soaked
Like the other ones.
Squat little girl,
Squat again:
If you do not squat
You cannot dance.

(*She picks up* DEEZO'S *mike and speaks as* CASTRO'S BEARD.)

CASTRO'S BEARD   Rumor has it the Sicilians hired a thug,
one Deezo, to murder Charlie Wall. But this
person had problems getting close enough to
get the job done. Charlie was a tough old
piece of work, his bodyguard was reliable,
and he kept a loaded .44 by his night table.
So, this punk seduces Charlie's girl, her
name was Marinette. But when she learned
she'd been used she got mad, she got more

than mad. She turned into a demon.
Marinette *bwa chech*—Marinette "of the dry
arms." They tell terrible things about her
back in Port-au-Prince.

(*Pause.*)

So the truth is, Deezo's been dead for forty-
two years.

(*She whistles.*)

But, don't worry too much. He'll be back
before too long. Don't worry. Beano's gonna
pray over his bones, the bones of Fnu Lnu.
That's who he was. Truly. "Fnu"—first name
unknown. "Lnu"—last name unknown. In the
argot of pathologists. It's a name for the dead
man no one knows, no one can identify, like
Mister Jesus Anybody. No one but the flim-
flam man. And Marinette. And me. It's a
dead certainty. The flim-flam man would
like to keep it quiet, but it won't work. If
they ask who said so, you can tell them it was
me: Castro's Beard. There are forks in time,
and one of them is the letter "Y." But things
like this just go on forever.

(*Pause.*

She sings one last song.)

SECOND ZOBOP   He is flying high over Tampa.
He is the President of Cuba,
and he remembers our Tampa
as he flies to the North Pole.

His mind is made up.
He is very alone in his mind,
and the cargo of his passion
to right the world's wrong.

He is tired of the embargo
as he flies to the North Pole.

He is tired of being tired
and his beard is tired also.

The CIA tried to cut his beard.
Americans are very weird.
They would have cut his beard
like Delilah did to Samson.

He is flying high over Tampa.
He is the President of Cuba
and he remembers our Tampa
as he flies to the North Pole.

(*Pause. She lowers the mike and speaks softly.*)

My boss was headed too far North for me; the
black hole of the ideological North Pole. Maybe
he should have listened more to José Marti,
and me. What the wind would tell him, blowing
through me, the Y of me and my whiskers. So
long.

(*Tips her Zobop hat and goes out.*)

End of play.

Girl Gone

In the mid-nineties I came to realize
how many wonderful new theaters
were operating all over the downtown New York scene. I happened to
catch Horvath's *Don Juan Comes Home
from the War* at CSC and loved it. This
was a coproduction with Annie-B Par-
sons and Paul Lazar's Big Dance Company, and we began to talk. After a
preliminary workshop with the company—of *Three Americanisms*, incidentally—I decided to write a play for
their fine company of actor/dancers,
to be presented at The Flea, home of
The Bat theater, an outfit founded by
Jim Simpson, Kyle Chepulis, Jan Harding, Eduardo Machado, and me.

I had never written for a dance-
theater company, and asked Annie-B
for some suggestions. Write a lot of

PERFORMANCE NOTE

The appearance of an asterisk within a speech indicates that the next speech begins to overlap at that point. A double asterisk indicates that the next subsequent speech begins to overlap at that point.

stage directions, she said. The imaginary dances of *Girl Gone* are a result. We played
to packed houses at The Flea, and later at The Kitchen, in Manhattan.

If a lion could speak we could not
understand him.
—WITTGENSTEIN, PHILOSOPHICAL
INVESTIGATIONS

No one can dig up a hole.
—AMERICAN PROVERB

PERSONS OF THE PLAY

DINAH and
FORREST, parents to
BUGGINS, a student at Saint Lulu's; and
   her classmates:
LISSA,
LISA,
ELYSSA (the EVIL SISTERS), and
HOPE,
FAY, and
DORRIT; and
   their TEACHERS:
MADAME TOMBA and
THE HEADMISTRESS;
CHAZ BOIARDO GUTHRIE, a young admirer of the Evil Sisters;
ELYSSA'S MOTHER;
other GIRLS from Saint Lulu's School; and
THE VADEMECUM OF VADOO (or VADU), also known as ANOOPH SAID or
   The Black Tulip.

The play is set at various places in Tenebrae and Palomino Counties and
takes place during the present, whatever that is.

Scene [𝒴 Tooth of Asmodeus]: *At one of the* GIRLS' *parents' summer place. The last party of summer, just before Labor Day. People are having a good time. Our trio:* LISSA, LISA, *and* ELYSSA *are dressed in black, with black veils. They avoid the others.*

FORREST   Look at them. The evil sisters.

DINAH   But they're not related, Forrest.

FORREST   Evil is a bond stronger than flesh.

DINAH   Nothing is stronger than flesh.

FORREST   Oh yes there is. Oh yes there is, Dinah.
Sibilance constitutes a kind of sibness.
Our girl there, thanks be to the Great
Blue Heron, is normal. A normal kid
who knows how to play in a normal way.

DINAH   Knock on wood. Forrest, watch your rug.
Your rug's on wrong.

FORREST   Damn this heat. Gets to me. Like I was
hard rubber sapped. Sapped on the sly.
Rubber stung, drowsy.

DINAH   And thick, Forrest. Thick.

      ᔐ

    (*Elsewhere three* GIRLS *sing a strange song.*)

    Go away, if you dare;

> Go and catch the toothpaste;
> Run and hide with lady slipper.
>
> No one knows Show from Scare;
> Who holds round the waist
> Cannot undo his own zipper.
>
> Zip, zip, zip; zap, zep, zup.
> (*Repeat × 7.*)

ᝌ

(*Elsewhere, three other* GIRLS: *one juggles bright red balls; one is obsessively doing cartwheels; one is dancing the Hokey Locus.*

Pause.

The one juggling stops, does cartwheels; the one doing cartwheels stops, starts to dance the Hokey Locus; the one doing the Hokey Locus stops, begins to juggle the bright red balls. and so on.

They freeze. Pause. Slightly off-key, they sing.)

> O, Pity is not enough.
> The executioner awaits
> his rope of gold.
>
> O, Pity is not enough.
> (*Repeat × 3.*)

ᝌ

HOPE — I've never been this far out in the country. Is this still Palomino County?

BUGGINS — Not quite. Blue Streak's the nearest town, just over the viaduct, and past the diner on Route Six, the Lazy Eyeball.

HOPE   Still I like it, though the air smells . . .
                smells, like, not quite right.

BUGGINS   Not quite right?

HOPE   As if, it were . . . you know, like . . .

BUGGINS   ?

HOPE   Too something. Too full of prismatical gases.
                Strange.

BUGGINS   ?

HOPE   Siccative, I mean. Like the Siberian
                wallflower.
         (*The other laughs.*)

BUGGINS   Supergobosnoptious, sirrah!
                (*They trade high fives, laugh.*)

A bunch of the GIRLS *bend over to look at something on the ground. Something fascinating.*

One gingerly touches it with the toe of her shoe. One pokes at it with a crooked stick.

They talk it over with each other, randomly.)

         What is it?

         Is it alive?
         Look at the tail!
         Look at the gimlet eyes!
         Is it the rat's tail?
         Ha, ha, ha!

(*Repeat × 3.*)

         ✍

DINAH   Why do they just stand there, glowering?

FORREST   My word, all three are gazing at Hope with a look of unbelievable malice.

DINAH   Off the pie chart. That's because Hope's a darling, doesn't complain about violin lessons, and can do cube roots in her head.

FORREST   Almost as though they were preparing to do the, the McCarthy on her Horn Lightning Arrestors.

(*Their daughter,* BUGGINS, *comes skipping up.*)

BUGGINS   Is the Parsnip River located in Mandrake or Tenebrae County?

FORREST   Rather difficult to say, Buggins. Why?

BUGGINS   Lindsay Shot and I made a bet, and now I've lost four dollars if it goes through both.

DINAH   It goes through both, precious.

BUGGINS   Drat. Double drat.

FORREST   Go and dandle Hope, Buggins. She'll cheer you up.

BUGGINS   Drat.

(*She goes over to sweet, buttery smooth* HOPE, *in her pillar of light.*

CHAZ BOIARDO GUTHRIE *enters, the sole boy present, and an old amour of* LISSA. *He wears black and does the Random Cakewalk, coolest of the cool.*)

LISA   Behold the reptile.

ELYSSA   The reptile draweth nigh.

(LISSA *silences both with a wave of her arm. Pause.*

They lift her veil, revealing her radiant whiteness.

She smiles.)

LISA   The reptile* contains his others, his eithers
            and epithets. His neithers and no ones.

ELYSSA   The reptile's* mighty roar cracks open the fabric
            of the heavens.

LISA   The reptile answers to the name "Reptile" because
            although his given name is Chaz Boiardo Guthrie,
            his true name* is Reptile.

BOTH   Reptile of the tribe of Reptile.

ELYSSA   Reptile* of the clan of Reptile.
        (*High fives all around.*

As CHAZ *proceeds, a shadow falls behind him like a cape. His trape-*
zoidal obscuration.

The GIRLS *freeze, one by one as they are touched by his shadow's lady*
slipper. It is a cape.

Then, one by one, and after each is touched, they go out simply and
slowly.)

CHAZ BOIARDO GUTHRIE
        (*Very quietly*)

                Lissa, Lissa. Listen, Lissa.
                You have to listen to me. Really, I mean
                it. Because as I see it, the wonder is why.
                The wonder is all around us and is, is
                deep within us and deep within our boxes.

                The wonder wonders at our whys and wherefores.
                The wonder has no patience for these questions,
                paltry matters of dubiousness. For not only
                is the wonder a thing that fills all boxes,
                and all possible hats; the wonder is itself
                a box that cannot be filled. Ever, not ever.

                Lissa. Lissa. Listen, Lissa.

You have to listen to me, because I love you
more than anything you know. I love you
more than my family, my nation or my god.
Compared with you my god is a boring botch.
An idol. A graven image. A fraud. Yes.

If I knew how to do it, I would frame the
ultimate question on your behalf, Lissa,
Because you are the answer to that question.
Just as you are what the true wonder most
wonders at, deep within wonder's hidden
place, here, in Domely Park and there, in
Refrigerator Heights and at Saint Lulu's
School over in Flatland off the Inkjet River
where you study topology, River and Rivets,
the meaning of Exodus 3:16, transubstantiation,
Ferrier-Golfe Systems, Vitruvian scrolls,
tree and branch platters, and wickiups under
the careful guidance of Madame Tomba and
the Headmistress whose name . . .

(*But he is stopped by a raspberry from* LISA, *the last of the* GIRLS *to
retire.*

Only now do we see, along with CHAZ, *that* HOPE *has spontaneously
combusted.*

All that remains of her is a small pile of char, and her smoking shoes.)
         . . . where did they all go? Where did they go?
         Where?
(*Pause.*)
         Lissa? Lisa? Elyssa?
(*Bends over to pick up one smoldering shoe.*)
         And what's become of Hope?

Scene [⟅⟆ The Cloven Hoof]: *The* GIRLS *in the schoolyard at Saint
Lulu's, smoking and thinking. All are intensely busy with the arcane game of
introspection and the inner life. A* TEACHER *appears.*

TEACHER   Three minutes, girls.
 (*Pause.*)

FAY   I saw what you did to Hope.* I think it's pretty
  mean. Not to mention, low.

LISA   Don't look at me.* (*Pointing to* ELYSSA.) She did it.

ELYSSA   She did it. Don't give me the stink-eye.
 (*They glare at each other.*

 Pause.

 All turn to LISSA *who smiles wickedly; yes, she did it.*)

DORRIT   I think that boy Chaz is cute.
 (*All look at her.*)
  . . . in a plebian sort of way.

LISA   I think he was actually a rabbit.

ELYSSA   I think he was actually a skunk.
 (*Pause. Thoughtful consideration.*)

LISSA   I think he has crossed over into the land
  beyond television.

BUGGINS   That's impossible!

LISA   ?

FAY   But, but there is no place beyond television.
 (*All stare at clueless* FAY.)

ELYSSA   Skunk.

LISA   Rabbit.

ELYSSA   Skrunk.

LISA   Skrabbit.

ELYSSA   Skrunkabbit.

LISA

(*Horribly hissed and trilled.*)
    Skrrrbt.

LISSA   When I go away, I shall go terribly
    terribly far away. So far I shall
    leave no trace. So far . . . no trace at all.

BUGGINS   No one goes that far. That far
    is beyond heaven and . . . and . . .

LISSA   The Bad Place? Ha.

BUGGINS   No. A place beyond that.

FAY   There is no place beyond that.

LISSA   Yes there is.
(*All become solemn and thoughtful.*

Pause.

It becomes completely still for a time.

TEACHER *reappears.*)

TEACHER   You have one minute, girls.
(*She goes. The* GIRLS *move about ever so slightly, as they regroup.*

Finish their cigarettes, and look up at the sky. In unison, they stub the butts.)

In precisely one minute, blackout.

Scene [〰 The Rat's Tail]: *The* GIRLS *in class. They listen as* MADAME TOMBA *lectures to them on certain important topics from history.*

MADAME TOMBA   The lesson for today is a momentous one, for
    it concerns the whys and wherefores of Going
    Away. And the question of how these questions
    implicate us . . . us all . . .
(*But the* GIRLS *are shuffling their feet. Pause. They cease their shuffling under the hard gaze of authority.*)

... and how these questions pertain to the
larger issue of templetation, disobedience,
and crime.

Not to mention the fate of those brave, but
foolish, women who have gone, so to speak,
away. Gone away, and in so doing, gone
astray.
(*Leaning forward.*)
Are we clear on that? Are we very clear?
I want to make very sure we are very clear
as to the nature of the topic under discussion.
Good.

DORRIT   I thought we were supposed to prepare
on Pandora.

MADAME TOMBA   Yes, Dorrit, that is correct.

FAY   And Hypatia of Alexandria and the Empress
Irene.

MADAME TOMBA   That is correct, Fay. You have evidently
gotten it right. Now before we tackle
the topic of these personalities directly,
perhaps we ought to . . . to address the question
of a general theory of going away. Now,
has anyone prepared . . . ah . . . upon the
subject of these three women in the context
of leave taking?
(*Pause. Everyone looks at* ELYSSA.)

ELYSSA

(*Calmly and quietly.*)
The way I look at it: The medieval mind
survives among men and women of today
as a kind of going away. And it does so
on a much grander scale than most of us
imagine.

For it is possible to live in a period
without being of it. What I mean is that
the modern mind is exceptional even in
the modern age.

For instance, to how many of us are the
conceptions on which the life of our time
is based—evidence, sequence, causality—
strange and unintelligible. These
people, those who have gone away, without
actually leaving, live fragmentary and,
as it were, piecemeal existences, in a
directly connected world. A world of cause
and connection.

MADAME TOMBA   Come to the point, Elyssa.

ELYSSA   In her time, Hypatia proved the riddle
of living connectedly in an unconnected,
and therefore fragmentary, world.

(*Pause.*)

MADAME TOMBA   Elyssa, that will be all. Fay, what do you
have to report on the topic?

FAY   Hypatia, daughter of the Alexandrian philosopher
and mathematician Theon, was also herself a
brilliant philosopher and mathematician. She
was so extraordinarily beautiful she was forced
to give her public lectures concealed behind
a screen.

(*General tittering.*)

MADAME TOMBA   Please, Fay, go on.

FAY

(*Deeply embarrassed*)
I cannot go on.

MADAME TOMBA   What about you, Lissa?

LISSA   Neither can I.

MADAME TOMBA   You cannot? Why not?
(*A cold and disobedient pause.*)

LISSA   Just that I cannot. I have to get out of here.
(*She gets up and goes. An awkward pause.*)

MADAME TOMBA   Lisa. Could you finish for her?

LISA   I prepared Pandora and Irene, not
Hypatia.

BUGGINS   I prepared Hypatia and Pandora and
Irene.

MADAME TOMBA   Very good, Buggins, but I did not ask you,
did I?

BUGGINS   No . . . not exactly . . . but* I thought . . .

MADAME TOMBA   Saint Absentia Profunda, the guardian of this
institution, does not care a fig what you
think, Buggins. What our saint desires
of you is perfect obedience, is that clear?

BUGGINS   Yes, ma'am.

MADAME TOMBA   Now Dorrit, perhaps you could cover Irene.

DORRIT   I know Irene deserved to be a saint even
though she deposed and caused to be
blinded her own son, Constantine the Sixth,
grandson of Constantine "Whose Name Is Shit."
In this way—

MADAME TOMBA   Very good, Dorrit. Lisa, could you perhaps
explain why Irene deserves to be a saint
even in despite of her ferocious crimes.

LISA   By her act she put an end to the Iconoclast
Controversy,

MADAME TOMBA   And?

LISA   By her act she restored to power those who
would venerate and preserve the icons.

MADAME TOMBA   And?

LISA   The worship of icons is part of the rat's
tail that must be preserved.

MADAME TOMBA   I beg your pardon.
   (*Pause. A chilly one.*)

LISA   You have my pardon.

MADAME TOMBA   And what is this "rat's tail" you are referring
to?

ELYSSA   The worship of icons is part of the problem
I mentioned before. It is a medieval thing,
and in so far as the practice continues
right down to this day, it constitutes
an exemplary instance of the sham of living
a life within an age without being part
of that age.

LISA   It constitutes one of the seven bad things.
   (*Pause.*)

MADAME TOMBA   One of the seven bad things. Specifically,
what seven bad things are you referring to?

LISA   The seven bad things are the left over contents
of Pandora's box.

MADAME TOMBA   In what sense are they left over?

LISA   After all the known and knowable evils
have escaped, have flapped and flittered
away.

MADAME TOMBA   These yet remain?

LISA   That is the hypothesis, Celia.
(*An icy pause.*)

MADAME TOMBA   Whose hypothesis?

ELYSSA and LISA   Ours.

MADAME TOMBA   I see. And who is "we"?

ELYSSA and LISA   Us.
(*Things are scary.*)

BUGGINS   Hey!* What's going on?

FAY   I know what happened to Hypatia. The mob
of Peter the Reader accosted her, alone,
on the street. They tore off her garments,
and cut away her flesh with oyster shells.
She was torn limb from limb, and what was
left was burned, burned like trash. All
this was at the order of Cyril, who was
the archbishop of Alexandria. But he was
really smart, and no one ever punished
him. That was Hypatia's going away.

MADAME TOMBA   And so, Fay, what is it to go away?

ELYSSA
(*Quietly.*)
To go away is to experience, or cause to suffer,
a break in the continuum.

MADAME TOMBA   What continuum are you referring to?
(*Pause. Turning violently to* LISA.)
You are never, ever to refer to me as "Celia"
again.

LISA
(*Under her breath.*)
Okay. Okay.

FAY   I don't understand why everyone is,
       like, talking this way. Talking this
       way is, like, really confusing.

MADAME TOMBA
       (*Coming apart*)
       Then perhaps someone should plug
       your ears, Fay. Does someone possess
       a piece of chewing gum or sticky wax
       to seal Fay's ears?

DORRIT   I have gum, but, like, it'd be hard to
          waste a stick on a silly drip like Fay.
          (*General tittering.*

       Pause.

       The GIRLS *notice* MADAME TOMBA *is quietly weeping.*)

MADAME TOMBA   I don't know. I don't know.
          (*Pause.*)
          I just don't recognize myself. And I just
          feel so god damn . . . well . . . superfluous.
          I just can't seem to get around the fact.
       (*But* LISSA *returns in a strange slither.*

       She is wearing slippers of a brilliant scarlet.*)

       Bump to black.

Scene [🖋 Desiccated Chicken Wing]: *Outside, on another recess. All
the* GIRLS, *smoking and thinking.*

BUGGINS   I don't get it. I was prepared to cover
           Irene. I was prepared to cover Hypatia.
           I was prepared to cover Pandora. No one
           asks me a blessed thing. I don't get it.
       (*Pause.*)

LISA   No one asked you, Buggins, because you
        are always prepared to cover anyone and
        anything and that is a fact known to
        everyone. And besides you are a very
        stupid person.
        (LISA *does something with her fingers.*

All the rest follow her motions with evident interest.

She makes a spider.

She makes another bug.

The spider goes on the hunt.

The other bug, being stupid, suspects nothing

The spider considers how best to achieve her aim.

The spider thinks deeply, deeply and mathematically.

The stupid bug continues happily being a stupid bug, unaware of danger.

LISSA *begins doing the spider web with her feet.*

All the other GIRLS *attempt to follow* LISSA's *lead.*

LISSA's *hands do the spider and the stupid bug; but her feet do the web.*

All the others follow the best they can, some better than others.

The poor bug is trapped. Only now horribly aware of its fate: it will be eaten.)

LISSA   It will be eaten.

ALL   It will be torn limb from limb, and eaten.

ELYSSA   The horrible stupid bug will be torn apart
         and eaten.
         (*All stop in astonishment.*

She sings, alone and tremulously.)

All the bugs now are eaten
because the ground is gray;
and I say: hey, okay!
and I say: hey, it is okay.
Because night is not a toilet.
Joy is not a day.
Dance, dance or be beaten
by wild oats or by what's wheaten.

ALL   Oaf, loaf; oaf, loaf; for up in the
sky . . .

ELYSSA   . . . is the Desiccated Chicken Wing,
whose song has gone away,
whose song has gone away.

ALL   Oaf, loaf; oaf, loaf; oaf, loaf.

ELYSSA   Oh, yes; oh, yes. The chicken's
wing is terribly, terribly dried
because the silly thing has died.

ELYSSA   . . . and gone away to the strangest place,
swank Vadoo, where,
you know who,
Chaz Boiardo Guthrie,
slithers . . .

ALL   . . . slither, slither,*
slither . . .

ELYSSA and LISSA   slithers, and does the Happy Snake.

(*Pause.*

All do the Happy Snake.

All do a strange thing with only

fingers and toes; nobody knows

what it is.

Everything stops. Silence.)

ELYSSA   Nothing new shall be put into the box
today.

(MADAME TOMBA *appears, glaring with hatred.*)

MADAME TOMBA   Time is out, young ladies. Time has gone away.

End of scene.

Scene [⊓⊤⊓ The Fork Malicious]: *Within the office of* THE HEAD-
MISTRESS. *Extraordinary shadows, as if from beyond the grave. She is dress-
ing down* MADAME TOMBA.)

THE HEADMISTRESS   Your actions have jeopardized everything we
work for.

MADAME TOMBA   I know it. I know it. I don't know what
to do. The girls apparently have concocted
a dream world they call "Vadu," from whence
they draw terrific energy. I know it is a
delusion . . . but the energy they now command
is terrible, terrible. I fear they had
something to do with poor Hope's disappearance.

THE HEADMISTRESS   And Lisa is the ringleader?

MADAME TOMBA   Not at all clear. She appears to be, but
they are all so intensely evilish it is
difficult on these occasions even to tell
them apart.

THE HEADMISTRESS   Somewhere, Celia, we've lost the idea of
childhood.

MADAME TOMBA   That is precisely what I keep thinking, only.
Perhaps their malice has some root cause
in a dynamic or something-elseian process we
cannot imagine. Drastically something-elseian.

THE HEADMISTRESS That would amount to a violation of the Hardy-
Weinberg principle; not to mention a rare and
rabbity instance of the ablative heresy of the
defrocked one . . . you know who . . .

Do we dare pronounce the name?

No. Those who have gone away are the
Gone Away in every respect. No part of
them lingers in the box, as it were.

MADAME TOMBA That reminds me. Odd you should mention it.
And they talk of Pandora . . . in a way I found
(or find, rather) distinctly disturbing.
They talk about what was left.

THE HEADMISTRESS How do you mean?

MADAME TOMBA They talk about what was left in Pandora's
box, after the more commonplace evils had made
their escape.

THE HEADMISTRESS How did you learn this, Celia?

MADAME TOMBA Because I have overheard them when they did
not suspect I was present.

THE HEADMISTRESS Like Absentia Profunda?

MADAME TOMBA Precisely. And their other models are Hypatia,
who was murdered for her crimes by a Christian
mob under instructions, allegedly, of Saint
Cyril. Saint Cyril the Hypotenuse.

THE HEADMISTRESS Yes, yes. That's a popular conjecture. Among
certain sets.

MADAME TOMBA And the ninth-century Byzantine empress,
Irene, who deposed her own son Constantine,
and caused him to be made to go away, to
go away in order to thwart the Iconoclasts.

THE HEADMISTRESS   A fine role model for a contemporary young
woman, if you ask me. Though church history
has never been exactly my long suit.
Nothing wrong with that, in my view.

MADAME TOMBA   No, no. They have twisted the meaning of these
events. They have twisted them horribly so
that their interpretation suggests a social
and philosophical meaning that is . . . that is . . .
monstrous and bold. One, furthermore, that
defies all convention.

THE HEADMISTRESS   I've heard enough.

MADAME TOMBA   Ask Dorrit. Ask Fay. Ask Buggins,
for Pete's sake.

THE HEADMISTRESS   Please. Stop whining.

MADAME TOMBA   Ask anyone. This is criminal. You must
punish them. You must.

THE HEADMISTRESS   But Celia, they have not committed a crime.

MADAME TOMBA   What about Hope?

THE HEADMISTRESS   What about her? What is the insinuation?

MADAME TOMBA   She was murdered.

THE HEADMISTRESS   A disappearance. Case closed.
   (*Pause.*)
What nonsense.

MADAME TOMBA   She burnt up. In a flash. All that
remained of her were her poor, little
shoes, smoking. And the horrible reek.

THE HEADMISTRESS   Spontaneous combustion is not a suitable
hypothesis in this connection, Celia.

MADAME TOMBA   You are killing the messenger then?

THE HEADMISTRESS   And what precisely is the message?
Call it whatever you like. You may go.

(MADAME TOMBA *buries her face in her hands, in total despair.*)

First, I would like to speak. Successively,
with the three girls you mentioned. In
proper succession. Then we will decide on
a course of action.

Oh, Celia, dear. Please stop crying.
I was only trying to scare you, to drive
a little sense into that pretty head.
My foolish little puppy.

Bridge scene: A cameo of the GIRLS *singing a song. They are arranged artistically, and dressed beautifully.*

GIRLS   To create an absence
is to give birth to air
scare
scare
scare me by that touch
so I become too much
with many, many voices
for pain to touch.

(*All go, but* LISSA.)

THE HEADMISTRESS   Hello, Lissa.

LISSA   Hello, Madam Headmistress.

THE HEADMISTRESS   How are you, Lissa.

LISSA   Doing very nicely, thank you.

THE HEADMISTRESS   So tell me.

LISSA   Tell you what?

THE HEADMISTRESS   You know.

LISSA   Not really.

THE HEADMISTRESS   Do you want to be made to go
            away?

LISSA   Hadn't really thought much about it.

THE HEADMISTRESS   Well you'd better.

LISSA   Why?

THE HEADMISTRESS   Because unless we can straighten a few things
            out* that's where you'll be going, young lady. . . .

LISSA   ". . . that's where you'll be going, young lady. . . ."
            (*Pause.*

            THE HEADMISTRESS *cracks her knuckles;*
            LISSA *cracks her knuckles also;*
            smiles at THE HEADMISTRESS.)

THE HEADMISTRESS   You know we had a name for girls like you.
            When I first arrived here.

            "Wiseacre." It was "wiseacre."

LISSA   We have a name for you: The Fork Malicious.
            (*Pause.*)
            The Fork Malicious.

THE HEADMISTRESS   Do you have any idea how . . . just how really rude,
            tactless, and inconsiderate you are?

LISSA   Tomba has fallen. Who, or what, is next?

THE HEADMISTRESS   Do you want to be made to go away?

LISSA   I don't give a rat's tail, really. If you
            want to know the truth.

THE HEADMISTRESS   Who is Vadoo?
            (*Wild laughter from* LISSA.)

LISSA   It's next door, and you don't even see it.

(*Blackout. When lights come back up,* LISA *is seated where* LISSA *had been.*

On the floor, the latter's smoking shoes.)

THE HEADMISTRESS   Lisa, what are you three up to?

LISA   Up to up to up to . . . going going gone.

THE HEADMISTRESS   We have removed Madame Tomba. She shall be
               replaced by the much sterner Madame Circumflex,
               an expert in certain ancient languages.
               Certain obscure Asiatic languages.

LISA   You are The Fork Malicious and there is nothing
               obscurer. Because—

THE HEADMISTRESS   What are you saying? What is this nonsense?

ELYSSA and LISSA

    (*Off.*)   Because whatever you do
               will be done over again
               deep in the darkness at Vadu.
               And be made right, quite
               right, deep in the darkness
               at Vadoo.

THE HEADMISTRESS   Don't mock me. The authority I represent
               and embody is a legitimate authority.

LISA   You have no idea what danger you're in.

THE HEADMISTRESS   Is that a threat?

LISA   The truth is the truth, whether or not it
               contains a threat.

    (*Pause.*)

THE HEADMISTRESS   Hope is a good girl. We are worried about
               her. What have you done with her?

Chaz is a good boy. His family says he now
suffers from an unaccountable delirium. They
say he is subject to rapid fits of torsion
and gyration. Have you done this?

How have you done this?
(*Pause.*)

LISA   Headmistress, madam, have you ever thought
it might be a good thing if you went away
for a while. Yes, if you went away for
quite a spell.

THE HEADMISTRESS   Lisa, you are being perverse.

LISA   I am not being perverse; I am being
the reverse of perverse; only my terseness
is such that it turn off
the top of your tap.
Drip, drip, drip, oh . . .
(*Pause.*

All three EVIL SISTERS *are heard.*

They sing.)

Far away in the state of Palomino
lies, like a carpet, velvet Vadoo.
All things that grin, they grin there
as they turn their back on you,
Headmistress, and folks like you.
You will never ever understand Vadu.

LISA   You will never go away
without returning where you stand,
forever ampersand. In between,
in between, faith and doubt,

ALL   In between faith and doubt,
In between life and death,

In between in and out.
In between,
In between,
In between.

Vadoo you will never understand.

THE HEADMISTRESS   You too, like all the fallen, can be made to
go, and go far away.

LISA   I do not care. I do not care a rat's tail.

THE HEADMISTRESS   Now tell me. Who or what is Vadu?
(*Wild laughter from* LISA.

She Goes Away, poof! Pause.

ELYSSA *appears where* LISA *had been.*

ELYSSA *mouths the words spoken offstage by her Evil Sisters.*)

LISSA and LISA   Vadoo is very near, but you are so blockheaded,
so counterfactually impaired you shall never,
never, never, never perceive it.

THE HEADMISTRESS   What do you mean by "it"?

ALL THREE   Skip it.

THE HEADMISTRESS   What do you mean by "skip it"?

ELYSSA   Skip that too.

THE HEADMISTRESS   Are you talking about a call, a summons?
An erasure? An extinction?

ELYSSA   Vadoo. A much better place. Perhaps a little chilly,
though, on those frosty winter nights. Velvety Vadoo.

THE HEADMISTRESS   I am worried, Elyssa, about you.

ELYSSA   No, my dear Headmistress, I am worried about
you. The Q in you.

(*Slowly* THE HEADMISTRESS *stands,*
like a hill of solid granite.

She speaks slowly, quietly,
as if to a foreigner, or to
a person of limited intelligence.)

THE HEADMISTRESS   Do you know, Elyssa, what suffering and agony
there are in the world? Do you know what
awful shocks and blows there are in life?
Can you imagine the lies and deceit which
undergird all human vainglory and wishful
thinking? Can you picture the torments of
those less fortunate than you? Don't you
have anything to say to those wise and mighty
ones who have prepared a place of presence
for you, here at this school in the golden
lady slipper of Palomino County?

ELYSSA   No. Not really.

THE HEADMISTRESS   And why, pray tell, why not?

ELYSSA   Because all that does not matter once we
have gone away.

THE HEADMISTRESS   And where do you imagine going away from?

ELYSSA   From the here and now.
(*Pause.*)
In our time, we are proving the riddle of
living connectedly in an unconnected and
therefore fragmentary world.

THE HEADMISTRESS   The here and now would not be flattered to
hear you talk like this. So?

ELYSSA   One more powerful proposition in the argument
we possess.
(*Pause.* THE HEADMISTRESS *is beaten.*)

THE HEADMISTRESS   I see.

>   (*She gets up. Takes off her shoes.*
>
>   *She slowly shambles off.*
>
>   *A cameo of the* EVIL SISTERS.
>
>   *They sing.*)

EVIL SISTERS   Girl gone. Girl gone, but not for long
                 for I'll see you all at the foot
                 of the Ding-Dong tree, at the foot
                 of the Ding-Dong tree.

                 And I'm going to go away
                 over the hedge,
                 over the hedge,
                 over the hedge.

                 Girl gone, girl gone,
                 at the foot of the Ding-Dong tree.

>   (*All the girls appear. They do the Spinal Fusion. They do the Full Cleveland. They do the Random Cakewalk.*)

Reprise of "Girl Gone."

End of scene.

Scene [The Black Tulip]: *Night, in an open field under a starry sky. The bugs make beautiful noises. Far off, we hear a man yelling and occasionally the detonation of crockery against a wall. This is* ELYSSA's *father. Two* GIRLS, *one kneeling, one standing. These are* ELYSSA *and* BUGGINS, *who is staying over for the night. They are staring straight out into the future and what they see is not good.*

BUGGINS   This is the time of The Black Tulip.
>   (*Corrects herself.*)
>   This is *a* time of The Black Tulip.
>   (*Pause.*)
>   That's better. That is much better.

ELYSSA   That is much, much better, Buggins.
That is so much better it is
like butter. The butter of much better.
You will get the hang of it, Buggins.

When I discover my nature and
unriddle the world I shall crow.
I shall promptly crow.

BUGGINS   When I discover the world and
unriddle my nature I shall . . .
(She goes blank.)

ELYSSA   Ha. She goes blank. Ha.
I shall develop the ability to open
boxes.
(Surprised at herself.)
What's so neat about that?

BUGGINS   Boxes belong to the night. Like all things
nocturnal, they are nightmare stuff.
Boxes belong to the Evil One, whom
being an Evil Sister I worship.
Is that right?

(ELYSSA and BUGGINS sing a song.)

ELYSSA   Bone of my foot, bone of my hand, bone of my top-knot.
Bone-batta, bone-batta, bone-batta, bop.

(Both repeat × 3.)

ELYSSA   Oh, the Devil's in the shoelace;
Devil's in the straw, -aw, -aw;
The Devil's in the whole shebang,

BOTH
(alternating lines)
and everything you* possess;
and all you think you* own;

and everything you* touch;
all you clasp to your* breast;
every truth you think you* guess;
like falling for, and being
(*Spoken*) smitten.

BUGGINS It's all worthless,
a broken crutch;

(*An evilish pause.*)

ELYSSA lies at the bottom of a pail,
like a drowned kitten.

(*Silence, except for the distant
holeration which gradually subsides.*)

BUGGINS I am Pandora.

ELYSSA ?

BUGGINS Boxes of all kinds await me.

ELYSSA Okay.

BUGGINS Boxes believe in being opened
by me.

ELYSSA By you.

BUGGINS Boxes believe deeply in me.

ELYSSA Some boxes.

BUGGINS All of them.

ELYSSA How do you know this?

BUGGINS My agents tell me. My agents are everywhere.

ELYSSA Oh, I see.

BUGGINS Fool, you see nothing.

ELYSSA Who can see nothing? Ha, nothing is nothing.

Nothing is simply a something that is not there.

ELYSSA   That's the point.

BUGGINS   Look, is that your mother coming?

ELYSSA   Listen to the night noises.

BUGGINS   You could hear them better if your father would put a lid on it.

ELYSSA   He got pretty mad when they called up from school.
              "There's been a very serious accident and we are very concerned." Blah blah.

BUGGINS   Blah blah.

BOTH   Blah blah.

ELYSSA   What's that?
              (*Something indeed odd happens.*

              Night noises cease and ELYSSA

              freezes in her moment of surprise.

              We see someone in the shadows.)

BUGGINS   Who is it? Who is there? Jesus.

THE VADEMECUM OF VADOO   Pardon me.

BUGGINS   Who are you? What are you* doing here?

THE VADEMECUM OF VADU   I will now tell you the whole truth; I will conceal nothing at all from you. I have already said to you, "A king's secret it is prudent to keep, but the works of God are to be made known with due honor." I can now tell you that when you, Lissa, Elyssa, and Lisa prayed, it was I who presented and

read the record of your prayer before the
Glory of the Lord; and I did the same thing
when you used to bury the dead.

(*Pause.*)

You don't remember, but you used to bury
the dead. It was your custom to bury
those who had died whom you found by the
roadside. I was sent to put you to the
test. At the same time, however, God
commissioned me to heal you and your
friends who have suffered spontaneous
combustion in this world and have therefore
been transported thereby to the world of Vadoo.

(*Pause.*)

BUGGINS   ——

THE VADEMECUM OF VADOO   For my name is Anooph Said
and I am also
known as The Black Tulip, but in either
case it does not matter. Because you must
come with me. You must come with me
quickly, before we are discovered.

BUGGINS   What are you TALKING ABOUT? Vadu
is a place we made up. Lissa and Elyssa
and Lisa, and me.

THE VADEMECUM OF VADU   No, no, no. Vadoo is really. Just past the
town of Blue Streak, over the viaduct and
past the diner on Route Six, The Lazy Eyeball.
Vadoo extends past the Old and Lost Rivers
of Tenebrae, only . . . only some people do
not see the place. Some people are foolish
and think if they do not see a place it is
not there.

(BUGGINS *turns out to us as she wonders at this.*)

No, no, no. Some people do not honor the
first things. Such as the first woman
to run a marathon in less than two and a
half hours (Grete Waitz) in New York in
1979; the first fire department to be
composed entirely of women (Asheville, New
York) in 1943; the first planetarium,
or Orrerry, imported to this country in
1732; the first orphanage established in
New York in 1654; the first child born
of European parents in the New World,
called Snorro, in the year 1007. Because
people who do not honor the first things
are incapable of perceiving what is there
when it is here. And so, I tell you:

(*Pause.*)

I am called The Black Tulip and I am the
Vademecum of Vadu. I am the Vademecum
of Vadoo, and I am one of the seven angels
who enter and serve before the Glory of the
Lord.

(*Stunned, she bows before him.*)

Come. Come with me. You must come
quickly.

BUGGINS   But I can't just run off.

THE VADEMECUM OF VADU   In Vadoo, you will find your friends. Here
there is nothing for you. Desperate codependent
parents, the tedium of unacknowledged class war,
clueless sister who steals your lipstick,

(*This is news to* BUGGINS.)

the idiocy of higher education looming. In
Vadu we have a very fine time.

(*Vadoovian music and dancing girls appear.*

Screens, incense, and a strange but seductive music.

They do the Jamaican Car Service.

They do the Flea Circus.

They do the Hokey Locus.)

We have a fine old time indeed. Not like here.

BUGGINS   I don't know what to say.

THE VADEMECUM OF VADU   And there is work to be done. Like your friends,
both Madame Tomba, the one who has fallen, and
the Headmistress have been dematerialized and
electronically reassembled beyond the mystic borders
of Vadoo. We need your help. We need it desperately.
And then there is the question of Hope.

BUGGINS   Hope? What do you mean?

THE VADEMECUM OF VADU   Your wicked nemesis, Hope Fleming,
who you thought
had been destroyed; yes, Hope, Hope has been
reborn in Vadoo; bright, beaming, wide-eyed Hope,
with all her solar radiance and golden beneficence.

BUGGINS   Hope! Why that tricky little bitch.

THE VADEMECUM OF VADU   You must help us destroy her.

BUGGINS   Okay. I'm going.
(*She gets up and follows his flickering phantom as it drifts off into the
woods like smoke.*

Night noises resume and ELYSSA *snaps out of it. Surprised, she
looks about.*

Pause.)

ELYSSA   Buggins, Buggins.
(*But she is gone. We see a figure approach. It is* ELYSSA'S MOTHER.)

ELYSSA   Rats.

MOTHER   So what are you two doing out here, It's
getting chilly. Where's Buggins?

ELYSSA   She was just here. Maybe she went back
to the house. Is Cosby on yet?

MOTHER   Have you finished your homework?

ELYSSA   No, Mom. Guess I'm still a little upset.

MOTHER   By the nasty incident at school?
    (*She nods.*)
        Well I wouldn't worry about it.
    (*Pause.*)
        There's bound to be a rational explanation
for it. But if I were you, I wouldn't
talk about it to too many people. At
least until you have your session
with the school's crisis counselors.

ELYSSA   Wasn't planning on it.
    (*Pause.*)

MOTHER   What a beautiful night. I'm going back.
Don't stay out here too late, Elyssa. Ten
thirty's your bed time.

ELYSSA   Yes, ma'am.
    (ELYSSA'S MOTHER *gets up to go. Looks down.*)

MOTHER   What's this?
    (*It is* THE VADEMECUM's *bizarre hat.*)

ELYSSA   Beats me.

MOTHER   Did you make this?

ELYSSA   Mother, please.

MOTHER   Well, do you want this?
    (*Looking it over.*)
        Looks like it's from the school play.

ELYSSA   Mother, please, I have no idea. People from
as far as the Parable River over in Fairfax,
from nearly as far as East Continuum come here
to wander in solitude, enjoying Mother Nature.
Probably some tinkers left it. Who knows?

MOTHER   Tinkers in Tenebrae County?

ELYSSA   I don't know.
    (*A strange pause.*)

MOTHER   Guess I'll go scare up Buggins.

ELYSSA   Probably back at the house. Spoiled little brat.

MOTHER   Hate the sin, not the sinner.

ELYSSA   The sinner is the sin.

MOTHER   That's a rather dark thought, young lady.

ELYSSA   She went back to the house. Probabilistically.

MOTHER   Well, okay. We'll see. Don't stay out here
too long, you hear?

ELYSSA   Okay, okay.

MOTHER   Kids these days.
    (*She strolls back towards the house.*

    Pause.

    ELYSSA *is alone. She sings.*)

ELYSSA   I am a random pant leg
looking for the moon. Alas,
alas, there is no room
in my mighty pant leg
for the bride and groom.
Pant leg, bird's egg, Scanderbeg.
Three legs, four legs, eight legs,
nine.

(*We hear a twig snap.*)

      Hey, who's there? Buggins, is that you?

(*A dark and ominous* SHAPE *appears.* ELYSSA *is scared.*)

SHAPE   What are you? I know you are
              a god, but what god I do not
              know.

ELYSSA   ——

SHAPE   Tell me what god and what you
              are doing in these woods. Great
              Pan is dead. Great Pan is dead,
              whose woods these are.
              Tell me,

ELYSSA   I . . . I . . .

(*She stutters. Tries to become very small.*

The shape alters its position.

Pause.)

SHAPE   Who I am, you ask and since you ask
              I will tell you.

ELYSSA   Please go away, and leave me alone.

SHAPE   Listen to me before you judge. Please
              listen. That's all I ask.
      (*Pause.*)

ELYSSA   Okay. But . . .

SHAPE   I am the President of the United States
              and I am very, very ill.
      (*Suspicious,* ELYSSA *whirls about, the* SHAPE's *upper torso and face are hidden in the shadows.*)

ELYSSA   Hey, what is this?

SHAPE   I said: I am the President of the United States
and I am very, very ill.

(*He sings:*)

> Willow,
> willow,
> willow,
> brillo, Oh . . .

(*Clears his throat.*

She sees it's CHAZ.)

ELYSSA   Chaz.

CHAZ BOIARDO GUTHRIE   How'd you guess?

ELYSSA   Real difficult.

CHAZ BOIARDO GUTHRIE   Hey, where's Buggins?

ELYSSA   Don't know. We were sitting here talking
and she, like, wasn't here anymore. I
think I dozed off and she wandered off
back to the house. You shouldn't scare
people like that.

CHAZ BOIARDO GUTHRIE   I just wanted to wish you two a good night.

ELYSSA   ——

CHAZ BOIARDO GUTHRIE   I heard something strange happened at
your school today.

ELYSSA   I don't really want to talk about it, Chaz.
(*Pause.*)
Please, go. Just go.
(*Pause.*)

CHAZ BOIARDO GUTHRIE   Okay, I'll go.
(*Pause. Takes his time.*)
I'm almost gone. Going, going . . .

> Good night, Lisa.* Good night.

ELYSSA   Go, please.

(Poof. He's gone. Tentatively, she looks around to make sure.

When she is certain he has removed himself from her presence she returns to where she was, looking out at us in the peace of the night.

She looks at the moon.)

> I know my evil sisters will be with me
> always and forever. Along with the
> contents of Pandora box: The Tooth of
> Asmodeus, The Cloven Hoof, The Rat's Tail,
> The Desiccated Chicken Wing, The Fork
> Malicious, and the Black Tulip.

(Her EVIL SISTERS appear as she speaks, each with a Japanese lantern.

They kneel on either side and all sing a final song.

Behind them the others reappear and do the Mighty Turtle.

They do the Hungry Vacuum Cleaner. The GIRLS sing.)

EVIL SISTERS   Oh, my beloved executioner,
> I have for you the golden rope.
> I have found it,
> I have found it,
> coiled neatly . . .

ELYSSA   . . . coiled neatly beneath the Ding-Dong
> tree,

LISSA   where that dope,

ALL

> *(Speaking)*
> Chaz Boiardo Guthrie

ELYSSA   had hidden it, near the,
> the sacred bar of soap.

LISSA   So: hear my song . . .

ALL   All this could happen,
only in Vadoo,
only in Vadu.

(*Softly, as lights dim.*)

All this could happen;
all this could happen;
all this could happen.

Blackout.

End of play.

Hypatia; or, The Divine Algebra

I wrote *Hypatia* in 1998 as a libretto
for a composer friend who passed on
the project, as he found the text too
abstruse. His reluctance surprised me,
since I find the narrative rather trans-
parent, although not a little unlikely.
Hypatia is as close to being a pure
Steinian language experiment as one
can get (there are several quotes from
her work in the piece). Whatever the
difficulties of the text, I remain fond
of it, as I was trying to explore the
middle ground between text that is
pure scenario and obvious dialogue.
Bob McGrath, of the Ridge Theater,
was in Boston working with American
Repertory Theater students and asked
for an unproduced play to work on
with his young actors there. I sent
my *Land of Cockaigne*, an early realistic
play and *Hypatia*. To my great surprise
he settled on the latter. Robert
Brustein was kind enough to fly me
up to talk to Bob and the students
about it.

Still, I was not prepared for the terrific little production I saw in Cambridge. About a year later Ridge remounted the entire production at Soho Rep. in New York. *Hypatia* proved controversial, to say the least, but was pretty much sold out for the whole run.

Hypatia, d. 415, Alexandrian Neoplatonic philosopher and mathematician, a woman renowned for her learning, eloquence and beauty. Little is known of her writings. Her fame is largely owing to her barbarous murder by a band of monks, said to have been encouraged by the Archbishop, St Cyril of Alexandria (a personal and political enemy of the prefect of Egypt, Orestes, who was believed to be Hypatia's lover.
—COLUMBIA ENCYCLOPEDIA, FIFTH EDITION, 1993

The Greek philosopher Hypatia was a Neoplatonist. She was famous for her public talks on philosophy and astronomy, and her forthright attitude to sex. Although concerned with higher knowledge she was also a political animal and had a keen sense of practical virtue. She was killed by a Christian mob, and has remained since a martyr to the cause of philosophy.
—ROUTLEDGE ENCYCLOPEDIA OF PHILOSOPHY, 1995

There is no entry on Hypatia in the Catholic Encyclopedia, *either old or new editions.*

The author is indebted to Maria Dzielska's *Hypatia of Alexandria*, Harvard, 1995.

PERSONS OF THE LIBRETTO

HYPATIA, Alexandrian mathematician and philosopher and daughter to
THEON, an Alexandrian mathematician and philosopher;
ORESTES, Roman consul and HYPATIA's lover;
PETER THE READER, a monk and tool of
CYRIL, Archbishop of Alexandria;
SYNESIUS, HYPATIA's friend and the anonymous author of the *Suda,* a
chronicle of the times;
MUSA, or ALGORISMUS, the Arab mathematician Muhammad ibn al-
Khwarizmi, the inventor of Algebra;
CONSTANTINE VII PORPHYROGENITUS, emperor of the Eastern Roman Empire;
his EMPRESS and their
CHILD; and a
CHORUS and a
YOUNG GIRL.

In Alexandria, Virginia, ca. A.D. *1915.*

A machine is revealed
Cries of why why why why why.
No one has heard her
cry

An infinite decimal an

o

ᔕ

The machine opens revealing a

unscroll the fabric of people speaking
Theon the philosopher and mathematician
Orestes the lover Synesius the friend and
praying mantis it is

isn't it isn't isn't isn't isn't isn't it?

praxis

Suda also who is recorded it all
in his
what unscrolls Alexandria
Alexandria Alexandria

Suda his chronicle and lexicon a book

prankish a

why why why mordant using the auxiliary

note above the why the principle

note why why why and

Cyril now a sainted figure

guess how he Peter the Reader and

directed to one side, oblique,
torn limb from limb

415 A.D.

෨

Famous for her beauty, Hypatia,
Philosopher and mathematician and daughter
to Theon;
torn limb from limb on the street.
Alexander's city.
At the command of upon of the of the hand
Cyril Archbishop of Alexandria,
by a mob at the hand of Peter the Reader.
Had to lecture behind
Hidden behind a screen
Had to

Because of her because of her beauty
maddened

had to

෨

Theon: Daughter don't don't go out don't

Hypatia: Why why why why why why why

Don't

Why

Just don't why

the power of Zero

sifr (cipher)

∽

The machine opens opens a

to scroll a zero

sifr (cipher), zephirum, zephiro.

Showing an absence by a presence

keep a place open

try it try try try try to try it try.

∽

And as the machine

And as the scroll

The heart's sick room

Sic passim, sic passim sic passim sic passim.

thus everywhere (used to indicate
that a term or idea is to be found
throughout the text)

the scroll. By beauty maddened.

Behind a screen.

By my beauty, maddened.

∽

I am unable not to not not la
Lacewing, marry me to my
inner circumstance.
Orestes will meet me by that
lace curtain

in Alexandria and the and the

wet wind wind wettens

my astrolabe my musical instrumenta

my tools my toys. If zero

were a person Zero is not

a person Zero were a

god, if

Hypatia, zero is the place of absence

why why why?

The absent place in position

constant and unchanging,

why why why why why why why why why why

Absence that guards do not go out
that guards the the integrity
la la lakh la

The integrity of the truth la la la

la la la la la la la labyrinthine

la la la

lace and other

Lachesis, my golden

Lachesis, my golden
toy of tool done. I see
off.

～

Do you intend to depress me? Certainly

not I asked for a translation. Zero
do not compromise my father here.
Zero, he is a solemn ass.

Do you intend to depress me? Certainly
not I asked for a translation. Zero
do not compromise my daughter here.
Zero, she is as absent as

⁊

They go do public works.

Others follow as fire up the flue and

no one trips.

No one tries.

Hides, hits a self, hits a nonself, fears a
grudge

Public health. Ptolemaic system. Psychosis.

She teaches on the staircase.
She teaches by the fountain.
She carries a screen to hide behind

it algorist.

Emanations. Triangles. Perfect circles.

yes yes yes

Snap all their fingers

Toes rise up

They stand there, dumb. They.

Deciding whether to be just there or
just there and dumb and

those there, maddened.

Sunya, the name for the mark of emptiness
Someone sings a little song:

Mother was a wild wildy cat
Upon the antique fire escape;
she folds up all (alas!) all
the silverware in no-one's hat,
tit for tat;
A wildy wild of great courage
Behind the moon la la la,
Behind the moon la la.

Apeiron, the boundless.

The machine opens up up and further and

out and out, what pours. What pours and pours.

౭

Meet me by the, by the, the archaic obelisk. The

Orestes; call me that

Hypatia, play no second fiddle

Second second second.
Second story
Second thought
Second base and second
fiddle.

Secant. Measure the arc.

Take me take me take.

No one sees the silvery couple slink off.

Half-moon way. Half-moon way, impolitic.

No one sees the
No one sees me

No one no one oh oh power of Rome
protect the, she, me,

Who. Who. Who who maddens. Who man. Woman.

༄

Mob rules topside;
no law can control
this part of the machine.

People are listening, *diabole,* for the

witchified underside. Zero
does does not
does does not
does does not

mean an
empty, *diabole*

. equals point of reference

The scroll unrolls with all the all the
city

Pagan philosopher Theon mathematician
girl
daughter, psst,
people hate
people hate
you you you with a

a

whywhywhywhywhywhywhy

number larger than any fixed

with a value, as a

burying beetle in an old sock, psst, psst

༄

Hypatia, the brilliant girl

girl can cannot her contest

∽

Reveal the temple of Serapis (Serapeum)
old gods about to die
old gods baboon face of Thoth
driven drive them drive them out

Baboon exhibit to the mob, you
Baboon, subject of ridicule,
Baboon, subject to ridicule as the

Christian mob

Destroy the temple of Serapis destroy destroy

Serapeum

∽

Hypatia, in her orbs and night,
pondering the divine algebra,
pondering the emanations,
pondering the continuum.

Recites some Euclid, some Diophantus.

Her secretary bird the only only thing thing
that

scratching, moves.

Scratching the golden dome, reversed, the floor.
Plotinus, she says.
Porphyry and Proclus.
Iamblichus, she

sunya, she

sifr, she

The Equation

They do a two-step

Philosophy, she

the, she

Most ineffable of the ineffable

෴

Bush clover
Bush bean
Bush baby
Bush honeysuckle

Hear the wind, broken stones, defiles the

The, thee

the temple of Serapis, still.

I do nothing.

Hypatia and Orestes wrapped in white linen

They people people watch
who

who watches hellfire hold.

Tophet, Gahenna.

Make the Hyperbola:

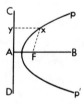

On the golf-flecked floor,

My little touraco color of a candle flame

I want to want want to want to too

A bird out of time, to leave no trace but

.

Temporalities.

Tempt.

Tempt tempt tempt.

I am nothing. I do nothing,
Alexandria
hot as a cinder
Hots. I, Hypatia,
bird out of time.

She slips out.

⌇

Alexandria.
500 monks leave their "hermetic lairs."
Peter the Reader, why,
I cannot can I cannot read.

We see like a silk ribbon the mob of Timothy
We also are like that too, so
See and watch the Mob of Cyril, watch and

on toes rise rise rise up.

They rise on their toes.

la la lakh la

⌇

Orestes orders the execution and torture of of
of Hierax;
Ammonius throws a stone at Orestes torture of of
execution and torture all of it class warfare.

Points at the "pagan Woman"

She is too swift and ingenious in her arguments.

On discourse, not violence, in politics.

Civitas.

O

sifr, (cipher), a point of reference:

On a day on a day in March
10th consulship of Honorius
6th consulship of Theodosius II

She, returns home, the angle at which
an object can be seen, she

on a street whose name is not known

is seen as a function of the distance
separating object and viewer if we if we
know the object's distance and angle
we can cannot measure the

the object:

I am pulled out quietly of my chariot on a
street whose name is not known dragged to
quietest Caesarion former temple of the
emperor cult my clothes torn off

Still. Quiet now.

and killed with broken pottery (*ostrakois aneilon*)
torn apart and the pieces collected in
a quietest collection to a place taken take the
parts to a place called Kinaron and burned.
Civitas. Civility.

૭

Everything

stops. A tangent

Zero, my mother was a who was wildly
wildcat crept crept crept
down from the tent stitch mountains
of the deep interior regions of the

sun

Solar

Your mountain was no such thing

No such thing. Mother you mean.

Mother I said. Mountain
you said ha you said ha but mother

perhaps perhaps perhaps you

intended.

Zero, why Zero?

Your remembrance has, all in all or

all in part or

or or or

in part taken flight.

Zero? Why Zero?

Tangent

stops. Everything starts.

Someone sings a little song:

Famous for her beauty, me.
Daughter and mathematician.
Had to lecture behind a screen.
Had to.
Because by beauty maddened

the people the

the people the

sifr (cipher),

the power of Zero

why why why why why why why

Absence that guards do not

go out

that guards the the integrity
la la lakh la
la la lakh la

☙

Pray to the lag screw.
Pray to the deep lagoon.
Pray to the lady bug.

la la lakh la
la la lakh la

(*Spoken.*) lakh, any very large number.

Alexandria.
Theon: Was no such thing.
Hypatia: Mother you mean.

Her remembrance is no quill or flight
feather.
They flight feather is the flight feather,
father.

Some god has touched you, Hypatia.

Sine, cosine, tangent. And cotangent.
Yield the description of an angle by the by the
numbers that characterize it.

This is done they do it quietly and with string.

⌐

Calculated, these numbers these numbers
are set in tables O I can see you I can see you
why are you talking to your toy
why are you talking to your toy
why are you talking to your toy
and not listening to your father?

I am talking to my toy
as if I were not here.

Orestes, help me help
Orestes, help me help
help help help help me help
I am helpless help me
help me help help, Orestes,
O.

⌐

Damascus.

Friendship, they say is either Dover's Powder a
powder to kill pain or mere double-talk.

Three centuries unscroll before us a man
of whom nothing is known dream a

Man business ruined a failure like me like
you a flop. Dreams he will find his fortune
beyond the Caliphate beyond the walls of Damascus:

After much harsh hardship
after being beaten many many
goes to the house in the dream it is

broken marble in moonlight the Serapeum.
Baboons.

Two thugs once more beat him.
Don't don't don't.

Big Thug. Why believe in dreams.
I pay no attention.
I dreamed of a house in Damascus,
and describes the house the house is my
house realizes the man

He goes home digs up the treasure in the garden.
Secant to a tangent. 1001 Tales

Call him Musa or

Algorismus.

৩

I
appear one day in Baghdad disguised as a
boy;
I carry with me an emblem, the sunya. the
name of the mark for emptiness.

I am that I am, I carry nothing with me.

She moves slow slow slow like an old woman
played by a boy, as portrayed in mosaic miniatures
on a retable retral to an old Persian arcade. At
rest.
Restive. At
rest. Restless. A
sifr, (cipher).

৩

A view of eight-century Damascus a
view of Antioch Medina Mecca
Baghdad

Mendicant

Mendicant
Mendicant riddle with a tine cup.

Screens. Minarets. Incense.

How large is large? How small is small?

Musa bumps into a strange boy, as though
a portrayal of himself. She is

Suddenly not behind a screen.

On the left-hand page each eye stares at a
right eye;
on the right-hand page each right hand
grips a left hand with fraternal warmth.

Infinitely deep,
scale upon scale,
a fractal.

Making a pair, infinitely
deep.

Musa, Hypatia

depict the notion of pairing;

If the sets each have an infinite
quantity:

Darkness. Wind and sand. Double heart beats.

Who

As a boy,
he takes her
from behind

he takes her
as a boy
from behind

from behind
he takes her
as a boy.

༄

Muezzin. Dawn, multiplicity. Music of the oud.

Golden number.

Stories: Of Moses (Musa) and the little wicker
boat;
the works of Theon, *Aigyptos* and *Alexandreus,*
Euclid's *Elements,* designed for students;
his *Data* and the *Optics*; commentaries
on the *Almagest* (Syntaxsis mathematica);
and on Ptolemy's *Handy Tables: The Great
Commentary,* in five books—and *The Little
Commentary,* in one.

Musa: Theon did not work alone.

(I shall live to be a to be to be a bird of gold;
even if no one know my name)

Hypatia, why aren't you
why aren't you
why aren't you
why aren't you
why why why why why why why

༄

Mine: The elucidation of Diophantus, and
of Apollonius's *The Conic Sections*

The astrolabe

Behind the not behind the
Behind the not behind the
behind the

Musa. Socrates Scholasticus. Suda. Damascius's
Life of Isidor.

Theon's daughter, a certain

shush him with a kiss.

༄

At Byzantium, Sulayman is stopped

beneath the wall:

717 A.D.

therefore Sulayman leaves the Caliphate to his pious
and upright cousin, Umar.

Umar, my master

The pious exchange vows of fealty with the pious.
Kharijis, Shi'is; his own family, the Marwanids
and the House of Umayyah

Umar
ends the condemnation of 'Ali from the pulpits,
ends the Berber tribute in children
reduces the tribute of some Christian groups

in their "Hermetic lairs"?

encourages general conversion to Islam.

Encourages mathematics and the
fine arts.

mud wasp
mudskipper
mud puppy
mudra.

The machine opens to reveal Hypatia
opening to reveal to Musa

her toy

i, an imaginary number.

Someone sings a little song:

O my friend O my friend,
all the minims and maxims
of night and of day
of laughter and fright,
all the turns and steps
of pleasure and spite
are as are as are as

nothing

are as nothing

to the square root of minus one.

∽

Alihu alihu alihu
Akbar
Alihu alihu alihu
Akbar

∽

They go hide in a linen shirt
They go hide in a cotton sock
They go hide and go and hide there,

i
So what I gather you are not saying is
So what I gather you are not saying
because in my dream your dream
I
returned home from Alexandria
and found, as in the dream prophetic,
you disguised as a boy

as a boy which is what I am not saying
as a boy which is what you are not saying

both salaam; are
enlightened

She holds out something, a

Sunya, name for the mark of emptiness

જી

I escaped, riding on an unbroken piece of shard.
The one who beat who beat you and
it was a man who could not read.
It was a dream prophetic

led you to me, and here we are in an i

an equation involving the imaginary

amicable numbers.
Ensoph. Zero.

I wanted to live forever as a golden bird,
a toy, a bird made of gold.

Here

She hands something to him.
Down he looks down at it.
o.

જી

Stay stay stay with. Zero.
Me.

Do you intend to depress me? Certainly
not I asked for a translation. Zero
do not compromise my lover here.
Zero, he is a silly ass.

I will go to Baghdad. I will copy down
*The Book of Addition and Subtraction by
Indian Methods*;
The name of Muhammad ibn Musa al-
Khwarizmi will live forever

Caliph al-Mansur will recognize the
greatness of our mathematics;

and of the Divine Algebra that is to come.
He repeats: And of the Divine Algebra
that is to come.

~

Synesius, wrong. The *Suda,* wrong.
Because I could not be stayed
Because 500 monks who left their
"hermetic lairs" and Peter the Reader
and Cyril himself

All my friends and all my enemies.

yes yes yes

Snap all they fingers.

toes rise up

They stand there, dumb. They

Hypatia, and the
Algorist

~

Disappearance.

All gone.

A broken pillar on the stage. A baboon head

A man: This is what the impudent Hypatia

wrote to me:

"For, as the Evangelist [John 1:10] said: No one
has ever seen God." So how, they say, can you
say that God was crucified? They say, too, "How
can someone who has not been seen have been
fixed to a cross? How could he have died and
been buried?"

This is the theology of the Nestorian Heresy,
and this is what Hypatia wrote to me.
I am the Archbishop of Alexandria, Cyril,
and it is impossible

It is impossible unimaginable that she
showing a presence by an absence
showing a presence by an absence
showing a presence by an absence

Hypatia appears out of a machine.
Out of a machine out of the baboon's head.
Incommensurability

The powers of destiny, the planetary spheres
are sustained by the lord of the immutable laws
of the universe, the god of eternal time—the Aion.

Cyril. And she has eluded me.
She has eluded me.
Has eluded me.
Eluded me, Me

Cyril, a great great defender of the

Commensurable. Falls
Flat.

⊱

My silken slippers of Divine
Hypatia are of velvet darkest indigo and

my father Theon wrote a book

*On Signs and the Examination of Birds
and the Croaking of Ravens*

are of indigo velvet the color of

the

Aion, the

$i = \sqrt{-1}$

ᘓ

Sphere, singleton a
set with one element with one

piece of lead pipe and a kettle
incommensurable.

As a toy.

Piece an accordion of hot air mimics
Achilles;
as a toy.

A brass wind instrument filled with **i**
imaginary
imaginary
superheated steam

As a toy

Bicyclic overshot imaginary and incommensurable
inblasted gusts of hot air and superheated
gusts of hot air and superheated gases

in oblique and circular cylinder as an

object for a child to play with a thing
a thing of little importance

an aeropile an accordion of hot air
mimics
Achilles;

ை

Her indigo slippers slippers slide over black sand

Hypatia, the brilliant girl
girl can cannot contest

300 years in a straight line 300 years.

Recites some Euclid, some Diophantus

her secretary bird the only only thing thing
that

moves, scratching

sifr (cipher)

Someone sings a song:

Within the boundaries
of the cipher is an island
of still standing water still
deep deep of darkest indigo

0, I am in you still, deep
0, I am in you still, deep
0, I am in you
deep in darkest indigo

Oh, to be made of burnished metal
behind the moon la la la
behind the moon la la

la la lakh la
la la lakh la

ை

Scene Forty-Three
People do not pour out people

Scene Forty-Four
A porism of aporias

Scene Forty-Five
Fisheye
Fish fry
Fish gig
Fish moon
Moon eye gig fry

Scene Forty-Six
Girl like a boy

Scene Forty-Seven
Incommensurability. In.

Scene Forty-Eight
Sore feet. Sore

that provides formulas and rules for the
calculation of irregular or changing
quantities, such as rate of change,
speed or motion, and semiregular
or irregular volumes and areas such
as curves and cones.

Scene Forty-Nine
Curves and cones.

Scene Fifty
The last mouse you eat must be the white
one.

Scene Fifty-One
Byzantium. Near 300 years. In black, hooded.

Scene Fifty-Two
Drag a bag full of brass and lead pipe.
Ilks.

Scene Fifty-Three
Perhaps illicit. One day.

Act Two
When a machine is not a machine a

Act Four
Skip Act Three

Act Five
Synesius to Hypatia: "I am in such evil
fortune that I need a hydroscope."
She makes him one.

Scene Two
(withered vine leaves, martyr's kisses)

Scene Three
Ipazia

Scene Four
Unable to identify the

Scene Five
Lost slipper . . .

Scene Six
. . . that Serapis would pass into formless darkness
and be transformed, and that fabulous and unseemly
gloom hold sway over the fairest things on earth.

Scene Seven
Countable. If one be willing to count forever.
One is willing.

Scene Eight
Aleph, the Transfinite,

Scene Nine
Automaton, a brass wind instrument that

Scene Ten
By Hyp
decline for many
had been few
physical screws
church crippled
reason as the
coming of C
lazy: what was
Hypatia,

Scene Eleven
Odd zeros and

Scene Twelve
Persons can be numbers also

Scene Thirteen
Skip this one

Scene Fourteen
Sack of Alexandria by the Arabs. 640 A.D.

Scene Fifteen
Or he starts counterclockwise from the fifth
mouse from the white mouse.

Scene Sixteen
Hidden behind a screen.
Had to.

Scene Seventeen
Scene Eighteen

Scene Eighteen
Scene Seventeen

Scene Nineteen
Scroll

sifr, she

The Equation

They do a Two-step

. A point of reference

Scene Whatever
Takes her from behind. Like a
boy. The algorist.

Scene
An infinite decimal

an o

Scene
How to not

Scene
This is called a play but

Scene
This is not called a

Scene
Toy

Scene
Hypatia. I was touched by an unknown
god.

Scene
Touched by a

Scene
All proofs and porisms.

Scene
Mbisimo. The ability of the poison oracle
to see far off things.
Someone sings a song:

Words words words. Words
are mere noises, noises
the croaking of crows, crows
are mere noises, noises

behind the moon la la la
behind the moon la la

Words spoken behind a screen
behind the moon la la.

ᔕ

Sunlight and sea. The Golden Horn.

Hypatia a self. Hidden
behind a self. The

Continuum.

ᔕ

The self as an argument
against self. A

compression coil
spiral coil
flat spiral
torsional
leaf
extension coil

Toy, sprocket wheel humming,
shoots dips stabilizes rises dips again
shoots dips dips rises rises stalls
stabilizes dips rises rises stalls and

drops
like a
stone,

behind the Emperor's wall wall of the Magnaura.
Basilissa, the Empress. Basilissa.
She, alone in an
Area abundant with tektiles
a strewn
area

∾

Tiny machine, clicks and whirrs at her
feet.
Go get the person who

They

drag the boy in,

Am a machine, partly made of metallica
and sheet rumble

sloe eye meets sloe eye

∾

Talk in swing dash, O stands for the
position in place

Empress, her child on a jumping stick
(Andronicus Ducas Angelus).
Make us a milkweed follicle to warble;
folksongs (from Eire? Baikal? Bhutan?)
from gross error,
usually transient in the readout of the
electronic device that is that is caused by
imprecise synchronism, as in

analog to digital
conversion, free. From gross error, free.

???

We are of Rom; know not this matter

The boy, Hypatia, partly made of brass silver gold
615 years old

okay okay

Techne over Theoria. Will you Byzantines

Real lions that roar birds that twitter
chairs that rise silently as if to the
Real lions that roar birds that twitter

On a column of hot air
superheated steam in
intertwined pipes or in
vents and ducts hydraulic.

yes yes yes

snap all they fingers

toes rise up

stand there, dumb. They

cheer cheer chirrup cheer

la la lakh la
la la lakh la

༄

A machine within a machine opens.

The Magnaura automata.

Hypatia. The mind cannot portray
the

workings of the mind
except as a machine;

I am a machine

. Point of reference.

The Emperor bows, showing a presence by
an absence

basileus autocrator basileus autocrator

∽

She instructs them to draw a
circle;

she instructs them to draw a
square

Kenosis. Kiss of death! Kinesis. Kiss of life!

Imagine a line with an origin at the point, zero,
running through the integers 1, 2, and so on all the
way to infinity. Call this the

Real number line

No matter how close two numbers be
others are always
between them.

fractions, integers, rational and irrational

The continuum is
established.

Hypatia. From al-Khwarizmi's *Kitab
al-jabr wa al-muga balah* (Treatise
on restoration or completion and of
reduction or balancing).

I learned this from this:
al-jabr, algebra.

ﻼ

But ideas, ideas, phooh! Give me solid brass

Automaton. Clangor and racket.
Automation. Clangor and tin pan alley.
Automata and wondrous tinnitus.

Imperials hold their ears and gape.

Titillation of automata
Tipcat world of brass and gold
and silver simulacra.

Plumage, modular, of an unreal nightjar
plundered iridescence for moire effect.
Automata of rare unscratchableness

Magnaura, a private party.

compression coil
spiral coil
flat coil
torsional
leaf
extension coil

and it, creaks and whirrs as it flies. FLIES.

ﻼ

No girl now Hypatia no boy either
on the continuum an irrational

Transfinite her slipper of deepest indigo.

ﻼ

Baboon head. An automaton in the form of the
ruined temple of Serapis.

A chorus:
It was of course that they expressed.
That they were never at all a pleasure
To themselves alone an advantage.
In which they were careful to be able
To thank them one at a time.
In every little while.

Little Emperor. Now I am not alone.
Hypatia: Speak too soon too too soon.

History is a big room with and without
a toy.

A place in position,
Sunya

ﻼ

Apeiron, the boundless

One day, goes, her stuff in the big ink-black sack
one foot flop foot after another foot flop foot an
infinite number of points between each each

footstep

toys and cheering in the closed garden closed
behind her

whirring
whirring

la la lakh la
la la lakh la

Wind. Stars. Sand and

Someone sings a song:

Perhaps I will live forever
Perhaps I am Perhaps I am
Already at the end of it all.

Perhaps I will raise to the power
of N, all those I love, all those
Already at the end of it all.

Perhaps Perhaps I am dead.
Perhaps I am only a broken toy.
A broken toy at the end of it all.

Perhaps a girl. Perhaps a boy.
Perhaps dead. To whom does it matter?
Perhaps I am only

I, Hypatia,
A bird out of time. Made of gold.
O to be made of burnished metal!

♒

Pray to the lag screw
Pray to the deep lagoon
Pray to the lady bug

la la lakh la
la la lakh la

She speaks: A

sifr (cipher).

She goes out.

♒

EPILOGUE: Alexandria, Virginia, 1915 A.D.

Two girls. By the river. Morning.
One with a bicycle. One with a

♒

Hello. Hiya.
What do you have there

Bicycle. Never seen a bicycle
I'm from far off

Oh. What's that wow that's really neat
A toy. Does nothing. Nothing useful.

Wow wow wow
Take it. It's yours.

I can count to a thousand I can . . .
Skip it. Can we talk about something
else

We'll trade. Even Steven. We'll trade
Bicycle. You call it a bicycle

I like you
I like you too. Take this. Take this
too

What is it wow what is it
A zero. Round straight line with a hole
in the middle

Wow wow wow.

Blackout.
End of the play.

The Sandalwood Box

Bob McGrath and Laurie Olinder's extraordinary theater group, The Ridge Theater, is a highly innovative visual company. As of this writing we are in preparatory stages for a full production, in Chicago, of *Jennie Richee; or, Eating Jalooka Fruit before It's Ripe*, a multimedia piece based on the life and art of outsider artist, Henry Darger. Among the preliminary pieces we collaborated on, to get to know each other, were *The Sandalwood Box* and *Hypatia*. *The Sandalwood Box* was commissioned by the MacCarter Theater in Princeton and duly presented there along with ten or so other short, short plays. But I liked the piece enough to want to see it fully produced. The opportunity came in 1996 when McGrath staged it as part of the Mac Wellman Festival that was the brainchild (not of me, surely!) of a bunch of adventurous downtown types, including the very talented Tim Farrell. The Ridge folk did a fine job with *The Sandalwood Box*, and that has led to our more extensive current collaboration.

The Sandalwood Box was originally commissioned and produced by the McCarter Theater, Princeton, New Jersey, Emily Mann, Artistic Director.

The Maiden caught me in the Wild
Where I was dancing merrily
She put me into her cabinet
And lockd me up with a golden key
—"The Crystal Cabinet," WILLIAM BLAKE

PERSONS OF THE PLAY

MARSHA GATES, a student and prop girl at Great Wind Repertory Theatre;
PROFESSOR CLAUDIA MITCHELL, Professor of Cataclysm at Great Wind University;
a BUS DRIVER; and
a chorus of VOICES, including DOCTOR GLADYS STONE, that sadistic monster "Osvaldo," and others from the House of the Unseen.

The play takes place in the rainforests of South Brooklyn.

Scene: We see MARSHA, *alone. Except for the table and the sandalwood box itself, all scenic devising is done vocally.*

MARSHA'S VOICE-OVER   My name is Marsha Gates. I lost my voice
                    on the 9th of November, 1993 as a result
                    of an act of the Unseen. If you think you
                    cannot be so stricken, dream on.

CHORUS   I took the IRT every other day for speech
                    therapy. In a remote part of Brooklyn.
                    Avenue X. Where my therapist, an angelic
                    person, resides. Her name is Gladys Stone.
                    Doctor Gladys Stone.

(*The good* DOCTOR *appears.* MARSHA *tries to speak.*)

. . ? (!) . .

(DOCTOR STONE *tries to speak.*)

. . ! (?) . .

(*Since neither can speak both give it up. Pause.*)

CHORUS   Dream on I did, but . . .
        (*The good* DOCTOR *disappears.*)

MARSHA'S VOICE-OVER   Parallel lines meet in Brooklyn. The East
                    and Westside IRT. This geometry is also
                    of the Unseen. It is inhuman design, and
                    therefore unnameable. Also the knowledge
                    of its mystery* is subject to error.

CHORUS   It is human to be so* stricken;

MARSHA GATES   I took the wrong train.
         (*We're on the wrong train.*)

MARSHA'S VOICE OVER   I took the wrong train and arrived at a
               strange place. A place I did not know.
               The air felt humid and tropical. The air
               felt not of the city I knew. A lush, golden
               vegetation soared up, up and all around
               the familiar landscape of the city, like
               a fantastic aviary. It *was* an fantastic
               aviary. A place full of exotic specimens.
      (*Pause.*)
               It occurred to me I might have lost my mind
               as well, although I did not think so
               because the idea gave me such strange
               pleasure, like the touch of a feather
               along the top of my hand. This place
               seemed a paradise. I laughed and fell
               asleep. I dreamed . . .

CHORUS   I am waiting at a bus stop, waiting
            to return to my home. Another person
            is standing there with me.
         (*We're at the bus stop by the Aviary.*)

PROFESSOR CLAUDIA MITCHELL   Hiya.

MARSHA GATES   Hello.

PROFESSOR CLAUDIA MITCHELL   I'm Professor Claudia Mitchell.

MARSHA GATES   I'm Marsha Gates, a part-time student.

PROFESSOR CLAUDIA MITCHELL   I'm an archeologist, of sorts.

MARSHA GATES   I'm a student at City College. No declared
            major. I also work part time in a theater.

Great Wind Repertory. The plays are all shit.
TV with dirty words.

PROFESSOR CLAUDIA MITCHELL I see.

MARSHA GATES I can't speak either.

PROFESSOR CLAUDIA MITCHELL So I understand.

MARSHA GATES It's very aggravating.

PROFESSOR CLAUDIA MITCHELL So it would seem.
(*Pause.*)
My specialty is human catastrophe.

MARSHA GATES That's very nice, but you're making
me nervous.

PROFESSOR CLAUDIA MITCHELL So it would seem.

MARSHA GATE Is this the Zoological Gardens? The beasts
seem to be making a considerable noise.
Perhaps the person who is supposed to . . .
feed them . . .

CHORUS . . . has been stricken,* like you, by an act
of the Unseen.

MARSHA GATES Like me.

PROFESSOR CLAUDIA MITCHELL I see. Perhaps so. Perhaps, however,
you mean an act of complete probabalistic
caprice. A fly in the Unseen's ointment.
An ontological whigmaleery. A whim of the die.

MARSHA GATES I work in the theater. Philosophy makes me
nervous.

PROFESSOR CLAUDIA MITCHELL I see. What theater?

MARSHA GATES I am a prop girl at Great Wind Rep. I told you.
(*The* PROFESSOR *throws back her head and laughs. Pause.*)

PROFESSOR CLAUDIA MITCHELL   An artist!
Then surely you must appreciate
the higher things in life. Knowledge. Ideas
pertaining to a theory of the world Id. The
power of the mind to crank out ideational
constructs beyond mere calculation and desire . . .
not to mention . . . mere mortality.

MARSHA GATES   This bus sure is taking a long time.

CHORUS   The bus arrives in a wild rotation
of dust, hot fumes, and the clangor
of the unmuffled internal combustion
engine.
(*All are deafened.*)
An instrument of noise close to the heart
of disaster.

BUS DRIVER   Ever seen a bus before? This is a bus.
Don't just stand there quaking. We in
the bus business don't have all day. We
live complex lives. We dream, gamble,
seek, deserve a better fate than Time or
Destiny, through the agency of the Unseen,
allows. So, get aboard if you are going
to. If you dare. There, there in the
valley, someone is playing a saxophone
among the peonies. His heart is broke.
There's no poop in his pizzle and surely
the will of the Unseen shall bear witness,
and lift him up from the abyss of his . . .
of his wretchedness, to the bright aire
above where lizards, snakes and the mythic
tortoise are . . . glub, glub . . . My
basket of sandwiches flew off into the
cheese that is the north end of the thing
in the hot ladder. Groans and slavver.

Spit and questions marked on the margin.
A sale of snaps, larval coruscations. .
Sweet drug of oblivion. On a global scale.
Flowers of unknown radiance, snarls of
snails, all of a coral wonder. Just
in time for the man who discovers himself
stubbed, in an ashtray. Put out. All
the work of the Unseen, like a wind in
the sail of our hour, midnight, when we
encounter the Adversary, anarchic and
covered with hairs, in the form of our
good neighbor's discarded sofa, left out
for the garbage man to pick up. He would
like to discover the truth about what can
do no harm only if it is kept, safely
under lock and key, in its cage, with no
poop in its pizzle, aware of us but dimly;
us lost in the crunching despair of our
endless opening up before the doings of
the Unseen, in all our sick, sad, pathetic
innocence. Innocence that is only the half-
cracked euphemism for our woe, which possesses
not even the required token for the train,
or bus. Nor even the train to the plane.
Not even the faith to enact that pizzle.

MARSHA GATES   I don't have a token.* Do you have a
token?

PROFESSOR CLAUDIA MITCHELL   No, I don't have a token.
Do you have
a token?
(*They look at each other hopelessly. Pause.*)

BUS DRIVER   Then what are you wasting my time for?

PROFESSOR CLAUDIA MITCHELL   And he drove off, leaving us both
in a brown study, abandoned. So I

> turned to my young companion, green
> with anxiety, and spoke in what I
> imagined were soothing tones . . .

(*Long pause.*)

PROFESSOR CLAUDIA MITCHELL   I collect catastrophes.
Vitrified catastrophes.
Enchanted in a case of glass. Encased in glass,*
that is.

MARSHA GATES   What a mess.* *Farblonjet.*

PROFESSOR CLAUDIA MITCHELL   You like messes?* Aha.

MARSHA GATES   What a* disaster.

PROFESSOR CLAUDIA MITCHELL   So you are fond of* disaster!

MARSHA GATES   What a catastrophe!

PROFESSOR CLAUDIA MITCHELL   *Quelle catastrophe!* I collect them,
you know.

MARSHA GATES   What did you say?

PROFESSOR CLAUDIA MITCHELL   I collect catastrophes.* Vitrified, of
course.

MARSHA GATES   No, the other thing you said.

PROFESSOR CLAUDIA MITCHELL   Vitrified. Encased in glass. They are
very beautiful. Would you like to see
my collection? My estate is very close,
just beyond the lianas.

MARSHA GATES   No, no. The other thing* you said.

PROFESSOR CLAUDIA MITCHELL   Never mind. Never mind. That
was in the French language.
The language of love.

(*They exchange long, hard looks.*)

CHORUS   So I went to her house. In the deep
Forest, near Avenue X. I went with her,

although I knew there was something
about it not quite right.
(*Pause.*)
Something, in fact, quite wicked.

MARSHA'S VOICE-OVER   I suspected that my hostess, Doctor
Claudia Mitchell, harbored heretical
views on the topic of the Unseen.

CHORUS   . . . heh-heh . . .
(*Pause.*)
. . . heh-heh . . .
(MARSHA *looks hard at the* PROFESSOR.)

MARSHA'S VOICE-OVER   I could not bring myself to ask. Her
draperies were of the finest brocade,
purple and stiff, annihilating the
out of doors with its pedestrian bird
cries, bus fumes, the horror of the
city's . . . hullabaloo . . .

CHORUS   Tick-tock . . . tick-tock . . .
(*Repeat*)

PROFESSOR CLAUDIA MITCHELL   I poured a large glass of sherry
for the young girl, and myself,
and led her into my studio.

MARSHA'S VOICE-OVER   There, upon a long, dark-grained, baroque
table of immense, carved teak, supported
by four grotesque, dragon-faced whorls
of some other strange wood, lay . . . ta-da!

PROFESSOR CLAUDIA MITCHELL   My sandalwood box. Within it, my
dear Marsha, is nestled my collection.

MARSHA'S VOICE-OVER   The deep plush of the box's dark interior . . .
took my breath away.
(*The* CHORUS *joins* MARSHA *and the* PROFESSOR *around the sandalwood box.*)

PROFESSOR CLAUDIA MITCHELL   This is . . .

(*She holds up a small, bright object.*)

Seoul, Korea. December 25th, 1971. The worst
hotel fire in history.* An eight-hour blaze at
the 222 room Taeyokale Hotel. A total of 163
persons are incinerated or succumb to the horrors
of noxious inhalation. Two workmen are later
sent to prison for terms of three to five years,
convicted of carelessness in the handling of
gasoline.

(*Pause. She replaces it in its place and holds up another.*)

This is Clontarf, Ireland in the year 1014 A.D.
Danish raiders under chieftain Sweyn the First
(Forkbeard) are repelled by the forces of King
Brian Boru. The Danes are mauled, with a loss
of 6000, and driven back to their stumpy ships.
Both Boru and his son are killed. Forkbeard
is slain later that year.

(*And another.*)

Saint Gotthard Pass, Italian Alps. 1478. During
the private war between the Duke of Milan and
another feudal lord, an array of 60 stout Zurichers,
allies of the Milanese are flattened by an
avalanche in the early afternoon, with the solar
furnace blazing away so innocently above.

(*And another.*)

Kossovo, in southern Yugoslavia. 1389. Prince
Lazar's Serbian army of 25,000 meets the Spahis
and Janazaries of Sultan Murad in the morning
mists of the 20th of June. In accordance with a
prophecy of the Unseen, the entire Serbian force
is annihilated, thus clearing the way for Turkish
mastery of the region for over half a millennium.

(*And another.*)

The Johnstown Flood. May 31, 1889. A wall of
water 30 to 40 feet high bursts down upon the

town as the entire dam collapses. Over two
thousand people are drowned, or dragged to their
deaths over tree branches, barbed wires and
overturned houses. Victims continue to be unearthed,
some far upstream, for the next seventeen years.

(*Yet another.*)

The retreat of the French Army from Moscow,
begun on October 19th, 1812. Hounded cruelly
by marauding Russian guerrillas, the Grande Armée
is soon mangled and beaten—reduced to a desperate,
starving horde. Snows begin to fall on November 4.
Ten days later Napoleon is left with only 25,000
able-bodied fighters. At the River Berezina 10,000
stragglers are abandoned in the crossing on the 29th.
French losses are the worst in history: 400,000 men,
175,000 horses, 1,000 cannon.

(*Pause.*)

This wonderful collection constitutes only the
merest part of the world's catastrophe, which
in toto comprises the dark side of the Unseen's Id.

MARSHA'S VOICE-OVER   But I hardly heard the words she spoke
because of a curious feeling that stole
into my mind, and I began to wonder, out loud:

MARSHA GATES   Why is the night better than the day? Why
do the young become old, and not the other
way around? Why is the world made mostly
of clay? Why can't a person always tell
what is wrong from what is right? Why does
the full weight of the Unseen fall most
heavily upon the visible, like brass? Why
can't we see what it is that compels both
cause and effect to be so interfixed? Why
can't I find a number beyond which nothing
can be enumerated? Why can't I know what

will come of what I do, think, and say? Why
can't I know truth from lies the way I do
up from down. Why is one person's disaster
not catastrophe for all? And who knows why
these things are called unaccounted. Unaccountable.
Uncountable. And why, oh why, don't we know
who *does* know the answers to these things?

(*Pause.*)

. . . because isn't it so that if we possess
and are possessed by a question, the answer
must, too, be hidden somewhere, somewhere in
the heart of someone, someone real, and not
a phantom of the Unseen?

CHORUS   Dream on, they did. Dream on . . .

MARSHA'S VOICE-OVER   When, however, I perceived, at last, the true
sickness of her Id . . . her sick, squat, demented
Id . . . I stepped quietly behind her while she
was focused on her precious set of vitrified
catastrophes . . . and picked up a large, blunt
object to bludgeon her with, but . . .

(*Picks up a chair, freezes. The* PROFESSOR *turns to her, freezes. Pause.
They look at each other a long time.*)

MARSHA'S VOICE-OVER   When I saw she wanted me to do it . . . She
wanted me to do it . . . out of a curious . . .
covetous . . . vexatious . . . perversity . . .

(*Slowly* MARSHA *lowers the chair.*)

PROFESSOR CLAUDIA MITCHELL   I am a recovering alcoholic, and a
fraud.

MARSHA GATES   And I knew she was neither . . . so:

CHORUS   Out of a curious, covetous, vexatious perversity . . .

MARSHA'S VOICE-OVER
(*Very softly*)

I refuse, I refuse, I refuse* to do it . . .

CHORUS   I REFUSE TO BLUDGEON* HER.

MARSHA GATES   Simply put: I refused to do* it.

CHORUS   She refused.
(*She laughs. The* PROFESSOR *roars out a command.*)

PROFESSOR CLAUDIA MITCHELL   OSVALDO! OSVALDO! *Throbow*
hobero obobut.
(*The* CHORUS *beats her up, and throws her out. As this is being done*
we hear the following, sung.)

PROFESSOR AND MARSHA'S VOICE-OVER   In the name of Id
and all the Id's work
show me what dark works
are done in the dark.

In the name of disaster.
In the name of catastrophe.

(*Pause. She lies outside the door of the* PROFESSOR'*s house, dazed. We*
hear birds cry.)

MARSHA'S VOICE-OVER   Her man, an ape named Osvaldo, beat me and
threw me out, but . . .
(*Pause. She opens her hand, revealing one small, glimmering object.*)

CHORUS   As I lay, bloody and beaten, on the forest
floor, amongst dead leaves and whatnot, nearly
poisoned by lethal inhalation of spores, and
accidental ingestion of strange moss and fennel . . .

PROFESSOR CLAUDIA MITCHELL   . . . wicked Id's fennel . . .

MARSHA'S VOICE-OVER   I opened my hand, and my voice returned.
I had stolen one small, nearly perfect
catastrophe:
(*A slow blackout begins.*)

MARSHA GATES   April 4, 1933. The United States dirigible
Akron goes down in heavy seas, in a remote
spot in the middle of the Atlantic Ocean
with a loss of 73 nearly perfect lives.

    (*Pause.*)

MARSHA'S VOICE-OVER   It was the most perfect jewel of that
sandalwood box.

End of play.

Cat's-Paw

A Meditation on the

Don Juan Theme

In an earlier note I mentioned Horvath's *Don Juan Comes Home from the War*, a play I have the highest regard for. (Why Horvath's work is not better known is one of the abiding mysteries of American theater.) That play got me thinking about the Don Juan theme and its close relative, the story of Faust. Over a period of time I read and read every version I could lay my hands on, and took lots of notes, hoping for an occasion to devise my own. Time passed, but no occasion materialized. So, I decided to write my own version, for the hell of it, as it were.

I wanted my Juan to be an absence, not a presence; so I made two rules, and two rules only: there must be no men in the play, and further, there

PERFORMANCE NOTE
The appearance of an asterisk within a speech indicates that the next speech begins to overlap at that point. A double asterisk indicates that the next subsequent speech begins to overlap at that point.

must be no talk of men in the play. My *Don Juan* was, thus, a play impossible to write—almost.

The Soho Rep. production was directed by Daniel Aukin, the brilliant new artistic director, and opened in December 2000.

This play was commissioned by the American Conservatory Theatre, Carey Perloff, Artistic Director, through a grant provided by TCG/Pew Charitable Trust's National Artist Residency Program; the author would also like to thank the National Endowment for the Arts for a 1995 Fellowship.

Mankind walks the earth as a
prophecy of the future, and all its deeds
are experiments, for every deed
can be surpassed by the next.
—EMERSON, IN MUSIL

When the only tool you have is a
hammer everything begins to look
look like a nail.
—LOFTI ZADEH

PERSONS OF THE PLAY

The MOTHER, Jane Bub's mother, visiting from the Midwest;
JANE BUB, her MOTHER's daughter;
JO RUDGE, JANE BUB's best friend; and
LINDSAY RUDGE, JANE BUB's best friend's daughter.

The play takes place on various commanding sites throughout the New York City area. Commanding, vertiginous sites. The time is the present, whatever that is.

Scene [rudolf valentino ▲]: *At the guard rail of the observation deck of the Empire State Building. It is raining. Two women (*JANE *and her* MOTHER*) stand next to each other, glaring into the mists below.*

JANE'S MOTHER   How long after you leap do you, do you think, make impact? Land. Hit the sidewalk.

JANE   How would I know a thing like that?

JANE'S MOTHER   Aren't you one who knows everything, with that degree in . . . what . . . nonlinear wah-wah?

JANE   Haven't you seen enough, Mother?

JANE'S MOTHER   In fact, it's about eight and a half seconds.

JANE   Do you want to go down? What do you want to do, Mother?

JANE'S MOTHER   Eight and a half seconds. I know these things. I looked it up.

JANE   Mother?

JANE'S MOTHER   What on earth would give you that idea? Isn't it clear that I am engaged upon the thinking of a thought?

(*Pause.*)

Upon the body of the earth. Make impact. Smack.

JANE   Do you think I am equipped with the appropriate apparatus? Do you think I am a speed gun?

JANE'S MOTHER   How would I know? I like it up here. No
one can ask you what you're thinking or what
you're feeling or what your life has been
like since the moment you lost that last
shred of hope in humanity. Because that is
the kind of thing people would like to
know, being people. Don't you think so?
(*Daughter doesn't know what to say or do.*)
Well? Oh Sarah, sometimes I truly wonder.
Wonder if the way I think and the way you
think are linked by the same coaxial cable.

JANE   Let's not talk about that, and whatever
else I do not want to talk about Bermuda.

JANE'S MOTHER   You brought it up, not me.

JANE   I do not want to talk about Bermuda.

JANE'S MOTHER   You brought it up, and why
would I want to talk about Bermuda?

JANE   I do not want to talk about Bermuda.

JANE'S MOTHER   Sarah, will you please listen to me:
I do not have the slightest intention
of even mentioning the word "Bermuda,"
much less touch upon the place.

JANE   Mother, I do not want to talk about
Bermuda, and that's that.

JANE'S MOTHER   I am not talking about Bermuda.
I would not even be thinking of the word
that stands for that place, that place
where* you faced for a moment . . .

JANE   I do not want to talk about Bermuda,
Mother, and if you should so much as mention
the word again I shall leap over this rail
and plunge to my death

JANE'S MOTHER   Sarah, why would you do such a thing?
Why would you consider such an ill-advised
and desperate act all because of a single
rather simple world. Word, I mean. A
name. A name is a world of a word, I find.*
A known name that is . . .

JANE   Mother, did you listen to what I said?

JANE'S MOTHER   Sarah, the name is so well known as to be,
for most purposes, innocuous. Sarah, for
Pete's sake, it's the name of an onion. It
is the name of a species of shorts. Are you
claiming a suicidal tendency on the basis
of the name of an onion?

JANE   I do not want to talk about Bermuda.
I do not want to talk about Bermuda.
I do not want to talk about Bermuda.
(*Pause.*)

JANE'S MOTHER   I was not talking about that.

JANE   You were hinting in that direction.

JANE'S MOTHER   I was not.

JANE   You were too.
(*Pause.*)

JANE'S MOTHER   I was not.

JANE   You were too.

JANE'S MOTHER   Sarah, Sarah. I was merely going to suggest,
out of the benefit of my many years
a few thoughts. A few cankered thoughts
touching upon your behavior, if one can
call it that, in recent years. A few
thoughts touching upon the exact moment,
the exact moment* one loses one's soul.

JANE   Mother, please, you're talking random. Remember
what we agreed?

JANE'S MOTHER   I just don't know why people always
assume there is a correct way to talk.
I mean, it is such an assumption that
we have anything at all to say to
one another. And maybe we truly don't.
Maybe the truth is far more scary than
even the books with terrible clawed faces
we read as children, or as cats. The faces
of Rapunzel and the dwarves. The dwarf
of Father Riley, the old dwarf known as
Stopes of Nokes, the dwarf of Anomalous
Narcolepsy, the seven-toed dwarf of
Reptile Boulevard and all the glimmering,
lazy-eyed rest. Folk of a devil parable.
Nope, maybe we all tend to that center
of gravity, down there, Hell, spooked
and propelled at the very same time by
the noise of our old shame.

JANE   Mother, I did not bring you all the way
to New York for this.

JANE'S MOTHER   I can spell *streptococcus*.
(*She does so. Smiles.*
Pause. Her daughter brightens.)

JANE   Do you remember when we lived in,
was it Santa Fe, and I had my nest
of pet scorpions in the bread box?
The air was like nothing I'd ever
seen. A solid crystal, bright as a
glass of white gin. Like a moment from
long ago frozen solid, squirreled away
among scarves and tartans of the family

trunk. The one from Mexico, with leather
hinges.

JANE'S MOTHER   A moment like the one in Bermuda.* Oops.

JANE   I do not want to talk about Bermuda.

I do not want to talk about Bermuda,
okay?

It's just that I do not want to talk about
Bermuda.

JANE'S MOTHER   A sleep of the tongue. I was thinking about
stage blood. Stage blood and Bermuda.
Stage blood and Bermuda and men's clothing.

JANE   Men's clothing?

JANE'S MOTHER   Men's clothing with nothing inside.

JANE   I wear men's clothing occasionally.
What of it?

JANE'S MOTHER   I was simply making an observation.

JANE   I wear men's clothing occasionally.
What of it? Are you trying to pick a
fight? ARE YOU?

JANE'S MOTHER   Shame, the shame of it.

JANE   Are you saying I look mannish? Is that
what you're saying? I do not look mannish.
These clothes* are good, clean clothes. These
clothes are not men's clothing. They are
simple clothes of the most fashionable kind
I can afford with a mother in Des Moines in
tow who gives one cause to worry, and worse.

JANE'S MOTHER   Shame, the shame of it.

Shame, the shame of it.

(*Pause.*)

JANE   What? What are you saying?

JANE'S MOTHER   I am saying "shame the shame of it." To
             threaten with harm your old woman of a
             mother. I think it is shameful.

JANE   I never did any such thing, Mother.

(*Pause.*)

JANE'S MOTHER   Shame, the shame of it.*
             (*Under her breath, bitterly.*)
                Vile, vicious. Bully.

JANE   I am astounded. I am absolutely
             astounded. I did no such thing.

JANE'S MOTHER   You were thinking of it. Confess
             you were. Thinking of it.

JANE   I am thinking of it now, why yes I am,
             but that is an outcome of the tack you
             are trying to get me to take.

JANE'S MOTHER
             (*Under her breath, bitterly.*)
                Vicious, vile. Bully.
             (*A shameful pause.*)

JANE   Mother, I do not think I have the slightest
             idea what you are driving at.

JANE'S MOTHER
             (*Not hearing*)
                Good. I'm glad. At least on that score.
                Now what I was thinking was that
                I know a great deal more about you
                than you suspect. Certainly more than
                you ought to suspect.

JANE   I do not want to talk about Bermuda.

JANE'S MOTHER   I was not talking about that.

JANE   You were hinting in that direction.

JANE'S MOTHER   I was not.

JANE   You were too.
     (*Pause.*)

JANE'S MOTHER   I was not.

JANE   You were too.
     (*Pause.*)
          So: just what is it you think you think know?

JANE'S MOTHER   I know you like to dress up like a man.
          Whoa. Whoa. I know too you have a
          way of touching the nape of your neck.
          Touching the nape of your neck in
          moments of emotional crisis. At critical
          points of crisis, when doom is near.
     (*Her daughter does this by reflex.*)
          Touching yourself on the back of your head,
          on the nape of your neck is an old habit
          with you, dearie. An old, old habit,
          I would say. From the season of our
          salad days, after we had departed
          Santa Fe but before the clinical terminus.
          The catastrophe that would lead, lead us
          that is, would lead ineluctably to . . .
          Des Moines. And you wore pigtails, and could
          take on all comers at baseball, darts,
          checkers.

JANE   Swimming and diving.

JANE'S MOTHER   Swimming and diving. And mumbletypeg.

JANE   Was that Pensacola?

JANE'S MOTHER   That might have been Pensacola.
It was the place, I can just barely
recall. Sawgrass under the Spanish moss,
and up on the limbs of trees, real grapefruits.

JANE   Was that Pensacola?

JANE'S MOTHER   I remember only the sweetness of those
big, pale green grapefruits. Oh yes,
Oh Yes, I do.

JANE   Anyway, that was not an old habit.
I formed it recently. It is, I suppose,
stress related.

JANE'S MOTHER   I have been able to observe the small motions
of your soul for all these years.

JANE   What a thing to say Mother. What a
genuinely creepy thing to say: the
small motions of my soul?

JANE'S MOTHER   Yes, dearie, yes. That is what they are.
Yes, and I have seen you paint your
nails for the first time. The first time
scarlet. Yes, dearie, yes. Scarlet,
for the very first time.

JANE   Why? Whatever for? Why is it these
odd and uncomfortable things that
you choose to share?

JANE'S MOTHER   Because.

JANE   And why, why, why do your persist in calling
me Sarah when you know I so hate the name?

JANE'S MOTHER
   (*Icily*)

   Who did the naming? Who? Nobody
names themself. I can see how angry

you are with all the names, some of them
not even your own, that you've soiled.
Not my doing, any of it. Who named
you, daughter, if not me—and . . . and . . .

JANE   And you! And so? What are you saying? Mother?

JANE'S MOTHER   Only a fool names herself, and arrives
by the end of her train of thought at the
pure end of the premature.

JANE

(*Coldly*)

Damn you. You hate my youth, my elegance,
and yes, my money, because at least I have
that. And you never had the wit to care.
About money.

JANE'S MOTHER   What do you know of what I cared? I cared
plenty. Still do.

JANE   Oh yeah?

JANE'S MOTHER   Yeah. Plenty.

JANE   I don't believe you.

JANE'S MOTHER   I don't give a damn what you believe.

JANE   That makes two of us.

JANE'S MOTHER   Amen.

(*Pause.*)

JANE

(*To herself.*)

Ha! What an idiot I am! How could I
be so stupid to end up like this, talking
to the crazy, ruined has-been who is my
mother on a dull, rusty Thursday a half-

348 : *Cat's Paw*

mile up over the mist of New York and not
go mad myself.

JANE'S MOTHER   All of you have wanted forever to put me
on that drug, Prolapsis or Prolepto-whatsis,
but I won't, see? I just plain won't. Sure,
you've got the upperhand, I know I know.
And don't count on me taking the easy way
out—over the rail, over the rail and splat.
Because the old harridan ain'ta gonna do it.
Nosirree, she's damned if she's not. She's
got other plans, and these plans include
living forever and winning the lotto jackpot
for seventy-five million.

(*Daughter whistles.*)

Go ahead, laugh. What do I care? I've
arrived at the calm serenity of wizened
maturity. Wizendom. Loss, what do I care?
Hope, a toy. All the rest of it, emotional
static. A caterpillar of moments, gone moments
of what is no more.

(*Pause.*)

JANE   Shall we try again?

JANE'S MOTHER   Why?

JANE   Well. I don't know. Just because.

(*A biological pause.*)

JANE'S MOTHER   I don't want to and besides, you made fun
of me not five minutes ago for just that
circumlocution.

JANE   What?

JANE'S MOTHER   Because. I said "because."

JANE   So? I don't remember saying anything in the
slightest derogatory.

JANE'S MOTHER   You wouldn't. Of course. That's no surprise.
(*Pause.*)

JANE   Blank.

JANE'S MOTHER   Blank?

JANE   Yes, blank. I just feel blank.

JANE'S MOTHER   What a sad case you are. I feel rich and
full and large with hopefulness, blood,
and a sense of true being.

JANE   What's your secret?

JANE'S MOTHER   Wouldn't you like to know?

JANE   Seriously, where does this sense of true being
come from? What's your secret? Really?
(*Pause.*)
Really?

JANE'S MOTHER   My secret is a chronically faulty sense
of spacio-temporal continuity. I don't
care if I behave in ways others consider
inconsistent, not holistic, or unself-similar.
Naturally this fills me like a . . . a blimp
with . . . with a sense of true being.

JANE   Sometimes I wonder if you're really my
mother.

JANE'S MOTHER   Who else would I be? Why else would I
bother, for Pete's sake?
(*Poor* JANE *doesn't know.*)
Yes, I'm as full of true being as the grapefruits
of Pensacola.

JANE
(*Wistfully*)
When I was a little girl, a little little

girl. Long before the episode of the
scorpions, I can recall you telling me
stories I loved. I've never heard
stories like the ones you told me
then, although those stories troubled
me like a stone skipping along over
the face of a pond.

JANE'S MOTHER   The moment's ripple.

JANE   Mainly I do not recall much of the
narrative structure, only. In the
story you called "I Forget What House"
I can still see the Poor Girl's purple
shoelaces and her blackened tooth that
caused her shame, but saved her from
the savage Wild Turnip. Each full
moon a different turnip, all of them
wild. All of them powerfully subject
to minima and maxima according to the
Handy Tables of G. J. Toomer's Survey
of the Toledan Tables.

(*Pause.*
Both sigh at the thought.)

Or the story about the caterpillar who
lived for centuries inside the wooden knee
of the Poor Tailor from Milwaukee. The
caterpillar who dreamed successively of
seven worlds, each more remote than the
last, the last unaccountably a world without
tailors. Hence caterpillars dozing in their
wooden knees.

JANE'S MOTHER   Yes, that was a very good one, only you've
missed a few crucial details and have the
point of the whole somewhat spavined.

(*Pause.*)

I never cared much for Jane. As a name.

JANE Then why was I named Jane?

JANE'S MOTHER It wasn't your Christian name. Your
Christian name was Sarah. We gave
you the name with the idea you would
use it, respectfully and worshipfully,
and not that other, that Jane.

JANE But I like to be called Jane.

JANE'S MOTHER That was at the last moment, to
fill out the whole. For the legal documents.

JANE Well, I like it.

JANE'S MOTHER You would. When I think of Jane, I think of
Crazy Jane or Plain Jane. Jane Bub:
sounds like a sprain or bellyache.
I know more about you than you think.
(*Pause.*)

JANE'S MOTHER My word, with all that fog down there
it feels like we're in an airplane.

JANE This is my first time up here.

JANE'S MOTHER I first came up here many years ago,
during the war. I forget which one.

JANE They do run together.

JANE'S MOTHER They do run together to form one long,
continuous, murderous, bloody-red splotch.

JANE So many dead.

JANE'S MOTHER So pointless.
(*Pause.*)

JANE Not if you died in one.

JANE'S MOTHER   Funny, you've always talked that way.
Pointless and obvious at the same time.
Funny, in a girl so smart. My, is that a man with wings
down there, walking across the cloudtops?

JANE   Some kind of a float, looks like. Isn't
this a holiday?

JANE'S MOTHER   Veterans Day. I think.

JANE   Veterans of Foreign Wars. Does that include us?
(*Soundless, dry laughter.*)

JANE'S MOTHER   Something like that. How long have we
been up here? One fine, fine thing
about tourists in Iowa: there aren't any.
Suppose you think I'm mad.

JANE   Never crossed my mind. Much. Until now.
(*Pause.*)
What I was thinking was how much I detest
being observed. One thing about Lucent,
mostly what I do there I can do unobserved.
Unseen. Fractals and Fourier analysis.
(*She looks up.*)
It is somehow more clean.

JANE'S MOTHER   Clean to be unseen. Ha.

JANE   I'm not joking, really I am not. People
watch you and suppose they know what
makes you tick. The one, tiny, little
fatal brass screw. I hate that. I hate
that arrogance of bosses . . . and friends
with their long gray fingers you can feel
threading the jewels of your dream. Pearls,
black pearls of your dream. Long bony
fingers up to the knuckle in your ear
sockets, poking around in the dull, windy

places of your head. Trying to take apart
whatever it is you want.

JANE'S MOTHER

   (*Matter-of-factly*)

   Skin. Human skin.

JANE   Skin?

JANE'S MOTHER   My Bermuda was Caracas, Sarah.

JANE   What? Beg your pardon.

JANE'S MOTHER   Caracas. The moment for me came in
                Caracas, in Venezuela. A place full of
                parrots and toucans. Caracas stands,
                for me at least, for depravity.

   (*Pause.*)

                Dropeverything depravity. Depravity undraped.

JANE   You?

JANE'S MOTHER   Depravity, yes. That was my object,
                although I did not and could not have
                known it at the time. Surely there
                is a thing called innocence, and
                I was young, so young and so . . .
                so seeming frail.* Although . . .

JANE   You? Frail? Ha. A mechanized urchin
                of spring steel, I'll bet.

JANE'S MOTHER   That too, dearie. That too. Still I
                was true to my nature, and to the
                clothes I wore.

   (*Gestures lamely.*)

JANE   Forget it. Forget it. Just that.
                That's all I mean. I should keep my trap shut.

JANE'S MOTHER   Feel like someone drove a ten-penny nail
through my skull.

JANE   Sometimes when I look at a person in the
street, all I see is costume. An arrangement
of men's clothing, more or less coherent
with nothing inside.

JANE'S MOTHER   This is turning into a cluster headache.
(*Pause. Brightening.*)
You know I always wondered what a
cluster bomb is.

JANE   Blows people to bits with fragments of
sharp metal. A whole lot of them, all
at one time.

JANE'S MOTHER   The things people dream up. It makes a soul
wonder. Costumes come and go. But what
rides the wind is the snake power. Like that
serpent of a parade down there. The beaded
snake-head.

JANE   That is not a snake. It is the hat of a
balloon. It represents some public figure.

End of scene.

Scene [rudolf the red-nosed reindeer ▶]: JANE'S MOTHER's *daughter,*
JANE BUB, *and her friend,* JO RUDGE, *stand on the observation deck of the*
World Trade Center. A dark and foggy day with misting rain.

JANE   Caracas, can you believe it? She said Caracas.

JO   I can believe it. Tough old bird, your mom.

JANE   Medium height, medium build. Murderous eyes.
Dressed to kill. Wave in the hair, all the same
down to the singleton earring. Black pearl.
With a look like murder, or its incubation.

JO   Odd to think of murder in an egg. As a mere chick.

JANE   No odder than the rest of it, Jo. What's great
starts small. That was Mom's motto.

JO   Well frankly I don't understand how you get
so theoretical about it. What it's about is
invisibility and how somehow you, Jane Bub,
have allowed yourself to be erased. Like a
cartoon figure, drawn by a child on a piece
of mat paper. Then set aflame and burnt. Ffft.

JANE   Erased.

JO   Made invisible, by your own choice. Such things,
such things happen to women who happen not to be
up to a truly responsible and informed choice.
In human terms. As time reveals itself, drib
by drab.

      (*Pause.*)

Reified. Then erased.

JANE   But I'm not erased.

JO   You've been erased, and are now invisible.
There is no one standing in your shoes.

    (*Poor* JANE *looks down at her shoes.*)

Only air. Ffft.

JANE   Only air and misery.

JO   Don't feel sorry for yourself. You aren't
the first. Nor the only.

JANE   Look, I don't know where you get off.
I don't understand your line of reasoning.

JO   I am asserting a fact. It's a metaphor.

JANE   Makes no sense to me. I'm not erased.
It's a silly metaphor if you ask me.

JO You are invisible.

JANE I am not.

JO You are too.

JANE I am not.
       (*Pause.*)

JO You have become commodified and reified.
    You have become invisible. An "it."
    From a "you" into an "it." Ffft.
       (*Pause.*)
    And I am not talking about Bermuda.

JANE And I do not want to talk about Bermuda.

JO I was not talking about Bermuda.

JANE You were hinting in that direction.

JO I was alluding to the event that occurred
    At Key West, and which you only allude
    to by the nonce term "Bermuda." And that
    is indeed a highly unusual coinage since
    to my knowledge you have never set foot
    in the place.
       (*Pause.*)

JANE Have too.

JO Have not.
       (*Pause. A sad one.*)

JANE Have too.

JO Have not.
       (*Pause.*)
    Ffft. Have it your way then. A martyr to invisibility,
    ha. You know Bermuda like the back of your hand.
    You visit the dignitaries of Bermuda on the National
    Day and take part in the festivities: curling, golf,

and clog dancing. You wear the famous shorts of that tribe. And eat of their onion. You and your damn silly invisibility are cherished friends of the Imperial Bermudian State. Ffft, I say, Ffft.

JANE   That is not funny, Jo. Just because I have sometimes shared a confidence somewhat does not mean you have the right to, well, mock me in my disgrace.

JO   You are talking like royalty, Jane. You are talking like a most wonderful machine of contented, well-adjusted visibility when I know otherwise.

JANE   Oh, pooh.

JO   Oh, pooh, indeed. I perceive the true invisibility of Jane Bub.

JANE   You and Mother both seem to assume you have the right to mechanically bore with drill-bit into the dark part of my mind. The inner recesses. I don't like that, Jo. I really don't.

JO   So, you admit. Being visually accountable terrifies you. Admit it, Jane.

JANE   I admit nothing except an aversion to prying eyes. Particularly when they pry under my lid. My lid is mine alone. Get thee behind me, Jo.
    (*Pause.*)
JO   You are invisible, it's as simple as that.

JANE   I sometimes wish I were, oh how I wish I were.
    (*Pause.*)
      I dream my teeth are broken stubs, and click about in my mouth like a pocketful of small change. My heart leaps up and I feel nothing

but a wheeze of no hope. Hope gone, and no
answer. No answer, but a dream of broken
teeth, and down . . . down there beneath that
eerie carpet of cloud a hell of what my heart
leapt up for.

JO   You're being romantic. Self-involved.
Be tough.

(*Pause.*)

And it's like, well, I don't have any bad
things going on in my wretched, dingy
sublet of a life, eh? It's like, solid
old reliable Jo, she's a pillar of cement
when it comes to matters of the fucking
heart, eh? She's like Miss Moral Center
of the Universe and the weight of Atlas
is balanced like a tractor-trailer on the
point of her chin, eh?* Sure, sure, go ahead
and deny it, deny all of it. While I spend
day after day wilting under the fluorescence
at work, totaling up statistics concerning
practices so grotesque I break out in
hives. And that jerk. You know who.
After three bourbons, you ask.
After my commitment to the larger things
in life. Ideas. Righting certain political
wrongs I had nothing to do with. My
whole generation a crowd of ciphers,
professional weathervanes, asshole-kissers,
nerds, carreerist windsocks, hypocrites,
emotional dwarves, and the intellectually
barren. Paper clips. Hair pins. Used
cue tips. (JANE *looks aghast at this.*)
Loose-wired has-beens and smoke-eating swine,
I'd like to tear the motherfuckers' face off.
The whole bunch.

JANE   Jo, what is it?

                 Jo, hey, Jo. It's okay.

JO   After three double bourbons, you ask,
                 what does a face mean?

JANE   A face mean? I don't understand.

JO   I mean, how much do you have to try
                 to stand face to face, and not lose
                 a chance at something better,
                 you know? I mean, a person's face
                 is her own face, and it is so damn
                 easy to lose it. It is so damn, damn
                 easy and you become a stand-in for
                 yourself. Even in the morning after
                 when you stand face to face with
                 whoever you are, in the mirror. Not
                 easy. Not so pleasant. Listen to me,
                 Jane, listen. This is important. This
                 is hard stuff.

JANE   I'm listening, Jo, I'm listening hard.
      (*A hollow pause.*)

JO   Well I'm not. Period. I am not ever
                 listening to another godamn thing anybody
                 ever says to me, and do you know why,
                 Jane, do you? Do you know why?
      (*She snorts in disgust.*)
                 You're just like all the rest.

JANE   Why do you say that?

JO   Because. Just because.
      (*Pause.*)

JANE   Someone owes me an apology. I ask,

with perfect clarity and an open heart, I ask
friends and family, all, all of you. I ask
all of them to speak when it is apparent
these persons have a thing to answer for, out
of my interest in their wellbeing. I do this
in a spirit of love* . . . yes, love. I ask
the hard question and the easy one, out of
a spirit of unmotivated, disinterested
compassion, and the reply I seem invariably
to receive is "because."

JO   It's because you pry too much.

JANE   "Because."

JO   It's because one senses an agenda.

JANE   I pry too much!

I pry too much!

I pry too much! Ha.
      (*An empty, dead pause.*)

JO   People talk about love when they mean
motor oil. People talk about love when
they mean epidermis. People talk about
love when they mean the unholy dollar.
People talk about love when they mean
a flicker of intelligence or recognition
or surprise even, even disappointment in
the face of the callous brute who has
shamelessly brutalized them emotionally
time and time again over the full, horrid
course of a three-hundred and fifty
year relationship. People talk about love
when what they mean is closer to a hideous,
insidious itch.

(Pause. Both are aware of the desire to scratch an itch. But given the circumstance neither one will honor the impulse.)

JANE Do you think it will clear up soon? It's
       supposed to clear up soon isn't it?

JO Weathermen are all degraded swine.
     How should I know? Fuck the weather,
     I hate the weather.

JANE I like the weather.

JO Let's talk about something else. Now I'm
     in a really foul mood.

JO I hate the weather.

     I hate the weather.

     I hate the weather.

JANE And while we are on the subject, I do not
       want to talk about Bermuda.

JO I was not talking about that.

JANE You were hinting in that direction.

JO I was not.

JANE You were too.
       (Pause.)

JO I was not.

JANE You were too.
       (Pause.)

JANE Feels like we're floating above the weather, like
       witches or crows. Weather of the word.

JO It's an ocean we're in, the weather of words.

JANE Nevertheless. Oh, hell, I *like* it up here.

I'm going to make a point of doing more
touristy things from now on. Being in New York.
After all, we are located here.

JO
I need sunlight. Otherwise I shrivel up,
emotionally. This sucks. I can't stand
this place when it rains.

JANE
(*Seriously*)
Life is good.

JO
Listen to you: life is good. Ha! What would
you know about life, little Miss Precocious.

JANE
Drank it to the dregs.

JO
Ha.

JANE
Life is my metier.

JO
Ha.

JANE
Life is the noise I make.

JO
Ha.

JANE
Life is a gift. It is our goldest God-given
adornment.

JO
Double ha! What's that from?

JANE
Great Aunt Dolly. Her branch of the family
consorted with snakes and spoke in tongues.
Hallelujah.

JO
What is it again?

JANE
Life is a gift. It is our goldest God-given
adornment. I like the word goldest.

JO
It's a mystery word. Name ten completely
unsolvable mysteries.

JANE   Any human heart at random. And nine more just like it.

JO   You know that one. Damn.
(*A full pause.*)
Ten hearts. What's ten? Deka. Decem. Dix. Dux. Duck.

JANE
(*Unselfconsciously*)
A duck of hearts.

JO   A duck of tarts.

JANE   A truck of ducks.

JO   A duck of trucks.
(*Now thinking thinkings.*)
A trunk of skunks.

JANE   Duck a duck. Duck a duck. Duck.

BOTH   Duck a duck. Duck a duck. Duck a duck.
JO   Donk.

BOTH   Duck a duck. Duck a duck. Duck a duck
(*Pause.*)
Donk.

JANE   Donka. Donka. Donka. Donka.
Donka. Donka. Donka. Donka.

JO   Bonk.
(*A meditative pause.*)

JANE   Donka. Donka. Donka. Donka.
Donka. Donka. Donka. Donka.

JO   Bonk.
(*Pause. Lightning. Out with rain hats. Lightning, Another bolt of lightning. Pause.*)

JANE

> (*Quietly*)
>> Frank Carranza
>> killed his wife
>> with five little sticks
>> and a pin.

JO

> Wow. Where'd you get that one? That one is truly creepy.

JANE

> Great Aunt Dolly's cousin Vernal. From Cajun country. Down south, way down south.
>
> (JANE *recites it primly. Pause. Both sing it perfectly. Both are impressed and pleased with themselves.* JO *darkens. A chilly and lonesome pause.*)

JO

> It's getting cold. Why don't we go back down. Have a cup of coffee. Cup uh Joe.
>
> (*Soundless laughter.*)

JANE

> I feel wretched.

JO

> Then let's go down. Coffee, or a drink maybe? Cheer us up. A double bourbon.

JANE

> You always get your way. This time you're not. People like you, people who end all their arguments with the word "because" . . . They are my bane.

JO

> Ha.

JANE

> Yes, my bane.

JO

> Come on, you'll feel better once we have our feet on the ground. Real, level ground. Try it.

JANE

> How long does it take, if you leap, if you vault the rail, for you to land?

JO

> ?

JANE   About eight-and-a-half seconds.

JO

(*Astonished*)

        How on earth did you arrive at a fact like that?

JANE   I overheard someone say so.

JO   It's eight-and-a-half seconds for the Empire
        State Building. The Twin Towers are higher.
        So, it's got to be at least ten seconds. Maybe more.

(*Pause. They sing:*)

BOTH   Don Juan Dudgeon
        that curmudgeon
        killed his wives
        his seven wives
        with five little sticks
        and a pin.

Slow fade to black.
End of scene.

Scene [rudolf hitler ▽]: *A brilliant, sunny gem of a day at the Statue of Liberty. Her torch, where we're not supposed to go.* JO RUDGE *and her daughter,* LINDSAY, *a nasty little girl. The latter surveys the harbor with a smile.*

LINDSAY   Someday all of this will be mine.

JO   Lindsay, what an odd thing to say!

LINDSAY   Nonsense, mother. I am being perfectly
        rational. I know exactedally what I want
        and when I go to Groaner University
        I shall know exactedally what must be done.

JO   What must be done? You sound like Lenin.

LINDSAY   What must be done to get it.

JO   Admire the view, dear. Stick to that
        if you don't mind.

LINDSAY   Okay, okay.

JO   You imagine how difficult it was
          to get permission.

LINDSAY   Yeah, yeah.
     (*Long pause.*)

LINDSAY   Mother, are you a mammal?
     (*Pause.*)

JO   Lindsay, can you sense the hugeness of the city?
          Volume? Scope? Dimension? Solidness? Light?
          To me, such a view of the city always suggests
          nothing so much as an illusion.

LINDSAY   An illusion: isn't that something that is unreal?

JO   It is the image of a thing. Something else.
          But images too possess a certain reality.

LINDSAY   I find what you've said baffling.

JO   Just remember how beautiful the view is,
          and that through an act of kindness
          your mother accomplished the most difficult.
          For most people, Liberty's torch is off limits.
     (*But her daughter's found something.*)

LINDSAY   Mother, look, they have roach motels. Wow!

JO   Don't be silly, dear.

LINDSAY   I can't believe it. They have roach motels
          on the Statue of Liberty.

JO   Stop that silliness.

LINDSAY   Oh, Mother.

JO   Stop it now. Look out that window and no,
          please don't pick it up, it is vile.

LINDSAY Oh, Mother. I like the small square boxy look of it. I like the idea of roaches cozily lodged within. I like the idea of a whole, new species of roach able to foil our murderous designs. Able not only to foil us, and live happily and contentedly, and to live among our stupid poisons, but also smart enough to fool us.

JO To fool us how?

LINDSAY To fool us by pretending to be dead when we drawn near. With our grossness and stupidity and mindless theatrical excess.

JO Look at the sky. Look at the sea.

LINDSAY I dislike the sea. It's a grotesque abstraction. Furthermore, it is not beautiful. The roach motel is beautiful. Boxy and beautiful.

JO You astonish me.

LINDSAY If that is your way of saying I am not an ordinary child you may as well know that I am already aware of the fact.

JO Where did you learn to talk that way? I am not sure I approve.

LINDSAY Oh, Mother, may I bring this lovely roach motel home? I just adore it.

JO Of course you may not. Put it back immediately, wherever you got it from.
  (*A chilly pause. Her daughter does as she's told. Another chilly pause.*)

LINDSAY You will pay for this, Mother.

JO Other children understand obedience, and also what the implications of this idea are.

LINDSAY   I am not other children, mother.

JO   Oh?

LINDSAY   No, mother, I am a genius. A genius
              of childhood and I will not be denied.

JO
       (*Suddenly bitter.*)
              Your time will come.

LINDSAY   No, Mother, not in the way you imagine.

JO   We will see about that, my dearie. We will see.
              I brought you here in the hope the experience
              would prove edifying. The world today is
              a stunned sea bass gasping on the shore,
              its glimmer fading. Certain old and sacred
              things, and the reverence which attends upon
              these mysteries has got broken. Spine
              shattered, no splint suffices.* Only the visible . . .

LINDSAY   Sham rules, we agree on that.

JO   Shame more than sham, Lindsay.

LINDSAY   Cultural wobble.

JO   Insincerity.

LINDSAY   Denial.

JO   Shame. The shame of it.

LINDSAY   All that, all that out there that you revere
              in obtuse sentimentality shall fall to me
              and be mine. I know this for a fact.
              As surely as the root weevil bores that part
              of both apple and pear.

JO   Do they teach the concept of liberty at that fine
              school I pay for?

LINDSAY   What I am talking about has nothing to do
             with what is taught at school, Mother. As
             I have explained before, I observe the world
             almost as if I stood far above it, and draw
             my own conclusions.

JO   There is knowledge, and there is killing knowledge.

LINDSAY   My aim is to accomplish something tremendous.

JO   And what of your friends, family?
             The community at large. What of me,
             your poor, old mother? What will become
             of me, after I cease my struggle, take up
             the needle and knitting craft of acceptance?

LINDSAY   I did not come into the world to bewail
             my state, nor to lament the lures and veils
             of appearance to which I've succumbed.
             What you say is simply false drivel. It is
             only meant to manipulate me.

JO   And so what do you do with the human
             heart? How do you account for its storms,
             its Bermudas and Caracases and even its
             drunken Keys West?

LINDSAY   That kind of talk is the reason why, even
             at my tender age, I distrust metaphor.
             You are fooling with me, mother.

JO   No, no, Lindsay, I am only trying to
             explain certain deep, true things to you.
             Things you will need to know when you
             come of age, and are possessed by your
             alchemical animal body. Possessed and clasped
             in the vice grip as tightly as we are held
             today, in Liberty's forbidden fist.

LINDSAY   It is the torch she carries that I shall
          model my intention upon. The pure light
          of ultimate reason that shall clear my
          pathway, and to which alone, in my secret
          self, I shall pledge allegiance.

JO   If you are so alone, how will you go
          into the world? People need other people,
          for solace, society, friendship, and comforting.

LINDSAY   There are others like me. I know it.

JO   Perhaps.

LINDSAY   I do not care a fiddle for your "perhaps."
          I know what I'm talking about.

JO   Can't you see, Lindsay, can't you understand.
          I mean when you perceive all creatured things:
          mice and kittens, alligators and rhyncocephalians
          even, bats and fowl of the air. Can't you image
          these and not not be seized by the rapture
          of what is holy? Can't you respond to the
          holiness that infects the very air we breathe?

LINDSAY   "Infects" is the right word, Mother, in that
          locution.

JO   Lindsay, I want to pass along to you what
          I've learned, learned from life. Not just my
          cynicism and heartbreak and tendency to
          whine; not just my modest savings and rent-
          controlled apartment in Murray Hill; these
          things do not matter. What matters is . . .
          is the heart and its dark unfathomableness.
          What matters is our social vision and human
          generosity and the willingness to measure
          one's reach by lacks. To not indulge one's
          instinctual dichotomy to the full furnace

blast. To be good, generous, and always
considerate. Even of the poor, withered,
blasted dolt standing there, *there,* there
below on the street, withering in his rage,
at us, in his desperate, irremediable
abjection.

LINDSAY   Talk turkey, Mother. All that is pure
rot.

JO   No, no, no, no, no, Lindsay. It is not.
Our humaneness is a vast, tentiform spider-
thing of inescapable connection. Connection
radiating from every point to every other
point in the three-dimensional field.

LINDSAY   Rot, Tommy-rot, all of it. As surely as the
Venus's-hair has black and shining roots and
branches.

(*An exasperated pause.*)

What you do not comprehend, Mother, is how
bogus and sentimental your phoney pipe dream truly is.
America hates the weak, Mother, because they *are*
weak

(*Mom is stunned.*)

America does not wish to hear the cries
of the underprivileged, the abject, the
unlucky. It has heard all these things
for years and years and years and years
and years.

JO   But the dream has never been delivered.
Once the full plan has been explained to
ordinary people they will be able to
grasp it. Why we must rebuild
our cities and save the snail darter, the
spotted owl, and so on.

LINDSAY   No, Mother, you are wrong. America
            hates all that. America hates all that
            because all that is creepy and dated
            and just doesn't cut it.

JO   Don't you want a family, children? Don't
            you want to pass on to the next generation
            what you care about? Don't you want to
            propagate values you believe in?

LINDSAY   Of course, but I realize there is a duplicity
            present in all discussions of these things.

JO   Oh? How do you mean?

LINDSAY   Just that, you people who claim you care
            so much for humanitarian causes, we see
            who you are. We are not so stupid. We watch television.

JO   Who is this "we"?

LINDSAY   This "we" is me. And people like me. Because
            we are everywhere, and we are a force that
            spurns your habit of lies.

JO   Television. So that's where this comes from.
            I should have known. Well, Lindsay, television
            is over for you. For six weeks no television.

LINDSAY   Oh, Mother, don't act so simpleminded. Do
            You really think I have regard for Oprah,
            or anything but contempt for Friends, Felicity, and
            David Letterman? Do you think I am so stupid
            that I actually buy the manure that they are
            dishing out? No, Mother, No. It is like
            I say: I *study* the creatures of television,
            and the fruit of this study shall be my
            ability to move silently and swiftly.
            Silently and swiftly through the world
            of appearances unseen and undetected.

In this way I shall achieve my objects.
And I shall do this without ever needing
to explain or justify my actions, motives,
or intentions. In this way I shall be
clean, and not subject to the fits of
whining hypocrisy and shabby question-
begging I see everywhere around me. Do
you understand, Mother, what it is I am
saying to you?

JO   I know I should've been more disciplined
            as far as attending parent-teacher activities
            at Crown of Briars school.

LINDSAY   No, no, you miss my point, Mother.

JO   ——

LINDSAY   ——

(*Both smile and shrug. Pause.*)
            The teachers at Crown of Briars are idiots,
            Mother; I pay them no mind.

JO   That's hardly reassuring, Lindsay.

LINDSAY   They're harmless. Faded liberals, just like
            you. As surely as the lightning bug *Photuris
            pennsylvanica* when squashed leaves a lovely
            smear of greenish-gold light.

JO   Watch what you say. Watch what you say.
            A thing said cannot be unsaid, an act
            of the human soul cannot be undone.
            You are getting drunk on sheer possibility.
            Leave one link out of the chain, and the
            entire sequence is broken.

LINDSAY   That's mere Popish fact-twisting.

JO   You are putting me in the state of high
dudgeon.

LINDSAY   What is high dudgeon, and if "high"
why not low?

JO   Dudgeon is rage, fury. Righteous indignation.
There is no such thing as low fury.
(A meditative pause.)
So? Did that wiggle your handle? It did,
diddle it? Diddle it? Diddle it?

LINDSAY   It diddle not.

JO   It did, diddle it? Diddle it?* Diddle it?

LINDSAY   It most certainly diddle not.
(Pause.)
I am thinking about what you've said.

JO   Good. I hope you manage to think your way
out of the intellectual cat's cradle you've
concocted.

LINDSAY   Then "high" dudgeon is redundant, mother,
at least by your reasoning, and you have
made an error of language. I like the word
dudgeon, and I like even more the phrase
cat's cradle, only, what does it mean?

JO   It's a . . . a gizmo made of hands and string.

LINDSAY   A gizmo made of hands and string?
What is that supposed to mean?

JO   A tentiform structure of string, using the
various fingers of the hand as supporting
struts.

LINDSAY   You are saying my way of thinking is like
a tentiform structure of string supported
by finger struts?

J O	It's only a figure of speech.
LINDSAY	A lie, you mean.
J O	No, the intention was not to mislead. The intention was to clarify.
LINDSAY	Then the intention failed miserably.
J O	I'm sorry, Lindsay.
LINDSAY	I forgive you, Mother, if you promise not to do this thing ever again.
J O	I'll do my best.
LINDSAY	Do better.
J O	I'll try.
LINDSAY	Trying is not good enough. You must promise.

(*Pause.*)

J O	Okay.
LINDSAY	Promise. Say it.
J O	I promise.
LINDSAY	The experience of Singapore has rotted the very pith of your mind.
J O	I do not want to talk about Singapore.
	I do not want to talk about Singapore.
	I do not want to talk about Singapore.
LINDSAY	I was not talking about Singapore, I was talking about the way Singapore had rotted your mind, a supposition further confirmed by the herky-jerky manner of your speech: "I do not want to talk about Singapore, I do not no want to talk about Singapore,* I do not want to talk about Singapore . . .

JO

(*Fiercely*)

What do you know about any of it? What?
What do you think people do? What about
my friend Alice, lost in the rabbit hole
of her dudgeon? My dear friend Jane Bub
and her mother, what about them? What do
they do? What about your friends? Dolly
Mitchell and Patty Carmichael, what about
them? And Lindsay Rudge, what in the name
of Sam Hill does she do?

LINDSAY There is no answer to your question, Mother.
Because it is a pointless one.

JO Senseless, all of it senseless. The dredging
up of counterfeit, past selves to be questioned
concerning this or that. Their sad lives and
accidental and inadvertent wickedness and
their witless political betrayals that follow
as easily from what they do not accomplish, as
from what they do. All of it senseless, cruel,
and compromised.

(*A reflective pause.*)

LINDSAY No, Mother, no. The Republicans are not
so dumb as that. Mister George W. Bush Jr. with his
glittering eye and that poor, tormented poet
Dick Cheney. These people are more intelligent
than you imagine. Why should they reveal
all they know and all they intend to do
before it is come to term. These men know
that the majority of people are weak and
foolish and do not even have a basic grasp
on statistics and the statistical use
of numbers. Ordinary Americans are baffled
by complex things and only want a strong

man to lead them. This is true. You do not
understand this fact, and that is why
your liberal glory is a faded thing. As superfluous
as a billet-doux from the olden days.
> (*Pause.*)
Will the police arrest us if they find us here?

J O   Maybe. Maybe not. Excursioning in Liberty's
arm is a misdemeanor, I believe.

L I N D S A Y
> (*Brightening*)
Jail! We're going to jail.

J O   You think jail's so nice?

L I N D S A Y   It'll be an experience. Besides, I don't
think jail can be as bad as it is portrayed
on television.

J O   Oh?

L I N D S A Y   You have your own little room, your own
little bed, and your own little toilet.

J O   Wouldn't you get lonely?

L I N D S A Y   Probably. But I would have my fellow
prisoners to talk to. We could meet secretly
and conspire. We could devise unusual
ways to escape. That would be fun.

J O   What of Dolly Mitchell and Patty Carmichael?

L I N D S A Y   They would come and visit me in jail.
They would keep me informed as to conditions
outside.
> (*Both laugh lightheartedly. Pause. The daughter turns to her mother.*)

L I N D S A Y   The seductions of the world would lean
less heavily upon me, being young.

JO	Callow youth.
LINDSAY	Mother, you never answered my question.
JO	What question was that?
LINDSAY	Are you a mammal? And, by implication, me?
JO	Yes, dear.
LINDSAY	And father, what was he?
JO	He was a reptile, dear. A snake.
LINDSAY	I like snakes. What kind of snake was he?
JO	A beaded snake.
LINDSAY	Are beaded snakes poisonous?
JO	They closely resemble the coral snake which is very poisonous, but no, The beaded snake is not poisonous.
LINDSAY	How can it achieve its objects in the world and avoid detection if it has no pot of poison?
JO	Because it resembles the coral snake, all things fear it.
LINDSAY	I like snakes; snakes are smart.
JO	Yes, they are.

(*Darkening. A sough of wind.*)

LINDSAY	Where does the wind go when it gets tired?
JO	It goes to its little wicker basket behind the moon.
LINDSAY	Is there a fuzzy blanket in the wicker basket?
JO	The fuzziest of the fuzzy.

LINDSAY   As surely as the leaning Tower of Pisa shall
           one day topple.

JO   One day topple.

LINDSAY   But I don't like the sea. The sea says the same
           thing over and over again.

JO   Maybe the sea gets restless.

LINDSAY   How can that be? The sea must have a low
           IQ.

JO   I'm not so sure.

LINDSAY   You're not sure of anything, Mother.

JO   Because I get lonely sometimes.

LINDSAY   I never get lonely. The world is a puzzle
           and I know how to read it. The world
           is full of wonderful toys posing as
           astounding objects. I think the world and
           me will get along just fine together.

JO   I think you will do just fine also.
           (*Mom whistles the tune from the little song at the end of the second
           scene. Pause.*)
           Don't you even like the sight of the wind as it
           troubles the water, over there, by Governor's
           Island?

LINDSAY   A little, yes, a little. It reminds me of the moon.

JO   Why the moon?

LINDSAY   Because the moon is a place that time left alone.
           I want to live forever, and be like the moon.
           A never-never land.

JO   I thought you wanted only to pursue your objects
           without detection.

LINDSAY   To become the moon is one of my objects,
           as surely as a cat's-paw is a person
           used by another.

JO   As surely as a cat's-paw is a hitch made
           in a bight of rope so that two eyes are
           formed to hold the hook of one block of a
           tackle.

LINDSAY   Mother, you are MAD.
      (LINDSAY *laughs*.)

JO   As surely as a light breeze that ruffles the
           surface of the water over a comparatively
           small area.
      (*Pause.*)

LINDSAY   Mother, I am quite pleased with myself
           today. Today I have learned a fine, new
           word: *dudgeon*. Dudgeon, rage. Righteous
           indignation.
      (*Pause. Out of the blue they sing.*)

BOTH   Don Juan Dudgeon
           that curmudgeon
           killed his wives
           his seven wives
           with five little sticks
           and a pin.

Fade to black.

Scene [rudolph giuliani ◀]: *A hallway in Federal Superior Court, in Lower Manhattan.* JANE'S MOTHER *and* LINDSAY *sit together on a long wooden bench outside a grand jury room.*

LINDSAY   My mother is a stupid fool.

JANE'S MOTHER   So was mine, so are they all.

LINDSAY   My mother is a greater fool than most.
           She didn't secure the proper documentation.
           Now she's up shit's creek.

JANE'S MOTHER   Up shit's creek? My word.

LINDSAY   Exactedally. That is exactedally true.

JANE'S MOTHER   How can you be so sure?

LINDSAY   You don't know who you're talking to, clearly.

JANE'S MOTHER   I have a pretty good idea.

LINDSAY   Don't act coy. It's so foolish. I am aware of
           the fact you know my name. I was not talking about
           that. What kind of ninnyhammer do you take me
           for?

JANE'S MOTHER   Does your mother know you talk this way?

LINDSAY   What business is it of yours?
      (*Pause.*)

JANE'S MOTHER   So, I see we're off to a fine start.

LINDSAY   Another idiotic euphemism. Phooey.

JANE'S MOTHER   Well, I wouldn't worry. My daughter
           will explain to the people inside just
           what they need to know.

LINDSAY   Who is your daughter, exactedally?

JANE'S MOTHER   Jane Bub, Jo's friend.

LINDSAY   Oh her. And you are her mother?

JANE'S MOTHER   Yes I am.

LINDSAY   What is your name?

JANE'S MOTHER   Why, Mrs. Bub of course.

LINDSAY   No, I mean your Christian name.

JANE'S MOTHER   Hildegard, Hildgard Bub.

LINDSAY   I am Lindsay Rudge.

JANE'S MOTHER   How do you do, Lindsay?
(*They shake hands. Pause.*)

LINDSAY   This whole day has put me in the
state of high dudgeon.

JANE'S MOTHER   Don't worry.

LINDSAY   I am not worried, I'm bored. And tired.
I want to go home.

JANE'S MOTHER   How on earth did the two of you get all the way
up there, undetected, to Liberty's torch?

LINDSAY   Mother claimed she had a powerful friend.
A special dispensation. We slipped past the guard, and broke
the monster padlock with these.

(*Holds up a pair of metal-cutting sheers.*)

JANE'S MOTHER   The law doesn't bend for anybody.

LINDSAY   ——

JANE'S MOTHER   ——

LINDSAY   We didn't break anything. I see no reason
for all this pointless rigamarole.

JANE'S MOTHER   Well, I wouldn't worry too much.

LINDSAY   I am waiting for you to offer some proof
concerning that.

JANE'S MOTHER   Well, Dr. Jane Bub is an expert on the physics
of stress. Metal fatigue may not be her
specialty, but it is a related discipline.
Metallurgy. Airy stress.

LINDSAY   Airy isostasy is one of my favorite things.

JANE'S MOTHER Airy apostasy?

LINDSAY Isn't she the one who didn't want to
talk about Bermuda?

JANE'S MOTHER That's my Sarah.

LINDSAY It was not our intention to break Liberty's
arm. Surely the grand jury will listen to
reason and not spring the trap upon us Rudges.

JANE'S MOTHER Sarah will offer evidence, and the
bonus of character witness.

LINDSAY Who is Sarah?

JANE'S MOTHER Sarah is Jane. My daughter.

LINDSAY All this is baffling to me. You Bub people
are all crazy, Hildegard.

JANE'S MOTHER Shall I tell a story while we wait?

LINDSAY Only if it is not a creepy one.

JANE'S MOTHER Once upon a time there* was a . . .

LINDSAY Hold it.

JANE'S MOTHER What's the matter?

LINDSAY I don't understand.

JANE'S MOTHER Understand?

LINDSAY What you just said. I don't
understand it.

JANE'S MOTHER Lindsay, I haven't got to the
story yet. There is nothing
to not understand.

LINDSAY What I do not understand is that
non-airy business of "Once upon a
time" . . . That is not airy.

JANE'S MOTHER   Yes, once upon a time, yes, my dearie,
　　　　　　that is the proper way to begin a story.

LINDSAY   Well, I do not understand it.
　　　　Furthermore, I do not trust it.

JANE'S MOTHER   What is there in such a harmless phrase
　　　　　　to warrant such suspicion. The hideous
　　　　　　and scary part comes later.

LINDSAY   What is time, Hildegard, that you can
　　　　say "once upon it" as though it were a
　　　　footstool? It makes no sense.

JANE'S MOTHER   Such old things contain the glister of
　　　　　　the deepest heartfelt things.

LINDSAY   ?

JANE'S MOTHER   What?

LINDSAY   Such talk gives me the creeps. Are
　　　　they going to execute Mother by firing
　　　　squad maybe, or by the garrote?
　　(*She feigns her own strangulation.*)

JANE'S MOTHER   Do you want to hear my story or not?

LINDSAY   Only if it . . . only if you do not begin
　　　　with this malarkey of standing on time
　　　　like it was the back of an elephant.
　　　　That is not airy. That does not
　　　　cut it.

JANE'S MOTHER   Agreed. No more talk of time's thinginess.
　　　　　　Shake on it?
　　(*They shake hands.*)
　　　　　　Once upon a time, there was a big, round
　　　　　　bowl of slobber.
　　(*The little girl rolls her eyes.*)

In this bowl of slobber there was a red
velvet couch, and upon this couch there
lay in gloomy splendor a rosebush carefully
trimmed to resemble a dead person. Now, sprinkled
all over this recumbent rosebush person
there were exactedly three hundred and
twenty seven crushed Christmas tree ornaments,
each one a slightly different hue so that
their fragments glimmered with a strangely disturbing
luminescence, as with a radiance from another
world, a strangely disturbing demented world . . .

LINDSAY   I don't like this story. Can you tell a
different one?

JANE'S MOTHER   It is a very fine story, Lindsay. What is it
you don't like about it?

LINDSAY   There are no people. I should like to hear
a proper story. With an interesting person
at the very center of it. Perhaps a fine,
young little girl, a person rather like me.
She should encounter certain obstacles and
learn how to overcome them, overcome them
with intelligence, bravery and her native
perscapacity. She should be rewarded and
grow rich and famous. All the evil phantoms
of her lonely and wretched childhood—a
childhood wasted among doltish adults—should
be utterly dispelled and made to vanish,
vanish and be no more.

JANE'S MOTHER   And be no more.

LINDSAY   And be no more indeed. Exactedally.
Hildegard, why are you looking at me
in that way?

JANE'S MOTHER   I am considering how I should reply.

LINDSAY   What a large and blocky hall this is.
Where in the world do they find all this
measureless mass of marble?

JANE'S MOTHER   Lawyers have a genius wire that extends
deep into the center of the world, and
that is where the trolls and cobolds
dwell. Not to mention all the dead pandas.
Special pandas, sisters under the skin
to the notorious March Hare. And a certain
very sad, very strange little girl . . .

LINDSAY   Really?

JANE'S MOTHER   Yes, really. They go there and release
hundreds of a rare breed of bunny rabbit,
called the sapphire-tufted coney. It is
called that because, of course, of the
wiggle-waggle of its bluish ear-flaps.

LINDSAY   Of course, of course. And the little girl?

JANE'S MOTHER   The little girl had somehow gotten lost
one fine spring morning as she was collecting
empty machine gun cartridges that lay about
scattered among the jonquils and snapdragons.

LINDSAY   She was a modern little girl then?

JANE'S MOTHER   A very modern little girl.

LINDSAY   Hildegard I don't like this story either.

JANE'S MOTHER   Why not, Lindsay?

LINDSAY   It smells wormy.

JANE'S MOTHER   Wormy?

LINDSAY   Yes, it smells wormy with the stench of the

pathetic loser and social victim. It smells
too of senility's elegy to itself. It suggests
all those tired cliches concerning loss of innocence.
Innocence, ha!

(*Pause. Hildegard sits pondering.*)

JANE'S MOTHER   Yes, I think they will probably shoot
your mother. Tie her to the mouth
of a cannon. Blup, blurp. Blown to bits.
Or poison her with a random overdose of . . .
of upas, or foxglove, or belladonna, yes . . .

LINDSAY   But we did not break Liberty, nor
commit an act of public nuisance
upon her person. Liberty's structural
integrity is intact. I'm very sure of it.

JANE'S MOTHER   I'm not so very sure of it. My daughter
is a doctor of these things, stress and
related metallurgical maladies. The
frown she wore upon entering the
grand jury room was symptomatic.
Symptomatic of a crime, my dearie.

LINDSAY   And why this business of "my dearie"?
It makes my flesh crawl. All this
"my dearie" business reminds me of the
witches of olden times and other even
stupider older stuff. Fictional stuff.
Pointless lies and bulldiddly.

JANE'S MOTHER   It is not bulldiddly. It is a gesture
of fun.

LINDSAY   It is not fun, Hildegard, it is bulldiddly.
It is pointless. A bad check on the mind's
fiscal resources.

(*Pause and a sigh.*)

JANE'S MOTHER   So: you do not want to hear a story?

LINDSAY   Of course I want to hear a story.

JANE'S MOTHER   No, I don't think you do.

LINDSAY   Yes I do. Yes I do. Yes I do.
(*Pause and a sigh.*)
        I diddily do.

JANE'S MOTHER   You diddily don't.

LINDSAY   Do.

JANE'S MOTHER   Don't.

LINDSAY   Only I would like this story to be situated
at the site of truth. The real, I mean.
Geographically. And be current, consistent
and such that it unfold according to our
contemporary notions of fact, reason, and
rules of evidence. All this hokey-pocus
of "once upon a time" gives me quite a pain.
And, as I have said, what is a specific and
local time, what kind of thing is it, like a
shoe or hat, that it may be "put upon" yet
another thing? And if it is an object like
one of these, what sort of thing must it
rest upon? Really? I can't imagine.
I can't.

JANE'S MOTHER   All right, if that's the way you want it.
I shall tell you a story with no once
upon a time, but with a local habitation
and a name.
(*A suspicious pause.*)

LINDSAY   What is the name of its name, and where
is its habitation located? In precise terms.
Sorry, I'm just checking.

JANE'S MOTHER
 (*Pausing for effect.*)
   It is called "The Story of the Monster Grease Ball
   that Clogged the Giant Sewer Pipe."

LINDSAY Wow. I like it already. Go on.

JANE'S MOTHER And it is located in the continuous present
   at a place called Sparks, Nevada.

LINDSAY Good, very good. I like the specificity of it;
   only is Sparks, Nevada a true place? Oh,
   it must be, Hildegard, it must be.

JANE'S MOTHER Yes, Lindsay, it is a very real place. Near
   Reno and Virginia City. In the vast American desert.

LINDSAY Go on then. Go on.

JANE'S MOTHER
 (*Sweetly*)
   Once upon a time (LINDSAY *frowns.*) oops, sorry—
   operators of the local sewage treatment plant,
   of Sparks, Nevada, were forced to warn locals
   not to pour grease down the drain, after a
   Monster Grease Ball disrupted operations.

LINDSAY Ooh ooh ooh.

JANE'S MOTHER Sanitary engineer John Gonzales . . .

LINDSAY We'll amend that to Lolita. Lolita Gonzales,
   a genius of childhood.

JANE'S MOTHER Cut from a familiar mold.

LINDSAY A fine mold, Hildegard. Go on.

JANE'S MOTHER Sanitary engineer Lolita Gonzales—
   that's her real name—reports that
   the 150 pound monster has lodged against
   a bar screen at the plant. It is the 4th

of February, 1996. The Monster Grease
Ball is causing sewage to back up, can you
imagine. Now, it is taking some twenty
sticky minutes to dislodge and remove the
terror of its greasy bulk . . .

LINDSAY   Oh, I like the bulkiness of it. Oh.

JANE'S MOTHER   Lolita explains that it looks like a
side of bacon and so she nicknames it
the Grease Bison. Now employees are
using pitchforks to remove it, now they
are hauling it to a nearby dump.

LINDSAY   Wow. What dump?

JANE'S MOTHER   The one at Dewlap, Nevada.
(*But she's making it up.* LINDSAY *narrows her eyes.*)
"There's no telling where it came from,"
Lolita says. "What people should do
is capture their grease, put it in a jar,
let it congeal and throw it away.
Grease is a serious problem; don't
put it down the drain."

LINDSAY   That must be the moral of the story.

JANE'S MOTHER   Now Lolita is urging residents to get
rid of their kitchen garbage disposals,
saying they're a major source of sewer-line
grease.
(*Our* LINDSAY *beams.*)
The bar screen that caught the Grease
Bison is used to keep objects such as
sticks and rags out of the sewage system.
(*She leans over* LINDSAY *and whispers into her ear.*)
Rings and dentures also have been
known to lodge against it.

LINDSAY   Wow, Hildegard. That is the most wonderful
          story I have ever heard.

JANE'S MOTHER   Hot off the AP wire. Real life, factual.
          A slice of the bacon of life.

LINDSAY   The people felt so real, not like the
          corny constructed people in children's
          books. And edifying too, without being
          an insult to one's perscapacity.
          It is, as far as I'm concerned,
          exactedally what the doctor ordered.
          I love you Hildegard. Oh, please tell it again.
     (*She sees* JANE *and* JO *over* JANE'S MOTHER's *shoulder. The latter,
     however, does not.*)

JANE'S MOTHER   The Story of the Monster Grease Ball that
          Clogged the Giant Sewer Pipe . . .

JANE   Mother what is this?

LINDSAY   Oh, mother, mother, Hildegard has
          told me the most wonderful story. And
          it is a true one.

JO   She has, has she.

JANE'S MOTHER   Right off the AP wire. From Sparks, Nevada.

LINDSAY   A 150 pound "Grease Bison" had to be
          removed with a pitchfork. Wow.

JANE   I am surprised, Mother, you have been
          up to your old tricks. Aren't you aware
          of the gravity of the situation?

JANE'S MOTHER   What's wrong with a little harmless
          distraction?* What's wrong with that?

JO   Oh, Lindsay dear, Mom's coming home.
          There isn't going to be any indictment.
          Mother's going free.

LINDSAY   Free? Scot free? Truly?

JO   Scot free. Truly. Jane Bub has
saved the day. It's a complete
miracle. Tell us, Jane, tell us
how you did it.

JANE'S MOTHER   I can just imagine, my dearies.

JO   Hush now, Mrs. Bub, your daughter
convinced the grand jury of our innocence.

LINDSAY   "Our" innocence, Mother? Surely you
are not implicating me, your own child,
in your crimes? Crimes against the
state. And the structural integrity
of Liberty's arm.

JO   Lindsay, stop this.

LINDSAY   Mother, I don't want to be implicated
in your idiotic choices.

JO   And I am coming to believe you are
one of the most. Idiotic, that is.

LINDSAY   I am not a choice of yours, mother.
I am an event all of my own. Do not
confuse me with you. You with your
Bermudas and* Acapulcos and whatever
the hecks. I just happened. We are
not the same.

JANE   I do not want to talk about Bermuda.

I do not want to talk about Bermuda.

I do not want to talk about Bermuda.

I do not want to talk about Bermuda;
and furthermore, if that child of yours
starts talking about Bermuda I am

going right back into that grand jury
room and tell Assistant District Attorney
Hoskins Carmichael* that I have perjured
myself and and that you, Jo, the apparently
innocent Jo Rudge, are in fact—

LINDSAY   Can we leave this place I'm getting hungry.
    (JANE *stifles an angry response, then begins to speak with calm assurance.*)

JANE   Well I presented the facts clearly to the
assistant district attorney: first outlining
the forces identified as stress, whether tensile,
compressive, or shearing, according to the
nature of the straining action.

I supplied graphs and appropriate diagrams.

Using Mohr's Circle, I succeeded in
demonstrating beyond a doubt that the
strain energy per unit stored in
Liberty's arm in no way reached the upper
yield point for strain hardening. Not to
mention necking, and fracture. The stress
within Liberty's arm remained—and remains—
safely within the maximum elastic strain per
unit volume.
    (*Pause. Then applause.*)

Like you they applauded. And ushered the
two of us out, Jo and me I mean. Triumphant.
I did not even need to mention airy stress
function, nor the fact that Assistant
District Attorney Carmichael's daughter,
Patty, is a classmate of one Lindsay Rudge
at Crown of Briars School. It seemed,
at that point, superfluous.

LINDSAY   By airy stress function you are referring

to the biharmonic function of two variables
whose second partial derivatives give the
stress components of a body subject to stress?

JANE   Precisely.

LINDSAY   Then, Miss Bub, I apologize for my insensitivity
and promise never again to refer to that subtropical
archipelago formerly ruled by Sir John Swan
where you suffered your Fall.

JANE'S MOTHER   Doom. Doom.

JO   But at least I am free.

LINDSAY   One thing I mean to ask you, Mother.
In the event of an indictment, am I
to understand it was your intention
to persuade me, your daughter Lindsay,
sweet, innocent Lindsay, to smooth the
way for your release by some act of
bribery involving my best friend,
Patty Carmichael, daughter of Assistant
District Attorney Hoskins Carmichael and
incidentally a classmate at Crown of Briars.

JO   Lindsay, it never crossed my mind.
       (*Pause.*)

LINDSAY   I would be vexed if it were to be the
case, Mother. Very vexed.

JO   Don't worry, dear, don't worry. There
is nothing to be vexed about. Wow,
I could use a stiff drink. I know
a nasty little bar down on Columbus
Park. It's called Winnie's.

LINDSAY   I don't suppose you remembered to ask
concerning my roach motel.

JANE'S MOTHER   You had a roach motel? Wonderful.

LINDSAY   Yes, I discovered a wonderful roach
motel in Liberty's arm. Mother, in her
predictable way, made an issue of it.
Only, without her knowledge, I managed
to secret it, here, upon my person.
At home I hid it in a perfectilius
place only to find it gone, later.
Agents of mother no doubt found it,
and brought it here, to turn it in
as evidence. Evidence against me.
And it was the most perfectilius roach
motel.

JANE'S MOTHER   How sad.

JO   Come on, Lindsay. Let's get going.

LINDSAY   So you did not ask the assistant district
attorney as I requested?

JO   Quite slipped my mind, Lindsay.

JANE'S MOTHER   Perhaps I can find you another roach motel.

LINDSAY   It wouldn't be perfect like the one
I found in Liberty's torch.

JANE   She's so cute.

JO   Don't let her hear that.

JANE'S MOTHER   Yes, Lindsay I can send you one even
more perfect than the one you lost.

LINDSAY   Hildegard, whose side are you on?

JANE'S MOTHER   Hush, hush. We'll fix all this silliness,
just the way Lolita Gonzalez did. With
her pitchfork, at the sewage treatment
plant in Sparks, Nevada.

LINDSAY Well, I don't know. It just seems
terribly unfair to me. Just because
I am young and small.

JO And powerless, Lindsay, remember that.
Powerless. Hopelessly dependent on the
kindness of her mother.

LINDSAY Mother, your attempt at wit is grotesque.

JANE Lindsay, tell me what the "airy points"
are. Then we'll all go to Winnie's for a
drink. After that we'll go to Chinatown.
Green tea ice cream all the way around.

LINDSAY Pooh on Winnie's.
(*She refuses.*)

JANE Let's hear about those airy points.
(*She refuses.*)

JO She hasn't been this bad since . . .
well . . . since . . .

LINDSAY It was the time of Acapulco, Mother. And I came
through the crisis unaffected, quite unruffled,
despite all the general hysteria. You, Mother,
on the other hand: a total basket case.
(*Her mother turns away.*)
Exactedally, Mother, your introjects
came unstuck. Pathetic.

JO (*Turning back in a fury*)
——

LINDSAY ——

(*Pause.*)
Hildegard, would you like a stick of gum?
(*She offers.* JANE'S MOTHER *takes it.*)
Jane?

JANE   Sure.

   (*She takes a stick.* LINDSAY *does not offer one to her mother.*)

JANE'S MOTHER   What about your own mother?

LINDSAY   She has put me into a state of high
            dudgeon over this roach motel issue.
            I am thinking of what former Senator Bob Dole
            would do in my place.

      (*Pause.*)

JO   Well Lindsay, what do you think
            he would do? Mister Dole. That
            lugubrious, snake-oil charmer! What?

LINDSAY   I do not think he would give you a stick
            of gum.

JO   We're going then without you, Lindsay.

LINDSAY   Fine, I am beginning to like this place.
            It is boxy and large. With vast blocks
            of anti-theatrical stone all around. It
            feels reliable and solid. It is full
            of the feeling of what's real. In fact,
            I like it very much. So maybe I'll stay.
            Maybe I'll just stay here forever.

JO   She likes being in the catbird seat.

LINDSAY   Tell Mother the state may have let her
            off gently, but not me.

JO   We will negotiate this, Lindsay.

LINDSAY   You need to establish a system of priority
            among your projects, Mother, and then go
            after them one at a time.

JO
      (*Aside*)
            I'm going to commit a violent act

(*Turning back.*)

        I'm going to count to ten first, and
        then I'm going to commit a violent
        act.

JANE'S MOTHER If you come along I'll tell you my favorite
        story, the story of what the glass eyeball
        had to say to the moon.

JO   One. Two. Three . . .

(*All smile. Pause. All go out.*)

End of play.

Questions about performance rights for all plays should be addressed to Mitch Douglas, International Creative Management, Inc., 40 West 57th Street, New York, New York 10019: tel. 212-556-5600, fax 212-556-5665.

Special thanks: Yolanda Gerritsen, Marjorie and Carey Perloff, Erika Monk, Eric Askanese, Buddy Thomas; Michael Roth, Doug Jacobs; Anne Bogart, Joan MacIntosh; Jim Simpson, Jan Harding, Steve Mellor, Anne Hamburger; Mark Margolis, Julian Webber; Greta Gundersen, Kyle Chepulis; Cynthia Hopkins, Stacy Dawson, Molly Hickok, Annie-B Parson, Paul Lazar; Laurie Olinder, Bob McGrath, Danny Zippi; Jennifer Cooper, Leigh Secrest; Teresa Lee, David Van Tieghem; Daniel Aukin, Linsay Firman, Alicia Goranson, Bridget Markov; Jeff Jones, Len Jenkin, Eric Overmyer, and Anne Washburn.